DiDA

D201
DIPLOMA IN DIGITAL APPLICATIONS

Molly Wischhusen
Janet Snell
Jenny Johnson

Heinemann

Inspiring generations

Heinemann Educational Publishers
Halley Court, Jordan Hill, Oxford OX2 8EJ
Part of Harcourt Education

Heinemann is a registered trademark of
Harcourt Education Limited

Text © Molly Wischhusen, Janet Snell and Jenny Johnson, 2005

First published 2005

10 09 08 07 06 05
10 9 8 7 6 5 4 3 2 1

British Library Cataloguing in Publication Data is available
from the British Library on request.

ISBN 0 435 45005 0

Designed by Lorraine Inglis
Typeset by 🅃 Tek-Art, Croydon, Surrey
Original illustrations © Harcourt Education Limited, 2005
Printed by Bath Colourbooks Ltd
Cover photo: © Stock Image/Pixland/Alamy

Acknowledgements
Every effort has been made to contact copyright holders of material reproduced in
this book. Any omissions will be rectified in subsequent printings if notice is given
to the publishers.

Post-it® is a registered trademark of 3M.

Travelbug and *travelbug.co.uk* are fictitious names and have no connection with
any company with such names at the time of printing, or in the future.

Websites
Please note that the examples of websites suggested in this book were up to date at
the time of writing. It is essential for tutors to preview each site before using it to
ensure that the URL is still accurate and the content is appropriate. We suggest
tutors bookmark useful sites and consider enabling students to access them through
the school or college intranet.

Screen shots reprinted with permission from Microsoft Corporation.

Tel 01865 888058   *www.heinemann.co.uk*

Contents

CANCELLED 1 9 AUG 2024

Acknowledgements

A very special thank you to Samantha Moss and Jeanette Theaker students at Croydon College, who assisted in the preparation of the Graphics Unit by producing designs for the CD Player, the MP3 Player and the lollipops and patterns used as examples of cloning. We are full of admiration for their attitude to their work and wish them all the best for the future.

BAA plc
Department of Health
Department of Transport
Gameplay GB Ltd
Haywards Heath College (now Central Sussex College)
Jade Teo
Lloyds TSB
London Borough of Merton
Long Tall Sally
Meningitis Research Foundation
Norwich Union Direct
Post Office
Starfish Design and Print, Heathfield, East Sussex
Steve Holmes of Signet Construction Ltd, Eastbourne
Thomson Holidays
VL Systems Ltd

Photo acknowledgements

The authors and publisher would like to thank the following for permission to reproduce photographs:

Canon Images – pages 216, 217
ePop – page 226
Getty Images/Photodisc – page 129
Sandisk – page 63

Dedications

I could not wish for better co-authors and friends to work with than Janet and Jenny. My very sincere appreciation to Janet for holding the fort for Jenny and me when we needed it. My thanks also to Elaine Tuffery and her colleagues for their understanding and support. As always the encouragement from my family and friends is invaluable and the arrival of Sophie Grace hardly delayed me at all!

Molly Wischhusen

My thanks to the team at Heinemann for their support and especially to my special friends Molly and Jenny, my husband Bob and all my family.

Janet Snell

I dedicate this book to my beloved husband Ray who died suddenly before it was completed.

My sincere thanks go to Molly and Janet and my sons Ian and Colin and my daughter-in-law Helen, without whose support I would not have been able to finish my contribution. Thanks also to the Heinemann team for their encouragement during what has been an extremely difficult time for me.

Jenny Johnson

Introduction

Welcome to the programme of study in digital applications. You may be studying for the Award, the Certificate or the Diploma in Digital Applications. These qualifications are designed to create confident users of digital applications, who are able to apply their skills purposefully and effectively.

Which units do you need to take?

- For the **Award** in Digital Applications (AiDA) you will achieve Unit 1.
- For the **Certificate** in Digital Applications (CiDA) you will achieve Unit 1 plus one other unit of your choosing.
- For the **Diploma** in Digital Applications (DiDA) you will achieve all four units.

Each unit is the equivalent of one GCSE. The assessment for each of the units is a summative project that is set by Edexcel, the awarding body.

This book provides you with the necessary knowledge and skills to complete Unit 1.

What do you have to do to succeed?

To enable you to complete the projects, you will need to use ICT efficiently, legally and safely. You will learn all about this in Part 2, Section 1 on standard ways of working.

You will also need to develop ICT skills in a wide variety of software applications, which you then apply to complete the projects. ICT skills are developed in Part 2, Section 2: see the Skills Checklist on pages 4–8.

TiP

In preparing for your project it is essential for you to build up expertise in each of the software packages that you will be using. The project will consist of a number of tasks, each of which will require careful planning and thoughtful implementation. Therefore it is vital that you work steadily, allowing plenty of time for each task. You will find some tasks cannot be completed unless you have finished others.

In addition, you must

- learn how to plan, review and evaluate your projects
- learn what is meant by an e-portfolio and create one
- understand the topics specific to this unit.

The aim of Unit 1 is to produce a range of materials that are aimed at a specific audience. Each final product must be fit for its intended purpose. Each of the separate activities will be given a range of possible marks. The quality and complexity of your work will determine the mark you receive for each activity.

The completed project will **not** be printed out in the traditional way. Instead you will create an **e-portfolio** that displays your work in electronic form. An e-portfolio is rather like a website where links lead the user to the different activities you have been asked to complete. The e-portfolio will be assessed by an internal assessor and an external moderator.

Features of the book

Many of the illustrations and activities in the book are centred around a fictitious company called Travelbug. Throughout the book you will find hints, tips and tasks to help you develop the skills, knowledge and understanding you need to successfully achieve your qualification.

Skills evidence – a general signpost to advise you when to save results in activities undertaken in the skills chapters, for possible inclusion in your e-portfolio

Go out and try! – practice tasks to help you develop the skills that have been described in that section of the book

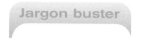

Jargon buster – explanations of some of the technical language which may be unfamiliar

Skills check – cross-references to related information in other parts of the book

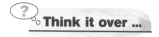

Think it over – activities to get you thinking about how you will go about or prepare for the practical tasks

Tip – guidance, notes and hints to help you

Skills builder task – practice closely linked to the skills you will need to complete your summative projects (not as demanding as the full project required by Edexcel, but it will be good preparation for learning how to develop an e-portfolio)

Assessment hint – hints to guide you on what would make the difference to achieving a merit, credit or distinction compared to a pass grade

We wish you good luck and hope you enjoy your course.

Molly Wischhusen
Janet Snell
Jenny Johnson

PART 1

Unit 1 — Using ICT

Introduction

Information is all around us. We find things out by watching and listening to television and radio; we talk to other people; we read books, newspapers and magazines; we search for information on the Internet, on CDs, etc. What do we do with this information?

- We gather it together.
- We reflect on what we have found out.
- We pass the information on, use or present it in various ways.

LEARNING OUTCOMES

After working through this chapter you should be in a position to

- ✓ search for reliable, up-to-date information from a wide variety of sources
- ✓ extract relevant information
- ✓ analyse and present the information in meaningful and effective ways.

How will I be assessed?

You will be given a project brief for this unit and you will be required to carry out research on a particular topic. The project brief will specify exactly what you will be required to produce, how you will present your findings, and to whom you will present them. You can expect to spend about 30 hours working on your project.

You will be assessed on **six** separate activities as follows:

1 Plan and manage the project
2 Select and capture information from a variety of sources
3 Collate and analyse data to produce information
4 Present and communicate information
5 Present evidence in an e-portfolio
6 Review the project.

The marks you will be awarded will depend on the quality and complexity of your work. Your teacher or tutor will be able to show you how the marks are allocated against each activity.

The project brief will give you hints and tips on successfully completing the assessment. The skills chapters provide help on the various software applications you will be using. In addition you will find detailed guidance throughout this chapter, and we strongly suggest you also read the following chapters, which contain specific help on completing the assessments:

- Project planning
- Review and evaluation
- Creating an e-portfolio.

Skills file

The table below lists all the skills required to complete this unit successfully. The pages where you will find these skills explained are identified in the Page column.

WORD-PROCESSING SOFTWARE	Page
enter, cut, copy, paste and move text	88
use page formatting features:	
headers and footers	107
margins	104
page breaks	106
page numbering	108
alignment	105
line spacing	109
tables	112
text boxes	119
columns	111
use paragraph formatting features:	
alignment	95
bullets and numbering	97
tabs	100
indents	102

○ format text:	
● font type and font size	91
● bold, underline, italic	93
● colour	93
○ create, select and insert components:	
● images	120
● lines and simple shapes	120
● tick boxes	123
● comments	123
● hyperlinks	124
○ use images/objects:	
● position	127
● crop	129
● resize	129
● group and ungroup	121
● text wrapping	128
● borders	114, 122
○ use spelling and grammar checkers	76, 132
○ use mail merge	132

SPREADSHEET SOFTWARE

	Page
○ enter, cut, copy, paste and move data	138
○ format cells to match data types	138
○ insert/delete rows and columns	147
○ enter formulas:	
● use operators	141
● replicate formulas	143
● use simple functions	150
● use absolute and relative cell references	143, 144
○ sort data	155
○ produce fully-customised charts/graphs:	
● titles	157
● axis and data labels	157
● legend	157
○ use headers and footers	161
○ print selected areas	162

DATABASE SOFTWARE

	Page
create simple flat-file database structures	167
set and modify field characteristics including name, data type, size and format	168
create validation rules	179
enter, edit and delete records	
• import data sets	182, 192
design and create data entry forms that facilitate data entry	174
sort on one field with a secondary sort on another field	185
create and use searches to extract relevant information:	
• single criterion	184
• multiple criteria	186
• relational operators	185
• logical operators	186
produce customised reports	188
export information from a database into other applications	191

PRESENTATION SOFTWARE

	Page
use colour schemes	197
use master slides	197
use slide formatting features:	
• frames	200
• alignment	201
• line spacing	201
• bullets	201
create, select and insert components:	
• text	201
• images	202
• sound	207
• lines and simple shapes	204
• hyperlinks	207
use images/objects	
• position	127
• crop	129
• resize	129

Using information sources

In order to complete your project you will need to undertake *research*, which means gathering *information*. Before you begin this, it is essential to decide on the purpose of your research – *what you need to find out*. The purpose may be to

- increase knowledge
- help with decision-making
- make recommendations.

Once you have established the aim of your research, you need to identify the *most suitable sources of information*. This is the key to successful research. To complete this unit you will use a wide variety of sources, both primary and secondary.

Primary and secondary sources

A primary source might be

- conducting an interview (Figure 1.1)
- carrying out a survey, possibly face-to-face or by email
- taking photographs
- recording sound clips.

Figure 1.1 An interview is a primary source

A secondary source might be

- paper-based – books, newspapers, magazines/journals, directories, maps
- ICT-based – Internet, CDs, DVDs, databases
- broadcast via the media – radio, TV.

Figure 1.2 A book is a secondary source

How can you decide what is a suitable source?

If you were asked to write a report explaining what software is, and to identify the various types of software available, the purpose of your research would be to increase your knowledge in that area. Undoubtedly you would already have *some* knowledge of software, but you would almost certainly need more detailed information to complete the report. In that particular case you would be able to find lots of information through paper-based sources and the Internet.

In contrast, if the head of a school were considering introducing this Edexcel qualification for the first time – perhaps as an alternative option to a GCSE in ICT – and you were asked to present a report about the programme, the purpose of your research would be to help with decision-making and to make recommendations. In that case you would probably use both primary *and* secondary sources. The primary sources might include interviews, or a survey with current pupils to establish how many would be interested in choosing this as an option. Secondary sources might include information from the Edexcel website, and reports in the educational press to establish whether the content of the course looked appropriate. As a result of your research you would be able to make recommendations and the head of school would be able to decide whether to run the programme.

Selecting appropriate sources and using suitable techniques

When using secondary sources you need to be confident that the information is

- reliable/trustworthy
- up-to-date
- unbiased.

It would be pointless relying on a ten-year-old textbook on software, as ICT changes so quickly. A very recent textbook would be useful to explain the general definitions – such as the basic *role* of the operating system – but a computer magazine or the Internet is more likely to have the very latest information on current operating systems. The Microsoft and Apple websites, too, would provide useful information – but they will be biased somewhat towards their own products and therefore might not present the advantages and disadvantages compared with their competitors' products.

Sometimes secondary sources are enough, as with the earlier example of researching software. On other occasions you will need additional information obtained through primary sources. The report relating to the possibility of the school head offering a new Edexcel programme of study is a good example. Secondary sources would be ideal to find out the content of the programme, but you would need primary sources through face-to-face interviews or an email survey to find out the interest level of students in the school.

Recording information and acknowledging sources

Go out and try!

Figure 1.3 Do you know what korfball is?

Look at Figure 1.3. Do *you* know what korfball is? Use a variety of secondary sources (such as your library and the Internet) to see what information you can find. Word-process approximately 200 words (about half an A4 page) about korfball and remember to record and acknowledge the sources you use.

Skills check

You will need to acknowledge all your sources, and you must respect legislation relating to copyright. Refer to the section starting on page 80 to remind yourself of the requirements.

During the course of your research you will gather information from a number of different types of source – information that will be useful for different sections of your e-portfolio. It is important to keep track of all this information, so that it is easily available when you are ready to use it. You may record it by

- *making notes* – listing key points can be more useful than writing long paragraphs
- *copying it into another document* – don't forget to put inverted commas around the text and to acknowledge who originally wrote it if you copy word-for-word

- *digitising and storing* – scan a map or a picture, or download a digital photograph
- *storing the URL* – keep a record of web addresses you have used, in order to acknowledge them
- *using bookmarks* – include any useful websites in your list of favourites to make it easy to find them again later.

Go out and try!

You will find it impossible to simply remember all your sources when your project is complete, so *immediately* create a new file where you will be able to list all the textbooks, magazines, journals, newspapers, URLs etc. you have used. Save the file as 'Sources'.

Skills check

If you are set this project as a mini project, you should think about *how to plan and manage the project*. Refer to page 279.

Skills Builder Task 1

At this stage you should be able to tackle this first task of a small project that will run throughout this chapter. The project scenario is set out below. Study the scenario carefully so you are clear about the project's objective.

The scenario

Your school Head or college Principal has received the following letter from a new mobile phone company.

Prelude is a new, innovative mobile telephone company. We are looking for partners in all parts of the country to host our up-to-the-minute service.

We are dedicated to providing a fair deal for young people. We ensure they receive a service that protects them from unscrupulous scams whilst enabling them to indulge their favourite pastime.

We are prepared to pay a substantial rent for a suitable site upon which to erect a new telecommunication mast in your area and believe your school has large grounds which might offer an appropriate location. We are sure the additional income your school would receive for hosting the mast would be most useful.

Our local representative would very much like to meet you to discuss this proposal and will contact you shortly to arrange an appointment.

DiDA

The Head/Principal is aware that there is considerable controversy over health issues relating to both telecommunication masts and the use of mobile phones by young people. He is anxious to study the facts before coming to any decision, so he has asked you to carry out some research on his behalf so that he can give guidance to the governors and parents.

Your first task is to use *secondary* sources to investigate the health issues surrounding the location of telecommunication masts and the use of mobile phones by young people. Produce a report of your findings.

Using surveys

Have you ever been stopped in the street by a researcher and asked whether you can spare a few minutes to answer some questions (Figure 1.4)? The researcher will be conducting a survey on behalf of an organisation, so he or she will record your answers to a series of questions on a questionnaire, and in some cases on audio tape.

Figure 1.4 A market researcher in action

Millions of pounds is spent every year on this *market research* by organisations that want to know the public's views on a variety of topics. A large proportion of this money will be spent on surveys. These are used by all sorts of organisations to gather information.

Figure 1.5 Topics of market research

Opinions

Market research is frequently carried out by manufacturing companies. For example, if a company is considering updating the brand image of an established product, the company will want to know the public's opinion of the proposed new image before investing considerable sums of money on promoting it.

Television companies sometimes produce *pilot* shows of work by new writers to find out viewers' opinions before commissioning a whole series. An invited audience will be asked to watch the show and complete a questionnaire recording what they thought of it.

Likes and dislikes

If a school headteacher was considering a change in the school uniform, a survey might be used to find out what pupils and parents would like or dislike when choosing a new uniform. For example, how many people like having a school uniform? How many people like the idea of girls wearing trousers rather than skirts? Would a new summer uniform prove popular? Is there a preference for a particular colour?

Purchasing patterns

Suppose a major high street clothing retailer is considering opening a new branch. A survey carried out in that town's shopping centre would reveal information about the shopping patterns of the local community.

The results of the survey could ultimately affect the decision on whether to open a store. If the results of the survey showed that local people generally went out of town to buy their clothes, the retailer may decide not to open a branch in that particular town.

Lifestyles

Some organisations conduct surveys on a national scale. These surveys gather information about our age, social class, marital status, housing, working life, income, leisure time, etc. Once analysed, the data provides valuable information on the lifestyles of groups with different jobs and incomes, and people living in different parts of the country. This data is then often sold on to other organisations that use it to target specific social groups with mailshots on products that would appear to fit in with their lifestyles.

Planning your survey

Your first step is to think about exactly what you need to find out and who the best people are to give you this information. Every survey should start with well defined objectives that state the reasons for carrying out the survey. When the objectives are clear, the questions can be drawn up and the questionnaire designed.

Questionnaires

Questionnaires fulfil several purposes:

- Most importantly they should enable you to gather accurate data.
- They ensure that each person is asked exactly the same question.
- They provide the easiest way of obtaining and analysing data by providing a structure from which the answers can be counted easily.

There is a skill in designing a questionnaire that will meet all of these requirements.

Question design

There are basically three types of question used in surveys: open questions, closed questions and scaled questions.

An *open question* allows the *respondent* to give any answer. For example, if 30 people were asked the question 'What is your age?' you could end up with 30 different answers. It is almost impossible to analyse the responses to questions of this nature.

A *closed question* will usually have anticipated replies.

Think it over ...

A publishing company is thinking of producing two new weekly magazines. One would be aimed at teenage boys and the other at teenage girls. How could the company research the potential markets? What information would the company be trying to find?

Jargon buster

A **respondent** *is the person answering a question.*

For example, the following question provides a set of answers that can be counted easily and then analysed.

Please indicate your age group	Under 18	☐
	18 – 29	☐
	30 – 39	☐
	40 – 49	☐
	50 – 59	☐
	60 or over	☐

If you use questions of this nature, make sure there is no overlap in the possible answers. For example, if you include two age response boxes '20–30' and '30–40', which box would a 30-year-old be expected to tick?

A *scaled question* is sometimes used to find out how much a person likes or dislikes the idea of something.

How likely are you to consider a weekend shopping trip to France by coach?

On a scale of 1 to 10 [where 1 represents very unlikely and 10 represents highly likely], please circle the number that reflects your thoughts

Very unlikely   *Highly likely*

1   2   3   4   5   6   7   8   9   10

This question will show you the scale of possible interest, *but be careful if you use questions of this type*. The secret is to include an *even number* of possible responses, such as 6, 8 or 10, so that respondents have to make a decision one way or the other. If you had a scale of 1 to 9 it is possible for all your respondents to choose number 5 – which is right in the middle of the scale and does not show any preference.

Once you have decided what types of questions to use, there are some other points to consider.

- Your questions should not be too long or complicated. Use simple language – you will not score points for using difficult words that people may not understand.

- Your questions should relate to the specific objective of the survey and should not be included just because you like the sound of them.

○ Your questions should definitely not influence the responses given. They should be unbiased and not lead the respondent to a particular answer.

○ Consider the order of the questions. They should flow easily from one to another, and questions on the same topic should ideally be grouped together.

○ Finally, be prepared to rewrite your questions. Your questionnaire will need to be thoroughly tested before it is used. Sometimes a question will not be understood in the way you intended. Don't rely on the comments of just one tester – ask several people to test the survey for you. Testing of this nature will also help you to find out whether you can collate the data easily, ready for analysis.

Go out and try!

You have already considered the sort of information a magazine would need before deciding whether to produce two new magazines (one for boys and one for girls) for the teenage market.

1 Write a series of questions that a researcher might use in a survey on behalf of the publisher.
  ○ Think carefully about the survey's objective. What exactly are you trying to find out?
  ○ What types of questions will help you to achieve this objective?
  ○ Try to write clear questions that will encourage an honest response.
2 Try out your questions on a friend.
  ○ Do the questions produce the types of response you expected?
  ○ Are there any questions missing that would help you to meet the survey's objective or to better analyse the responses?
3 Rewrite your questions if necessary and repeat the trial with another person.

Designing a questionnaire

The visual appearance of a questionnaire is important, and you should make use of plenty of white space so that it is easy to read. Use a standard (i.e. not fancy) font style and size so that the questions are clear, and make sure the spaces for answers line up with the questions. If you are including tick boxes or a scale – as in the previous examples on page 17 – make sure you give a clear instruction to tick a box or circle a number. Make it clear whether your respondents should tick just one box per question, or as many as they wish.

Use the features in your word-processing software to help you present your questionnaire. For example, use the **Tab** key to line up answers and boxes.

Consider using a table to produce a questionnaire. You could replace the standard borders with other borders of your choice. Figure 1.6 shows an example.

Please tick one box		✓
Please indicate your age group	Under 18	
	18–29	
	30–39	
	40–49	
	50–59	
	60 or over	
Please indicate your gender	Male	
	Female	

Please tick one box		✓
Please indicate your age group	Under 18	
	18–29	
	30–39	
	40–49	
	50–59	
	60 or over	

Please indicate your gender	Male	
	Female	

Figure 1.6 Part of a questionnaire produced using a table, and the same questionnaire printed with selected borders

Finally, think about producing a sheet on which to record the answers to the questions. When you count the answers, a useful way of recording them is to group them in fives. Use one vertical stroke for each of the first four answers and record the fifth answer horizontally, like this: ‖‖. You can then total them easily by adding up in fives. Figure 1.7 illustrates this.

Please tick one box		✓	Total

Please indicate your age group	Under 18	|||	3
	18–29	‖‖ |||	8
	30–39	‖‖ ||||	9
	40–49	‖‖	5
	50–59	||||	4
	60 or over			1

Please indicate your gender	Male	‖‖ ‖‖ ‖‖ ||	17
	Female	‖‖ ‖‖ |||	13

Figure 1.7 One method of collating data before it is entered into a spreadsheet

Questionnaire on underage drinking

- Please tick only one for each question that applies to you.

1. Male ☐
   Female ☐
2. age: 12–13 ☐
            13–15 ☐
            15–17 ☐

3. Do you drink alcohol?
   Yes ☐
   No ☐

4. How often do you drink alcohol?
   ....
   ....

5. Can u purchase your own alcohol?
   Yes ☐
   No ☐   Sometimes ☐

6. How do you usually get alcohol? ☐
   Parents ☐   Off licence ☐   Pub/bar ☐

   Friends ☐   People off the street ☐

   Other..

7. Why do you drink alcohol?
   Peer pressure ☐   Nothing else to do ☐
   To feel older ☐

   Other..

8. Do you think if there were more activities for younger people, you would drink less alcohol?
   Yes ☐
   No ☐
   Maybe ☐

   Please explain your answer, why? ....
   ....

9. If yes or maybe, what activities do you think should be provided for younger people?
   ....
   ....

10. What are your opinions on underage drinking in general? ....
    ....
    ....

Figure 1.8 A questionnaire produced by a student – some improvements are necessary

Go out and try!

There is concern amongst teachers that some students are not spending enough time on their homework or coursework. Your Headteacher/Principal would like to invite parents and guardians into school one evening to discuss the problem, but first of all she needs to investigate how the situation affects students in your school/college.

You have been asked to find out how students in your peer group spend their leisure time. For example, how much time do they spend in paid employment, doing homework, playing sports, watching television, and so on? You won't need the wide age range indicated in Figure 1.7, but choose a range that is most suitable for the students in your school or college.

Carry out a survey to gather together data that the Headteacher/Principal will be able to use as evidence when talking to parents and guardians.

⭐ Assessment Hint

To achieve top marks you must

○ *identify and use **at least three** secondary sources, also checking that the data is valid and reliable*

○ *identify and use **one** primary source, thinking carefully about how to ensure you gather the information you need*

○ *if you use a questionnaire, test it, and revise it if necessary before conducting your full survey*

○ *acknowledge your sources fully and accurately.*

Skills Builder Task 2

At this stage you should be able to tackle the next task of the mini project introduced in Skills Builder Task 1 on page 13. Again, don't forget to study the scenario carefully so that you are clear about the project's objective.

Conduct a survey amongst your peer group to find information on

○ current service providers

○ pay-as-you-go and monthly billing

○ how frequently handsets are updated

○ the average number of text messages sent and received each day

○ the average number of phone calls made and received each day

○ the average monthly cost of text and phone messages

○ who pays the bill

○ any other relevant information you can think of.

Collating and analysing data to produce information

Using a spreadsheet

Once you have finished your survey you need to collate the data in a spreadsheet. If the questionnaire has been prepared well, the design of your spreadsheet will follow closely the format of the questions.

You can then include formulas and functions to make calculations, from which you can analyse and interpret the results. You will then be able to produce meaningful information – some or all of which will probably be in the form of bar charts or graphs.

Figure 1.9 shows how a spreadsheet can be used to analyse the data shown in Figure 1.7 on page 19.

From the analysis of the data you can then produce useful graphs or charts to illustrate the information more clearly. For example, the bar charts in Figure 1.10 show that the majority of respondents in this particular survey are aged 19 to 39, and there are 14 per cent more males than females.

	A Age Range of Respondents	B No in each category	C % of Total in Each Category	D Breakdown by Gender	E No in each category	F % of Total in Each Category
1						
2	Under 18	3	10%	Male	17	57%
3	19 - 29	8	27%	Female	13	43%
4	30 - 39	9	30%			
5	40 - 49	5	17%			
6	50 - 59	4	13%			
7	60 or over	1	3%			
8	Total respondents	30				

	A Age Range of Respondents	B No in each category	C % of Total in Each Category	D Breakdown by Gender	E No in each category	F % of Total in Each Category
1						
2	Under 18	3	=B2/$B$8	Male	17	=E2/$B$8
3	19 - 29	8	=B3/$B$8	Femal	13	=E3/$B$8
4	30 - 39	9	=B4/$B$8			
5	40 - 49	5	=B5/$B$8			
6	50 - 59	4	=B6/$B$8			
7	60 or over	1	=B7/$B$8			
8	Total responden	=SUM(E2:E3)				

Figure 1.9 The spreadsheet data from Figure 1.7 and the formulas to analyse it

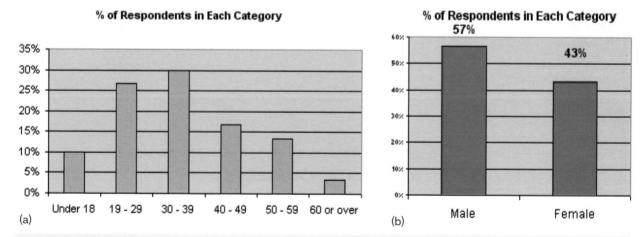

Figure 1.10 Graphs illustrating (a) the percentages of respondents in each category, and (b) the percentages of male and female respondents, for the data in Figure 1.7

Go out and try!

Create a spreadsheet based on the questions you have asked in your survey. Try to make the row or column headings much briefer than the actual questions. For example, the questions in your survey might all start with 'How many hours ...?' Instead of writing out every question in full as row or column headings, think about other options as shown in Figure 1.11. The heading 'No of Hours Spent On' has been centred across the columns relating to the questions asked.

No of Hours Spent On:		
Paid Employment	Homework	Watching TV

Figure 1.11 Possible heading styles to analyse the survey results

If the respondents have been asked to indicate their age in categories, as suggested earlier, then you can design the spreadsheet to establish (a) the total number of respondents, (b) how many are in each age group, and (c) the percentage of the total that are in each group. When you analyse the responses to the questions in your survey, you will be able to identify whether there is any significant difference in the replies depending on the age of the respondent.

Skills check ▶▶

As explained on page 165, databases are used to store large quantities of structured data covering a huge variety of topics – from stock control, to travel or theatre bookings, to medical records and much more. Make sure you read this information on databases.

TiP

*Remember that it is very important to consider the nature of the data to be stored and what information you hope to obtain from it **before** you start to design your database.*

Information handling

In order to complete your project for this unit you may be able to extract information from databases that have been created by someone else. Alternatively you might need to create your own database to store and analyse the results of your research.

When creating your database you will need to

- use validation rules when designing the fields – see page 179
- import given data sets – see page 192
- enter, edit and delete records – see page 182
- design data entry forms – see page 174
- use queries to extract valid and meaningful information for a specified purpose – see page 184
- use reports to present information clearly – see page 188
- export data for use in other applications, such as mail merge – see page 191.

Importing data

If you already have a set of data stored elsewhere, it may not be necessary to copy the data into the database records. Instead the data can be imported directly into the database. For example, if you have entered data into a spreadsheet file, you can import that data directly into your database.

Exporting data

If you are sending the same letter to a large number of people, you can use the names and addresses already stored in your database by *exporting* the data to use in a mail merge file.

Sometimes you may need to analyse data using both a spreadsheet and a database file, because these software applications provide different facilities for representing the data.

- The spreadsheet is the most suitable way to analyse numerical data and produce graphs and charts to visually represent that data.

- Whilst the *filter facility* of a spreadsheet enables you to extract particular information just as you would by creating a query in a database, the advantage of the database is that you can present that information more clearly by producing a report from the results of the query.

Therefore it may be appropriate and beneficial to import the data from your spreadsheet into a database file.

Skills check ▶▶

See page 192 for step-by-step instructions for importing data into a database.

Go out and try!

1. Having set up a spreadsheet to record the results of your survey of homework and coursework, design a database into which you can import the data from your spreadsheet. The fields in your database must follow the relevant column headings in your spreadsheet. For example, the small snapshot shown in Figure 1.11 (page 23) showed three relevant headings: Paid Employment, Homework and Watching TV. The field names in your database would match these and you would choose a suitable field type – in this case *number*. You need to consider whether it should be an *integer* (whole number) or *two decimal places* to allow for quarter or half hours.

2. 💾 Save the table and then import the data from the spreadsheet.

Assessment Hint

To achieve top marks you must

- *select and use the spreadsheet and database tools to produce relevant information clearly and efficiently, using more advanced formulas and a variety of data types in your field design*

- *review and modify your work, taking account of feedback from others.*

Skills Builder Task 3

At this stage you should be able to tackle the next task of the mini project introduced on page 13. Again, don't forget to study the scenario carefully so that you are clear about the project's objective.

(1) Analyse your results using a spreadsheet and create relevant graphs or charts to illustrate your findings.

(2) Record your results in a database and produce suitable reports for the Principal.

Working with information

Identifying the purpose

When you have completed your research and gathered the data together the summative project brief will identify the information you must obtain from it.

- Sometimes this might simply be a case of extracting relevant items and passing the information on in a straightforward way.

- At other times you might have to study a wide range of information and present it in your own words. You could be asked to draw conclusions or make recommendations.

You must learn to present your information in a way that will be immediately helpful to the readers, by providing answers to the questions that they are most likely to have. The information you provide may ultimately influence their decision-making in some way. If you are

- *presenting your own views*, remember that whatever you write or say should be justified or explained.

- *passing on information*, make sure you have the facts right and that what you are saying is accurate.

- *quoting from somewhere or someone*, you should put the quote in quotation marks and acknowledge the source of the information.

While you are writing, think about the purpose of your document and make sure that every word you write contributes to that purpose. The purpose helps to determine the writing and presentation style that is most appropriate, and you will learn to approach different purposes in different ways.

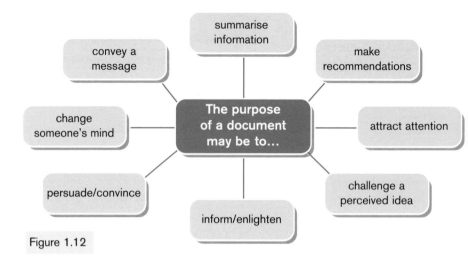

Figure 1.12

Let's look at each of these possible purposes in turn.

Conveying a message

Figure 1.13 shows how easy it is for a simple message to be conveyed incorrectly! It is essential that you learn to pass information on to other people in an accurate way without altering the facts or imposing any ideas of your own (unless your opinion is asked for).

The message you are passing on might be very straightforward, such as confirming the arrangements for a meeting. It might be more complex, such as the description of a technical problem with machinery. The consequences of passing on an inaccurate message could be disastrous. For example, a letter to clients advising them of

Figure 1.13 It is important to convey messages accurately!

a change in the arrangements for ordering goods must be accurate or the company could be liable to lose business worth thousands of pounds. One thing always remains the same: you must make sure that what you are writing is accurate.

Think it over...

This is something the whole class can do together or in two groups. Ask your teacher or tutor to write down in secret a message that contains several key points. He or she will speak softly and pass the message to one person in the group. That person will pass the message on to the next person and so on until everyone has been given the message. You are not allowed to hear the message repeated. The last person to receive the message will state it out loud.

○ Did the final message match the original message?

○ If the original message was different from the final message, why do you think it changed?

○ What steps can you take to ensure a message is passed on accurately?

Summarising information

Learning to summarise information is a bit trickier than just being accurate. You have to read through all the information you have gathered and then pull out the relevant facts from the various sources. You must then *reassemble* the facts in your own words without altering the facts or changing the meaning.

Look at the page from a holiday brochure in Figure 1.14 (page 28). It provides a summary of the holiday resort together with some local information on currency, local food specialities, etc. Relatively few words have been used, and information on the weather has been summarised in graphical form to make it much easier to understand.

Think it over...

Earlier in this chapter you used secondary sources of information to find out about korfball and wrote about half a page on the subject. At that time you were summarising information. Now compare your work with that of a friend.

○ Do the two summaries contain very similar information?

○ What differences can you find?

○ Is any of the wording exactly the same? That is, have any sentences or phrases just been copied from the original text?

○ Do you agree that both passages contain all the important facts about the topic? Refer back to your source material and see what relevant information has been left out.

Costa del Sol

"From the fine sands of exuberant Torremolinos to the chic allure of exclusive Marbella, the Costa del Sol is a vibrant mix of sun, sea and spectacular sights."

Costa del Sol

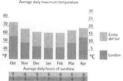

Andalucia embodies all that is typically Spanish...sun-soaked beaches, passionate flamenco dancers, Moorish castles, orange groves, proud matadors and sleepy whitewashed towns perched on dramatic hillsides. The Costa del Sol is the perfect gateway to this quintessential picture of Spain and offers so much more besides.

From the cosmopolitan marinas of Marbella to the top class golf courses of Fuengirola, from the glittering sands of Torremolinos to the lively tapas bars of Nerja, the resorts that make up Spain's 'sunshine coast' offer all ages a fascinating spectrum of sights and activities by day and night.

Averaging 300 days' sunshine a year, it's little wonder that the Costa del Sol is widely acknowledged as the playground of Europe. The coastline is famed for its miles of wide, sandy beaches lapped by the sparkling waters of the Mediterranean. Most offer a wide range of watersports if you're feeling energetic and sunbeds and parasols if you prefer to while away your days in the sun. Torremolinos has a 7km stretch of unbroken sandy shoreline while Nerja is known for its pretty coves tucked under cliffs - perfect if you're looking for a little more seclusion.

If you like to relax by day and party by night, you'll love the cheerful exuberance of Torremolinos, Benalmadena and Fuengirola. The streets are lined with an abundance of lively bars, discos and clubs where you can dance the night away. In contrast, evenings in Estepona, Nerja and Marbella are more low key. Visitors often prefer to enjoy the buzz of local tapas bars, romantic waterfront restaurants or the flamenco shows where you can experience the compelling rhythm of a Spanish guitarist and flashing moves of a dancer.

From small souvenir shops to smart boutiques, the Costa del Sol overflows with shops of all shapes and sizes. Marbella is the place to head if you're after classy designer wear while Malaga is home to a large shopping mall and a number of department stores. Fuengirola stages a weekly street market every Tuesday. Leather goods are particularly good value, as is Andalucian blue and white coloured pottery.

factfile Ask your travel agent for further information on accommodation in this resort. See A-Z guide.

Your Local Expert *"Some local knowledge to make you make the most of your holiday."*

Money There are 1.41 euros to the £1.00 as at 31st August 2004. Banking hours are Monday-Friday 08.30-14.00. Major credit cards are accepted at most shops, hotels and restaurants.

Meals Southern Spain is the birthplace of tapas bars. Sometimes called 'pinchos', tapas are small bar snacks that are usually served as an accompaniment to a glass of sherry, wine or beer. Even the smallest of villages in Andalucia play host to at least one tapas bar where locals head in the evenings to enjoy a drink, a bite to eat and of course a chat with friends.

Whet your appetite with 'jamon serrano', salt-cured ham that's dried out in the mountain air, or 'tortilla espanola', Spanish omelette made from potato and onions bound with eggs. Other tempting dishes include 'calamares fritos', deep fried squid rings drizzled with lemon juice, 'albondigas', meatballs served in a rich tomato sauce, and 'queso manchego', a mature sheep's cheese. Tapas are normally eaten standing rather than sitting down which adds to the vibrant atmosphere experienced in the bar.

Dress Code In most hotels and apartments gentlemen are required to wear long trousers.

Thomson 175

Figure 1.14 A typical page from a holiday brochure will include a summary of information about the resort. It may also include a graph or chart to illustrate the annual temperature and rainfall

Making recommendations

A recommendation usually follows a detailed investigation into a particular subject. For example, the decision to introduce the theory element to the car driving test was the result of a recommendation made following a study of driving standards in the UK and in Europe.

An idea to change the school/college year from three terms to four terms is quite topical. In fact some areas have already adopted the new proposals. If the Head Teacher of your school or the Principal of your college wanted to make the change, he or she could not just wake up one morning and announce the change. Any decision would have to follow an investigation that would take into account the views of parents and guardians, the local education authority, local employers, teachers, trade unions and students. The investigation would make a recommendation to the Head Teacher or Principal, who would then make the recommendation to the governors.

In business, recommendations are usually made in writing, such as a letter recommending a particular course of action, or a detailed report with recommendations in the conclusion. Sometimes a multimedia presentation will be used to support a recommendation. Whichever method is chosen, the facts will be presented and arguments offered for and against the proposal in order to support the final recommendation.

Go out and try!

You now know the facts about korfball. The Head of Sports in your school or college has asked you to make a recommendation on whether the sport should be adopted there. Make your own decision based on the information you have obtained, and then write about 150 words in support of your recommendation.

TiP

Sometimes graphs and charts are used to attract attention. They can demonstrate the highs and lows with far more impact than a paragraph of words and numbers. The tip is to make the image relevant and the words notable.

Attracting attention

If you are trying to attract someone's attention, the message needs to be 'short, sharp and to the point'. Posters and advertisements provide fine examples of publications that are designed to attract attention. Compare any selection of advertisements in magazines or on hoardings and try to analyse which advertisements are eye-catching and why. The chances are that the eye-catching ones will contain a relevant graphical image and few words – little enough to be taken in with a quick glance but sufficient to make you want to find out more.

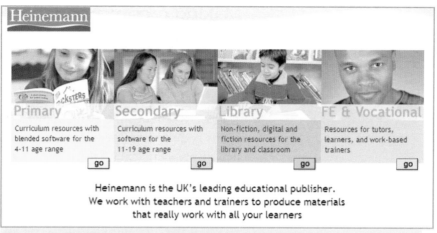

Figure 1.15 The front page of Heinemann's website is designed to attract attention

Skills check ▶▶

Refer to pages 285–286 for information on mind mapping.

? Think it over...

Whether this goes along with your recommendation or not, the Head of Sport has decided to introduce korfball on a trial basis and wants to arrange a meeting with students who may be interested in trying the new sport.

Get together with a group of your friends and brainstorm ideas for a 'catchy' phrase that will attract the attention of students and make them want to find out more. Use a *mind map* to organise your ideas.

Challenging a fixed idea

From time to time we come across people who have very fixed ideas about certain topics, but these ideas do not always agree with the widely accepted view on the same subject.

If you read a daily newspaper you will know that stories are often printed that cause a public outcry. When this happens, the story is followed by a series of articles and television and radio interviews where people have the opportunity to offer varying views on the topic. These people are challenging the original idea and presenting arguments based on evidence they have collected.

We are all free to express our opinions and to challenge the ideas of others, but we must support our point of view with true and relevant facts.

- Some radio stations raise issues of topical interest and invite viewers to phone, email or text their opinions on the matter being discussed.
- Many websites invite users to contact them with suggestions or complaints. The BBC website invites feedback from the public

Figure 1.16 Ideas are regularly contested in debates

not only on suggestions or complaints but also regarding factual errors. This allows someone to point out a mistake, but the validity of these comments must be backed up by evidence. The BBC is, of course, free to accept or reject these opinions.

? Think it over...

'Most people think that teenagers eat too much junk food and this is having an adverse effect on their behaviour.'

Do you agree with this statement? Discuss your ideas with a group of your friends and agree a list of arguments that you could put forward to challenge the statement.

Informing/enlightening

Many of the things we buy today come with a set of instructions, written to explain to the new user how the item works, how it is put together or how to care for it. Look in the information rack in your local library or post office and you will see leaflets that cover all sorts of subjects. The purpose of these is to make things clear to us or to let us know about something. They are written and presented in an unbiased, easy-to-understand style that passes information to the reader – but they do not represent anybody's personal views.

Persuading/convincing

Many businesses – both manufacturing and commercial – employ advertising agencies, whose job it is to persuade us to buy those businesses' products or services. Judging by the amount of money spent on advertising each year, it would seem that they are successful. Constant advertising ensures that products and services become household names. Before you know it, you have fallen into the advertiser's trap and parted with your money!

In order to persuade us to buy their products, companies tell us the benefits their products will bring to our lives and how much better these products are than the competition's.

Government agencies try to convince us that healthy eating is a good thing and recommend that we should eat five servings of fruit and vegetables each day. Similarly they try to convince us that smoking or excessive drinking is not good. To persuade us to change our habits, they must also tell us why! In order to be persuaded or convinced, we need to be provided with reliable facts and arguments that inform us of the advantages and disadvantages. Then we are in a position to make an informed decision.

Changing someone's mind

How often do you change your mind? Probably quite often! What makes you change your mind? What wins you over? Sometimes you will change your mind because of something you are shown or something you are told. If you are trying to make someone change his or her mind, your line of reasoning must be clear, concise and relevant to the purpose.

The target audience

When you are clear about the purpose of a document you intend to produce, you must ask yourself who is going to read it. In other words, who is the *target audience*? This might be the general public, colleagues at work who have some knowledge of day-to-day business operations, or specialists who are experts in a particular field. It could be a group of adults, young people or perhaps visitors from another country. You need to be able to produce documents that are directed towards different target groups in a way that will be helpful to them.

?₀Think it over...

Look at Figure 1.17, which shows pages taken from two different student books. Who would you consider to be the target audience for each book? Why did you reach that conclusion?

Figure 1.17 Pages from two different student books

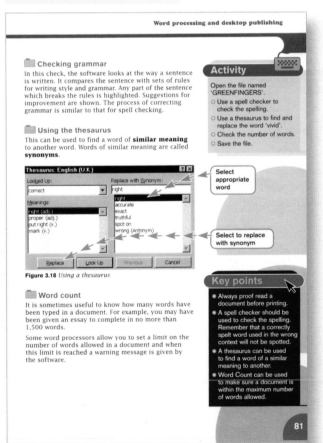

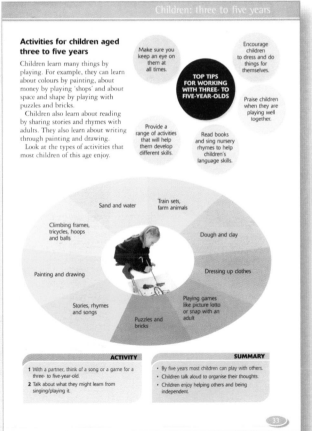

As you plan each project, always keep these questions about your readers in mind.

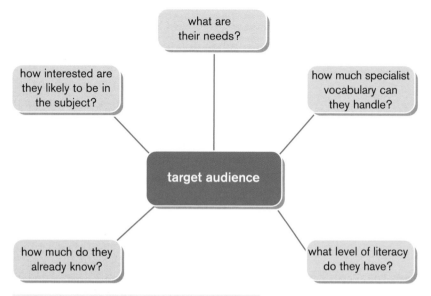

Figure 1.18 Thinking about your target audience

Go out and try!

Imagine you have been given the task of promoting an international junior korfball tournament in your home town. You have a variety of target audiences:
- VIPs – perhaps the mayor, whose presence at the event will add credibility to it
- the general public – who you must attract in order to sell tickets to help cover the costs of the tournament
- young people – who might be persuaded to take up the sport if they come along and watch some games
- potential sponsors
- travel and tour operators – who might wish to bring visitors from the other countries who have teams participating in the event.

Would you target each of these groups in different ways? How might your approach differ for each group? Work in small groups and brainstorm ideas. Compare your ideas with those of the other groups.

TiP

Sloppy work containing errors in spelling, grammar and punctuation is unacceptable, especially when you have tools such as the spelling and grammar checker to help you.

Presenting information

Most people with very basic skills can sit at a computer and produce pages and pages of text. The essential skill for you to develop is to be able to make full use of the ICT features available within the software to increase your document's *readability and effectiveness*.

The work you produce will give your readers an image of you or the organisation you work for, so it is essential that there are no mistakes and that it looks good. The initial impression of any document or on-screen publication is very powerful in swaying or influencing people. You must therefore make sure that on first glance your readers want to find out more.

A document's content and structure

If your document is going to be made up of more than just a few paragraphs of text, it is a good idea to sketch some designs on paper before you even turn the computer on. This can help you to visualise the finished document and will enable you to compare one possible design against another.

TiP

If you were to go for an interview you would normally dress to impress. Suppose you hand over a CV that is badly written, crumpled, stained, etc. What would that tell the interviewer about you?

Figure 1.19 Sloppy presentation style

Before you begin to draft any text to be included in your document you should consider the overall composition.

○ *What components are to be included?* Will there be text, charts, diagrams or graphics? If it's a slide presentation, will there be animation, video or sound? How can the message be conveyed to the audience in the most effective way? Will you rely on one component or combine two or three? Your final decision will obviously depend on whether your document will be published on paper or electronically, on the purpose, and on the audience.

○ *How will the key items be positioned on the page?* Think about headings or headlines, graphics, and buttons or other links. Remember that you want to maximise the impact of these elements in order to grab the reader's attention. It makes sense to think carefully about these features during the initial stages of planning. For example, from the reader's point of view it is useful if you position similar features in the same place on every page. This presents a consistent appearance and shows that you have given thought and care to the design.

○ *What is the relative importance of the various components?* The proportion of text to visual/audio information will probably depend on the target audience and their subject knowledge. It is often easier to learn about a topic by looking at pictures and listening to information rather than having to plough through pages of text. Make sure that any images you include are clearly labelled and positioned close to any text relating to them.

Writing style

Once you know the purpose of a document, who is likely to be reading it and the components you wish to include, you should be able to decide on a suitable writing style without too much difficulty. Good writing mostly depends on choosing the best style for the type of document you are producing so that you can get your message across in the most effective way.

Formal or informal?

Language can be *formal* or *informal*. Business correspondence is generally written in a formal style. Your aim then is to create the right impression to encourage the reader to read what you have to say.

TiP

Look at a wide selection of documents to get an overview of different writing styles. If you base your document on something similar, you should get the style about right.

A letter that begins

'Dear Sir, I refer to your recent advertisement in the Whychton Gazette for a travel consultant' is definitely more formal and more appropriate than 'Hey Mister Travelbug, I hear you've been looking for someone to do all your bookings and stuff and I'm just who you need.'

At other times a more informal language style might be appropriate or acceptable. A sentence that reads 'Travelbug are here to help you sort out your travel needs' is far more suitable and more likely to catch the reader's attention than 'The staff of Travelbug cordially invite you to attend their premises to discuss your travel requirements.'

Exactly where to pitch the level of language between formal and informal is not always easy to decide. As a rough guide, somewhere in the middle is pretty safe. Just remember to keep in mind the *reason* for the document and the *type of readers* and you should not find it difficult to produce a document that is entirely appropriate.

Simple or complex language?

If what you are writing is to appeal to a broad range of ordinary people, you should choose a straightforward and uncomplicated language style – one that can be understood by everyone.

If you are writing for a young audience, don't use words that they are unlikely to have heard before and so will not readily understand. On the other hand, if you are writing something of a more technical or specialist nature then it is quite likely that your language style will need to be more complicated. Even so, don't try to use complex language if you do not understand the subject well enough yourself, because you are quite likely to end up writing nonsense. If in doubt, stay on the cautious side!

✔ TiP

If you find it difficult to get the right words down on paper, try speaking them out loud first. More often than not you will find the sentences start to flow.

? Think it over...

Think about the writing styles you would use for the following:
- a letter to thank a relative for a birthday present
- a letter to the supplier of a faulty computer game
- a web page giving details of an art exhibition of work produced by students
- a letter applying for part-time work in a bookshop
- a leaflet advising students of various facilities available in a library
- a presentation to school or college governors designed to get their agreement to a group of students taking part in an international sporting event in France.

The tone

The tone you use can affect the way that people interpret your document. For example, if you feel angry about a subject, that anger may be reflected in the tone of your document and may prevent your readers from reaching an open-minded decision. In contrast, too much humour introduced into an important topic could give the impression that you are not treating the subject seriously – although a little humour might make a difficult or boring subject more interesting. You must learn to match the tone against both the purpose and the audience.

Presentation features

Remember that any document or publication that you produce is going to present an image of you. For this reason it is important to make good use of the presentation features in the software applications available to you. You will then feel good about the document you have produced.

Headings and sub-headings

Use headings and sub-headings to break a document down into sections, particularly if the document is long. This will help your readers (and you!) to navigate around the document and make it easier to read.

Layout and use of white space

Make full use of the available page or screen size to ensure that your documents are laid out clearly. It isn't always necessary to place text on every line of the page or screen. In fact, sometimes it is more effective to leave some areas clear – this is usually referred to as *white space*, although of course it might not be white! These clear areas can be a useful way of highlighting certain information.

Font type and size

It is usually accepted that most 'standard' documents – and particularly letters and reports – are produced in certain font types and sizes. The most common fonts are Arial and Times New Roman, simply because they are available on all modern computers. Arial is an example of a *sans serif* font, while Times New Roman is a *serif* font.

TiP

The rule-of-thumb to remember is: 'An uncluttered document is a clear document!'

Jargon buster

A **serif** is a small cross-stroke at the end of a main stroke in a letter.

Skills check ▶▶

There is more information on font type and size on page 91.

Times New Roman – Size 10	Times New Roman – Size 12	Times New Roman – Size 14
Arial – Size 10	Arial – Size 12	Arial – Size 14
Daves Hand – Size 10	Daves Hand – Size 12	Daves Hand – Size 14
Comic Sans - Size 10	Comic Sans - Size 12	Comic Sans - Size 14
Garamond – Size 10	Garamond – Size 12	Garamond – Size 14
Tahoma – Size 10	Tahoma – Size 12	Tahoma – Size 14

Figure 1.20 Different fonts and font sizes – which are serif and which are sans serif?

For printed documents the most common sizes are 11 and 12 point, but a slightly larger font size is helpful to very young or older readers because it makes the text clearer. Posters and flyers are easier to read from a distance if a much larger size of font is used.

As a general rule, do not mix several different font styles on the same document, or use too much decoration, such as WordArt. This can distract the reader from the purpose of the document.

Similar guidelines apply to screen-based publications, which also need to be clear and easy to read.

Line spacing

Text presented in single line spacing is the generally accepted standard for documents such as letters and reports. One-and-a-half or double line spacing can make text more prominent, especially if viewed on a screen or from a distance. Always keep the purpose of the document and the target audience in mind when considering which style of line spacing to use.

Skills check ▶▶

There is more information on line spacing on page 109.

Alignment

When we talk of alignment we are usually referring to the way paragraphs line up on the page. The default paragraph setting on most computers is left alignment, and this is used for most paper-based documents.

Full justification spreads the text between the margins and looks good for things like columns, newsletters and leaflets because the left and right margins remain straight and equal.

Centring of headings, text and whole paragraphs can successfully be applied to posters and flyers. In fact you might consider combining centred headings with fully justified paragraphs in documents such as flyers, to keep the margins even and present a unified appearance.

Skills check ▶▶

There is more information on alignment on page 95.

Skills check ▶▶

There is more information on bullets on page 97.

Skills check ▶▶

There is more information on text wrapping on page 128.

Bullets

It is sensible to use the standard bullet point for most text-based documents. This is represented by the character symbol •. You can be more imaginative with on-screen publications, advertisements, etc., but don't get carried away, and always keep the purpose of the document in mind.

Text wrapping

Various layout styles are available to wrap text around images and objects. Use these to avoid leaving unnecessary white space, but also remember the advice given earlier about the usefulness of some white space for clarity.

INTERNET FEATURE

SHOPPING WORLDWIDE
Background

According to many, shopping on the Internet is going to be a boom industry for many years to come. Experts have predicted that as our lives become even busier and the roads more congested, more and more people will switch to shopping over the Internet.

Although there are certainly signs that the number of people purchasing by this method is increasing, a degree of caution should be employed. This article sets out to discuss some of the implications of shopping over the Internet.

Using the worldwide web to source and purchase goods is not as new as you might think. It has been possible to purchase goods in this way for more than five years. However, during the last two years many new Internet stores have been created and many of our best-known retailers have invested heavily in websites. Is this really because large numbers of people are changing the way they shop, or is it because these retailers are frightened they may miss out?

Large sums of money have been invested in setting up brand new e-tailers, (the jargon used for

retailers who sell through a website). These companies exist purely to sell via the net. Although it is early days for these businesses it should be noted that few of them are reporting profits at present.

Many small specialist companies use the web to promote their goods which may be hard to find and highly sought after. It is, of course, possible to purchase from overseas which opens up many new choices for consumers.

Just how easy is it to locate goods and order through the Internet? Is it really time saving and convenient? Only time will tell in the long term, but we can look at how successful Internet shopping is today.

Supermarkets

Most of the leading supermarkets in this country are now offering an Internet service. You click onto the site, browse around a 'virtual store', choose the goods you require and then venture to the checkout. Here you check the goods you have ordered are correct, enter your credit card details and within minutes you should have received an order confirmation.

Many supermarkets offer same or next-day delivery but recent reports suggest that delivery is not always as reliable as one would wish. One tester stated that she was told there were no delivery slots free until the

following week! Not very useful if you need something for tea the same evening.

Other reports have claimed that orders have arrived incomplete or incorrect. On one occasion, the supermarket in question had to purchase some of the customer's goods from a nearby rival supermarket as they were out of stock!

Once the goods have been delivered to your door, they need to be checked against the order to ensure that the order is correct. If you have ordered a large number of items, this could take quite some time.

However, many users say that this service is 'the best thing since sliced bread'. They state that they save a

great deal of time and effort by using this service. It should be pointed out however, that most of the reports regarding Internet supermarket shopping have had testers ordering only a small number of items, say eight to ten. An average family's weekly shopping would include around fifty to sixty items. This in turn means that there is a much wider margin for error when receiving your order.

All in all, Internet supermarket shopping is obviously useful to many people, particularly those who make small, regular purchases. However, for those who enjoy picking out special offers and trying out new foods then the virtual supermarket will probably not be the most suitable way of shopping at present.

Specialist Items

If you have a hobby or interest such as collecting model cars or old records, then the Internet can be of great interest to you. You may find that companies who advertise in specialist magazines now boast a website, so you can immediately browse through their catalogue without delay. You will be able to e-mail these businesses with a question and receive a reply without too much delay.

You may also find that your hobby or interest has a chatroom. This

Sharon Spencer   4

Figure 1.21 An example of wrapping text around a graphic

Colour

Posters, flyers and screen-based presentations provide the best opportunities for using colour. However, if your viewers are likely to print out pages from a website you should make sure the font is dark so that it can be read when printed on white paper. Remember also that light text colours need to be presented on dark screens or dark paper.

Dark colours should be used on printed white paper.

Light text colours need to be presented against a
dark background to make them easier to read.

Paper-based documents are clearer to read and can be photocopied
successfully if the text is in black ink.

Tables

Skills check ▶▶

There is more information
on using tables on
page 112.

Numerical data is often easier to understand if it is presented in a
table, and lists of information can also be displayed in a table format
as an alternative to using tabs. Tables can provide a very adaptable
structure to help you present a wide variety of information. For
example, the questionnaire illustrated in Figure 1.6 on page 19 used a
table structure. Folded leaflets can also be produced in two- or three-
column tables. Remember too that you can remove lines from a table
and even include another table within a table cell.

Borders and shading

Skills check ▶▶

There is more information
on using borders and
shading on page 114.

A border and/or shading added to a paragraph of text
will make it stand out from the rest of the document.

You may choose to use borders in a table, or to remove them
completely. Use whichever style makes the table easiest to read.

You can be imaginative and apply different styles of lines to different
sections of a table, but don't get too carried away and detract from
its purpose. It is a good idea to check your document in Print Layout
view before printing to make sure the borders and lines are where
you expected them to be.

Use shading with care, especially if you are using a black and
white printer. Sometimes the shading can be so dark that the text
becomes unreadable. It can, however, be very effective to apply
dark shading to a selection of cells in a table and then to change the
font colour to white.

Jargon buster

Single-sided means that print appears on one side of the paper only. **Double-sided** means that both sides of the paper are used.

Skills check ▶▶

There is more information on setting margins on page 104.

Skills check ▶▶

There is more information on using tabs on page 100.

Margins

If you are producing a paper-based document that is to be printed single-sided, the left and right default margin setting of 3.17 centimetres (about 1¼ inches) in Word is quite suitable. If you are printing double-sided you might consider setting mirror margins (*inside* and *outside* instead of *left* and *right*) or, if the work is to be bound, you should set a gutter margin to ensure the binding doesn't cut through the text.

Tabs

Tabs provide a very useful way of lining up text across the page. Don't rely on the space bar because you will end up with an uneven line of text down the page. If you want to use tabs within a table, hold down the **Ctrl** key whilst using the **Tab** key.

Indents

A paragraph indent can be used to make a section of text stand apart from the rest of a document. There are three styles of indent that you might consider using, as shown in Figure 1.22.

This style of indent is called a **first line indent** because the first line of every paragraph is set in from the margin.
It can be used effectively to separate paragraphs of text if you don't wish to leave a clear line space in between.

This style of indent is known as a **hanging indent**.
It is often used in a document which has "side headings".
Each new heading starts alongside the margin making it clearer to read.

Sometimes a paragraph of text is indented within a document.

This paragraph has been indented from both margins.

It makes the paragraph stand out within the document.

Figure 1.22 Three styles of indent

Skills check ▶▶

There is more information on using columns on page 111.

Columns

Columns are generally applied to newsletters and leaflets, especially if the finished document is going to be folded. Work presented in columns usually looks more professional if you use fully justified margins.

To place text at the beginning of a new column, do not use the **Enter** key repeatedly to move it across! Instead, insert a column break by clicking on the **Insert** menu and selecting **Break, Column break**. Similarly, insert a column break if you wish to leave one column empty – do not rely on the **Enter** key.

NEWTOWN PRIMARY SCHOOL PTA NEWSLETTER

The PTA

All parents of Newtown Primary School are members of the PTA. The committee, elected by members, consists of 8 parents and 1 teacher representative. Committee members can serve for a maximum of 4 years. Meetings are held every 4 weeks and all members are welcome. The details of these meetings are displayed on the PTA noticeboard in the main school corridor.

The committee's officers comprise a chairperson, vice chairperson, treasurer and secretary. These posts are for a 2-year period. The officers must be serving on the committee and are elected by the committee members.

The main function of the PTA is to raise funds for the school. These monies help provide the more luxurious items such as IT equipment, musical instruments, library books and play equipment. It also subsidises school trips which means that trips are affordable by all. Funds are raised by 3 or 4 main events each year. These usually include a Christmas Bazaar, Summer Fete and Sponsored Spell. The children are actively involved in these events which prove to be educational and enjoyable.

As well as fund-raising the PTA also organises social events. Discos, barn dances, barbecues and quiz nights are a few of the events that have been held in the last few years. These are well supported and great fun.

If you would like to be involved in the PTA but haven't the time to join the committee don't worry! We are always looking for willing helpers to man stalls, make refreshments and, of course, wash up.

During the coming year we will need to replace 3 committee members as their children will be leaving the school. If you are interested in joining please contact Marge Lovell, the committee secretary.

Auction of Promises

Our next main fund-raising event should prove to be a great night out for parents and supporters of the school. We are holding an Auction of Promises on 23 March at 7.30 pm in the school hall.

The auction lots will consist of 'promises' made or donated by parents and local businesses. A promise can be anything from a pair of theatre tickets to receiving a freshly baked cake for a birthday party.

We have been given a number of promises but we could do with lots more. You can promise almost anything. Ideas include doing the ironing, walking the dog, looking after a pet hamster for a week, digging the garden, an evening's babysitting – whatever you can do. If you can persuade your company to give as well, so much the better.

We need to have your promise by the end of February as catalogues need to be collated. Please contact Jenny Riseman as soon as possible.

If you can't help, please attend the meeting as it should be lots of fun. Philip Malcolm, a local auctioneer, has kindly agreed to run the proceedings, giving his services free of charge. Refreshments will be available and there will also be a raffle.

Tickets will be available at the end of next week and will cost £1.50 per person.

School Clothing

We have been asked by the Headteacher to remind parents that we sell school clothing on Tuesdays in the dining hall.

From 3.30 pm to 4.15 pm you can purchase any of the school garments including sweatshirts, gym kit and polo shirts. These items are all embroidered with the school logo.

The garments are made from 100% cotton and we feel they represent excellent value for money. They are machine washable and can be tumble dried. These garments do not shrink and are very hard wearing.

We usually have all sizes in stock. Given below are examples of the low cost of these garments.

Item	Price
Sweatshirt	£9.50
Polo shirt	£5.00
Gym shirt	£4.50
Gym shorts	£4 00

Dates for your Diary

As well as the Auction of Promises we have some more events lined up for this term. On March 17 we will be helping with the annual Sponsored Spell. About a week beforehand your child will be given 20 words to learn and a test will be given on the day. Prizes are given for children who get all 20 words correct. Please help your child by sponsoring them per word. Last year we raised over £700.

A cake sale will be held on Friday 3 April. This is to tie in with the children's charity day. As you are aware, children are encouraged to raise money for a local charity and can help to do this by paying a fee to wear 'civilian' clothes on Charity Day. The proceeds from the cake sale will go to our local charity, the Homeless Shelter. Please send in cakes on Friday morning and come and buy after school at 3.30 pm.

Book week is another important event in our school calendar. This will be held the week beginning March 10. The PTA will be holding a book sale each day after school in the main hall. Please support this event by coming along and buying a book. The proceeds from the sale will enable us to purchase more books for the school library.

Figure 1.23 A multi-column newsletter – notice that each section starts with a dropped capital

✔ **TiP**

You can apply a dropped capital to the first letter in a paragraph through **Format**, **Drop Cap**.

Styles

If you look for the word 'style' in a thesaurus you will find a variety of alternative words such as *technique, elegance, flair, smartness, good taste,* and *design.* The Style feature therefore makes it simple to apply formatting styles to make your documents more interesting and stylish. You can apply paragraph styles, character styles, list styles and table styles to ensure that the style of presentation is consistent throughout a document.

Skills check ▶▶

There is more information on text boxes on page 119.

Text boxes

You can use a text box to position text anywhere on a page and can apply various effects from the *Drawing* toolbar. The use of these features can make a publication more interesting and professional. For example, you can use text boxes to label diagrams or add prominence to headings. In Figure 1.24 we have used three text boxes, changed the fill and font colours and applied a 3-D style.

Figure 1.24 Styles applied to text boxes

✓ TiP

If you wish to apply a water-mark as a background to a document, copy it into the header and then reposition and resize the image on the page. In that way you will be able to work on top of the image and it will appear on every page.

Skills check ▶▶

There is more information on headers and footers on page 107.

Headers and footers

Remember that anything inserted in a header or footer will appear on every page of the document. It is very useful to record the filename and date in the footer area of documents you are still working on.

Page numbering

Skills check ▶▶

There is more information on page numbering on page 108.

You should apply page numbers to multi-page documents. The bottom right-hand corner is a good place to put the number. Remember too that you can hide the number on the first page – this is especially useful when the first page is also the cover or title page.

Skills check ▶▶

There is more information on page breaks on page 106.

 TiP

A quick way to start a new page is to use the **Ctrl** *and* **Enter** *keys together.*

Skills check ▶▶

There is more information on image resolution on page 224.

Page breaks

Do *not* use the **Enter** key repeatedly to move text on to a new page. Instead insert a page break by using **Insert, Break, Page break**. Make sure headings remain with the following text, and try not to end up with just one or two lines of a paragraph on the following page.

Using images

It is very likely that you will include images in your final documents, so their *quality* is an important consideration. The skills section on artwork and imaging software introduces bitmap and vector images (page 224) and shows you why enlarging an image may impair its quality.

This section also compares the *file sizes* of various image formats and looks at the most appropriate format for print and screen-based publications.

Whatever you intend to do with graphic images, you must remember to keep in mind the overall purpose of the document.

Transferring information to different types of software

After carrying out research into a topic, it is highly likely that you will want to include the results in a document or presentation. Earlier in this unit you will have used a spreadsheet to help you analyse results, and may well have produced a series of charts or graphs. These can be copied and pasted into the new document or presentation.

Think carefully about any headings you want. For example, do you need to insert them in the spreadsheet software, or will you type them in under the chart or graph. If you paste spreadsheets, charts or graphs using the **Edit, Paste Special** function in Word and select the **Paste link** option, any subsequent amendments to the data in the spreadsheet will automatically be reflected in the pasted chart or graph.

Paper publications

Types of paper publications

Organisations use a range of styles of documents. These include

- letters
- reports
- leaflets
- newsletters
- posters and flyers.

We will look at each of these in turn.

Writing letters

A business letter is a formal, written communication from one organisation or individual to another organisation or individual. The first impression of an organisation is often established as a result of the letter sent out. In much the same way, organisations form an impression of you based on the letters you send them. Clearly then, a letter should be written in an appropriate style and be well presented.

Letter format

Jargon buster

The **house style** presents an easily recognisable look that creates an impression of a well-organised and efficient organisation.

Most organisations adopt what is called a *house style* to ensure that all their documents have a similar appearance. Many of these organisations have templates set up in their house style that employees are expected to use if they are writing letters. Nevertheless, each organisation has to rely on their employees' knowledge of how to compose a business letter.

Figure 1.26 (page 48) is a closer detailed look at one of the letters in Figure 1.25. This illustrates the most widespread style of layout and presentation. These are the main points to remember:

- Every line starts at the left margin – this is called *blocked style*.
- The only punctuation you will see is within the body or content of the letter. Notice that there are no commas or full stops in the reference or addressee details, nor after the opening or close. This style is called *open punctuation*.
- The postal town in the recipient's address is shown in capital letters with the postcode underneath (or on the same line if space on the page is tight).

Jargon buster

The **opening** is the line that starts with *Dear*. The **close** is the line, such as *Yours sincerely*, that comes before the signature.

Today, people with visual impairment can receive cassettes and CDs containing audio letters via the Internet. L-mail enables Internet users to submit typed text to its website, which is then recorded as an audio file and saved on the recipient's choice of media. There is a fee for using the service. Audio letters are posted from the UK to addresses worldwide. Braille letters can also be sent.

Think it over...

Figure 1.25 illustrates two letters produced in different writing styles.
- Can you identify the common features in each letter?
- What do you think is the purpose of each letter?
- Do you think the styles of the letters suit the target audiences?

Figure 1.25 Two letters produced in different writing styles

- Clear lines are left throughout the letter to separate the different sections or paragraphs. In most cases one clear line is sufficient. In order to leave enough space for the signature, five clear lines should be left. If a letter is short, you should leave bigger spaces so that more of the page is used – the spaces between the reference, date, addressee and greeting may be increased as long as the spacing is consistent. Within the letter itself you must keep to one clear line.

○ The close must match the opening. Did you notice that the two examples in Figure 1.25 are different in this respect?

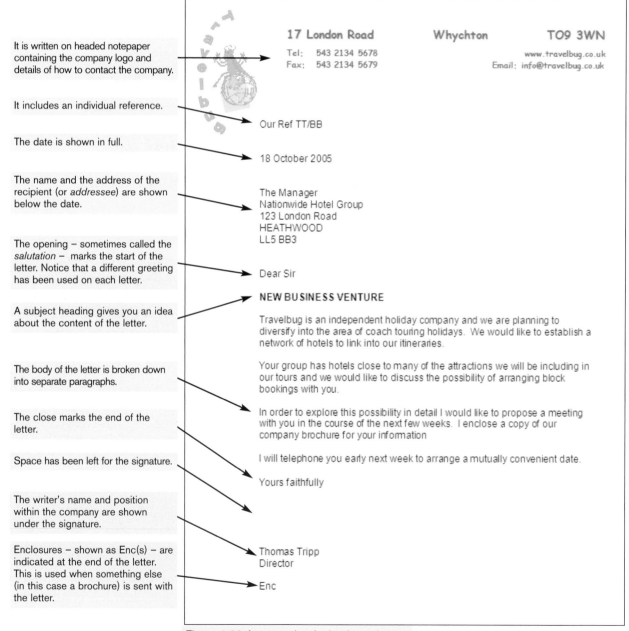

It is written on headed notepaper containing the company logo and details of how to contact the company.	**17 London Road** Whychton **TO9 3WN** Tel: 543 2134 5678 www.travelbug.co.uk Fax: 543 2134 5679 Email: info@travelbug.co.uk
It includes an individual reference.	Our Ref TT/BB
The date is shown in full.	18 October 2005
The name and the address of the recipient (or *addressee*) are shown below the date.	The Manager Nationwide Hotel Group 123 London Road HEATHWOOD LL5 BB3
The opening – sometimes called the *salutation* – marks the start of the letter. Notice that a different greeting has been used on each letter.	Dear Sir
A subject heading gives you an idea about the content of the letter.	**NEW BUSINESS VENTURE**
	Travelbug is an independent holiday company and we are planning to diversify into the area of coach touring holidays. We would like to establish a network of hotels to link into our itineraries.
The body of the letter is broken down into separate paragraphs.	Your group has hotels close to many of the attractions we will be including in our tours and we would like to discuss the possibility of arranging block bookings with you.
The close marks the end of the letter.	In order to explore this possibility in detail I would like to propose a meeting with you in the course of the next few weeks. I enclose a copy of our company brochure for your information
Space has been left for the signature.	I will telephone you early next week to arrange a mutually convenient date.
	Yours faithfully
The writer's name and position within the company are shown under the signature.	
Enclosures – shown as Enc(s) – are indicated at the end of the letter. This is used when something else (in this case a brochure) is sent with the letter.	Thomas Tripp Director Enc

Figure 1.26 An example of a business letter

Letter content

The first paragraph of a letter introduces the topic. You may be referring to a telephone conversation, a letter you have received or an advertisement you have seen. You are likely to start a letter with an opening sentence that begins like one of these:

> 'Thank you for your letter dated ...'
> 'I refer to our recent telephone conversation ...'
> 'I am writing to enquire ...'
> 'With reference to ...'

The next paragraph or paragraphs expand on the reason for writing. The final paragraph concludes the letter and often starts with a sentence like one of these:

> 'Please contact me if you would like further information.'
> 'I/We look forward to hearing from you.'
> 'Thank you for ...'
> 'I/We will contact you again in due course.'

Style of language

Business letters are written in a formal language style. Some organisations expect their employees to use the *plural* – 'we' and 'us' – if a letter is sent on behalf of the organisation. If you were writing a business letter as a private individual, you would use the *singular* – 'I' and 'me'. If you look at a selection of the business letters that come into your home you will soon get a good idea of the writing style to use.

Go out and try!

1 Write a letter to the marketing department of a car or bike manufacturer asking for information on their production processes to help you with a school or college project.

2 Write a letter to Tommy Tripp at Travelbug asking whether you can interview him at his office for information on a school or college travel project.

Skills Builder Task 4

At this stage you should be able to tackle the next task of the mini project introduced on page 13. Again, don't forget to study the scenario carefully so that you are clear about the project's objective.

Write a letter to parents and local residents to make them aware of the proposition from Prelude, also inviting them to attend a special meeting to discuss the proposal.

Assessment Hint

To achieve top marks you must do the following:

○ *Produce a range of suitable print and digital publications. The range will be specified in the summative project brief – make sure you cover the whole range!*

○ *Use appropriate structures and styles to ensure that the publication is suitable for the target audience and is the most appropriate way of presenting the information you are trying to get across.*
   - *Should the writing style and tone be formal or informal?*
   - *Should you be using simple or complex language?*
   - *How can the information be best presented (text, charts, diagrams, etc.)?*
   - *Did you check the spelling and proofread thoroughly?*
   - *Did you take account of feedback?*

○ *Respect copyright. If you quote someone's work, acknowledge it by using quotation marks and identifying the source.*

○ *Avoid plagiarism. Don't download material from the Internet or copy from a textbook and pretend you have written it. Finding a suitable source and identifying relevant information from that source does not make it your own work.*

Writing reports

A report is usually prepared following an investigation into something. The investigation might be necessary to find a way to put right a problem, to look at the possibility of introducing new working practices, or to pass on information following a study.

Report format

Reports are usually divided into four sections:

○ *Introduction*. This briefly explains the purpose of the report.

- *Methodology*. This provides details on how the investigation was undertaken.
- *Findings*. This records what the investigation revealed; that is, what the author found out about existing systems and practices. This section is often broken down under headings or divided into sub-sections.
- *Conclusions/recommendations*. The final section considers everything that has been found out. Where appropriate, the report will recommend suitable action to improve the situation that was investigated.

Unless it is very brief and simple, a formal report usually adopts a system known as *decimalised numbering*, as shown in Figure 1.27.

Skills check ▶▶

You can apply this style of heading numbering through **Format**, **Bullets and Numbering**, **Outline Numbered**. Refer to the exercise starting on page 98 in the word processing chapter to see how to do this.

? Think it over ...

Find out what report templates are available on your computer.

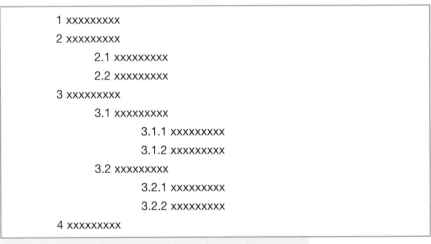

Figure 1.27 Decimalised numbering system used in reports

Creating leaflets

Leaflets are frequently used to provide general information. The leaflets illustrated here serve a variety of purposes.

For example, the leaflets in Figure 1.28(a) and (b) were issued on behalf of government departments, and are intended only to provide facts. Their purpose is to bring the public up to date on certain matters. The leaflet in Figure 1.28(c) was produced by the publisher of this book to advertise the range of products available and to persuade potential customers to purchase their books. Each of the leaflets in this series follows a similar design. Notice that different font sizes have been used on the inside pages for the headings.

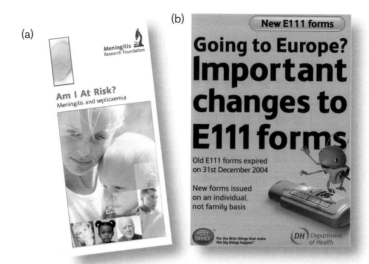

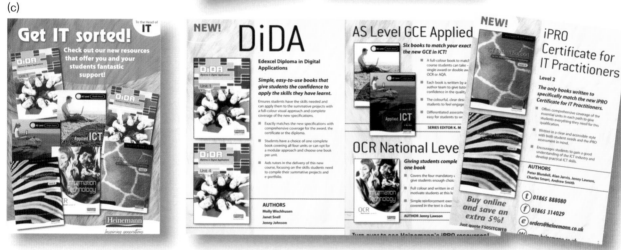

Figure 1.28 Leaflets issued (a) on behalf of a charity, (b) by The Post Office Ltd., and (c) by Harcourt Education Ltd.

Although these leaflets serve different purposes, there are some common features:

- They provide information on a product or service.
- They are colourful and include relevant images.
- The front page contains a short 'snappy' message.
- Leaflets from the same organisation adopt a distinctive house style.
- They include a contact telephone number or web address for further information.

Most such leaflets fold down to A5 size and open up to present more detailed information.

Front of sheet   **Back of sheet**

(a)

Back cover of Page 4	Front cover of Page 1

Page 2	Page 3

(b)

The page on view when opened	Back	Front

Inside 1	Inside 2	Inside 3

Figure 1.29 You must be careful to assemble the pages in the right order: (a) a single fold, and (b) a double fold

If you produce a leaflet it will probably be printed double-sided, and you must be careful to assemble the pages in the right order! Figures 1.29(a) and (b) show the principles of getting this right.

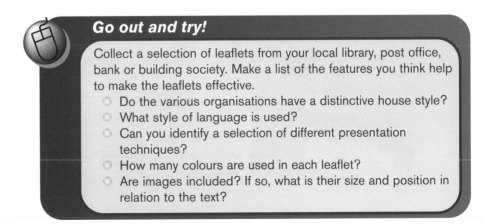

Go out and try!

Collect a selection of leaflets from your local library, post office, bank or building society. Make a list of the features you think help to make the leaflets effective.
- Do the various organisations have a distinctive house style?
- What style of language is used?
- Can you identify a selection of different presentation techniques?
- How many colours are used in each leaflet?
- Are images included? If so, what is their size and position in relation to the text?

Skills Builder Task 5

At this stage you should be able to tackle the next task of the mini project introduced on page 13. Again, don't forget to study the scenario carefully so that you are clear about the project's objective.

Prepare an informative leaflet for other students, to present the facts that you have discovered.

Creating newsletters

Newsletters are a popular way of keeping people up to date with what is happening in an organisation. Sometimes they are used within an organisation as a way of informing staff, and sometimes they are used externally to keep in touch with customers. They may be sent to customers in the post or by email.

A newsletter usually has a banner heading that stretches across the top of the page. The newsletter will have several headings and short paragraphs written on a variety of subjects, and will usually include relevant images. Newsletters are usually presented in columns.

Figure 1.30 A selection of newsletters

Posters and flyers

Posters and flyers are used to attract our attention. The message might be saying 'buy me', 'watch me' or 'visit me'. The poster or flyer will usually be short, to the point, eye-catching, colourful and designed to persuade the reader. They will almost certainly include a significant amount of white space and sometimes a border to help draw the eye towards the message.

Flyers frequently find their way on to our doormats or inside the local newspaper because they are a relatively inexpensive way for local companies to advertise their products or services. Occasionally new businesses opening in your area may hand flyers out to passers-by in an attempt to entice them into the shop.

Go out and try!

1 Collect some examples of flyers, possibly including those that are delivered to your own home. Compare the information they contain.
2 Look at posters on the noticeboard in your school or college, your library and other public places. What do you think makes some more effective than others?

✓ TiP

Flyers are usually printed on A5 paper. There is a very simple way to produce an A5 flyer if you do not have A5 paper. First produce the flyer to A4 size using your computer's word processor and then copy the contents onto page 2 of the document. Then select to print two pages per sheet, as shown in Figure 1.31. Each flyer will then be equivalent to A5 size after cutting.

Select this to print two pages per sheet.

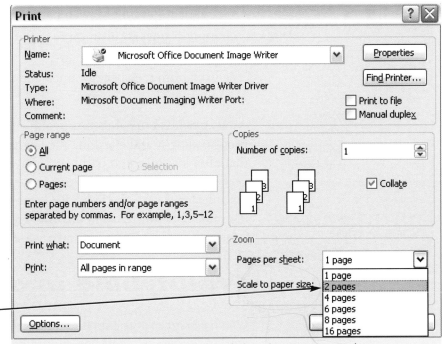

Figure 1.31 The dialogue box that allows printing of two pages per sheet

Skills Builder Task 6

At this stage you should be able to tackle the next task of the mini project introduced on page 13. Again, don't forget to study the scenario carefully so that you are clear about the project's objective.

Produce a poster to be displayed in local public places to invite the public to attend the special meeting.

On-screen publications

Nowadays more and more documents are being prepared electronically for viewing on a computer screen. These can be in many different formats, such as websites, slide presentations and information points.

The National Health Service (NHS) is introducing information points in a variety of public places including libraries, supermarkets and chemists, as well as hospitals. These are in the form of touch-screen computers and give a guide to common health problems.

Many on-screen publications use features that you will learn about if you study for the multimedia unit. These include

- creating and linking web pages or slides using hyperlinks
- using frames to position text and objects in a slide presentation
- using different backgrounds and transitions to enhance a multimedia production.

As always it is crucial to thoroughly test and check your work by proofreading it and checking the layout. It is essential that you ensure that all hyperlinks and pathways in a website or slide show work. It is very easy to edit your work and forget to ensure that the change has not interfered with the links. Remember also that not everyone uses the same computer system or browser. You must therefore check that your end product will work on a variety of systems.

Prototyping and testing

Quality assurance is explained in the chapter on standard ways of working (page 76), and you should be familiar with the many tools

TiP

Just because you can include video clips and blinking text, it does not mean that you should. Having too many features will detract from the information you want to put across, so use these effects only if they enhance your message. It is no use having too many gimmicks but little information.

that are available to help you present documents that are accurate and clearly understood.

However, these tools alone will not guarantee that you produce professional-looking documents. The final check must come from you – by carefully proofreading every document you produce to ensure that it is accurate, easy to understand, and says what you intended it to say.

You must remember to check everything you produce for

- accuracy
- clarity
- readability
- consistency
- layout
- overall fitness for its purpose.

In addition to the checks listed above, your on-screen publications will require additional testing to make sure that all the features (such as buttons and links) actually work, enhance the publication and do not detract by being too fancy or gimmicky.

When you are happy with your publications, remember to ask other people to review them for you. Listen carefully to any comments and feedback offered, and be prepared to modify your publications if necessary.

Skills Builder Task 7

At this stage you should be able to tackle these tasks of the mini project introduced on page 13. Again, don't forget to study the scenario carefully so that you are clear about the project's objective.

(1) Prepare a short presentation to be given at a special meeting of parents and governors to support the findings of your research.

(2) Design a single web page to present the same information you used for the poster and leaflet.

(3) When you have finished your project, review your work. Produce a short evaluation outlining how well it met the requirements explained in the scenario and any aspects you feel could be improved. Justify your comments. For example, if you say the poster is effective, explain what makes it effective. If something needs changing, explain why and how. You should attach to your evaluation the records of the feedback you received and the actions you took in response.

Skills check ▶▶

For more information on preparing your e-portfolio, including suitable file formats for saving your work, refer to page 298.

(4) Finally, present your work in an e-portfolio using suitable file formats. Your e-portfolio should show the following:
- Home page
- Table of contents
- Report outlining the results of your investigation using secondary sources
- Database reports
- Letter to parents and local residents
- Presentation to be given at the special meeting
- Poster informing the general public of the special meeting
- Leaflet for your peers.

You should also include some supporting evidence:
- Project plan
- References to secondary sources and links if appropriate
- Evidence of data collection using a survey
- Questionnaire used for the survey, including evidence of testing
- Evidence of the design and implementation of the database
- Spreadsheet showing the survey results and the formulas you used
- Storyboard for your presentation
- Review and evaluation of the project, including feedback from others.

★ Assessment Hint

You will find that the requirements for the e-portfolio, project planning, and review and evaluation are almost identical for each of the units.

PART 2

Section 1 Standard ways of working

While working on your projects you will be expected to use information communication technology (ICT) efficiently, legally and safely. So it is important to understand the need for good practice both in your studies and your future work. The guidelines in this section will ensure that you work with ICT in the correct manner and avoid problems that may cause you to lose your coursework at a crucial stage.

LEARNING OUTCOMES

You need to learn about

✓ file management

✓ personal effectiveness

✓ quality assurance

✓ legislation and codes of practice

✓ working safely.

File management

You may be absolutely brilliant at creating spreadsheets, designing complex databases and producing imaginative websites, but is your file management system just as brilliant? If it becomes so disorganised that you cannot remember what a file was called, waste time trying to find the right file, or have no backups, you may not achieve your qualification simply because you were unable to hand in the assignment!

In a work environment, your employer would become frustrated with you if, despite being very capable, you never met your deadlines because of poor file management skills.

So what do you need to do?

- Save work regularly and make backups.
- Use sensible filenames that indicate their contents.
- Use appropriate file formats.
- Set up folder structures.
- Limit access to confidential and sensitive files.
- Use effective protection against viruses.
- Use 'Readme' files where appropriate.

Saving work regularly and making backups

Probably the most obvious and simplest rule to remember is to *save* your work regularly. It is so easy to do, but just as easy to ignore!

You might be so busy designing a superb poster or flyer, thoroughly enjoying working with the graphics and using your imagination, that you forget to save the document. Then, when it is almost finished, you lose *all* the work because there is a power failure or you accidentally delete everything. If you are lucky, when you reopen the application software the file will be 'recovered' by the computer, but you can't guarantee this.

As well as saving your work regularly, it is important to keep backups. Information stored on a computer can be corrupted or lost through a power surge or failure, or by damage to or failure of the hardware. If 'disaster' strikes then you can use the backup copy. It might be slightly out of date, but at least it can be updated.

In business, backups are usually made at the end of every day. At the end of the week another backup is made, and stored separately from the daily backups. To avoid the damage done by viruses or other system-wide disasters, it is not enough to back up files into a different folder on the same computer – files should be regularly backed up onto external storage media. Here are some examples.

- *Floppy disks* are used for fairly small amounts of data – up to 1.4 megabytes (MB). However, files containing graphics quickly become too large to save on a floppy disk.
- *Pen drives*, *flash drives*, *keychain drives* and *memory sticks* (Figure 1) are portable devices that connect to a USB (*universal*

TiP

*As soon as you start a new file, save it with a sensible name. After that you can just keep clicking the **Save** icon 🖫 to update the saved version.*

TiP

It is a good idea to keep separate copies of your files each time you make major changes. This way you can record your progress in your e-portfolio. Also, sometimes you decide that an earlier version was better after all, so you can easily go back to it.

Figure 1 Memory sticks

serial bus) port of a computer. They can store between 32 MB and 2 GB (gigabytes) of data. These removable drives are the latest method of data storage and are automatically detected by the computer. You can use them to store or move files that won't fit on a floppy disk. These drives are extremely small so they are ideal for transferring files between work or college and home.

- A second hard drive can be installed, either within the same computer or externally. The disadvantage of a second internal drive is that it cannot be stored off-site or in a fireproof safe.

- *Zip drives* are another magnetic disk medium, with storage capacities of up to 250 MB. These are also suitable for domestic or small business use.

- *CD–R* (recordable) and *CD–RW* (re-writable) compact discs can store up to 700 MB. Most modern home PCs are now fitted with built-in CD–RW drives, making this a convenient and inexpensive method of backing up large amounts of data (such as the text and illustrations for this book).

- *DVDs* look the same as CDs, but can store up to 9 GB of data. Several different types of recordable DVD are available.

- A *tape streamer* is a magnetic tape generally used by large businesses. Cartridges that can store up to 300 GB of data are currently available. This method is the most affordable method of backing up the extremely large amounts of data required by large businesses. It also has the benefit that the tapes are small and, as they are removable, they can be stored off-site or in a fireproof safe. The disadvantage of making backup copies on magnetic tapes is that to recover a particular file you must search through the tape starting from the beginning until you reach the file you want – just like with a tape for music.

Jargon buster

One gigabyte (1 GB) equals **approximately** 1000 megabytes. One terabyte (1 TB) equals **approximately** 1000 gigabytes. Text of 500–600 pages uses about 1 MB of space.

By the time you read this book, the storage capacity of pen or flash drives, Zip drives and DVDs will probably have increased. Research the Internet (see Internet and intranets, page 241) to check out whether the storage capacities given above are still correct. Are there any new methods of backing up data?

Create a new word-processed document. Enter a bold heading called '**SW Activity 1**' and write a short paragraph describing the information you have found from the research in the task above.

 Save the file as 'Standard ways of working'.

Using sensible filenames

When working on any project, *as soon as you have written just a few words on the page*, save the file – naming it in such a way that it is easy to identify later. By having a sensible system for all your filenames, it is easy to find the right one without having to search through (and possibly open) several files.

Older operating systems limited filenames to eight standard characters, but modern operating systems allow more than enough space to identify each file clearly. That is why you were able to name your first file in this chapter 'Standard ways of working'.

With Microsoft operating systems, files usually have more characters, called *extensions*, added to the filename. Filenames are followed by a stop (.) and then an extension of up to three characters. When you save a file, the file extension is usually added automatically to the name you have given the file.

Why is an extension necessary? The extension tells the computer which program to start so that the file can be opened. For example, a Microsoft Word (word processor) document will be followed by '.doc', an Excel (spreadsheet) file by '.xls', and a bitmap graphic by '.bmp'. Another important extension is '.exe', which means an *executable program* – an application. Figure 2 is a list of the most common file extensions.

TiP

However clearly you name a file, it can still be difficult to find the right one later. So, for your coursework, it is excellent practice to include in the footer not only your name, the date and page number, but also the filename and path, like this: **F:\Digital Applications\Standard Ways\Standard ways of working.doc.**
Information on inserting footers appears on page 107.

Extension	Application or type of file
.bmp	Microsoft Paint bitmap image
.doc	Microsoft Word document
.dot	Microsoft Word template
.exe	Executable program
.gif	Graphics interchange format image
.html	Hypertext markup language (web page)
.jpg	Joint Photographic Experts Group (JPEG) image
.mdb	Microsoft Access database
.pdf	Adobe portable document format
.ppt	Microsoft PowerPoint presentation
.pub	Microsoft Publisher publication
.swf	Macromedia Flash vector graphics
.tiff	Tagged image file format image
.tmp	Temporary file
.xls	Microsoft Excel spreadsheet
.xlt	Microsoft Excel template

Figure 2 The most common file extensions

Choosing appropriate file formats

In most cases the file format is automatically selected by the software application. For example, Excel will always use the extension **.xls** for spreadsheets and **.xlt** for templates.

When saving images you often have a choice about which format to use. The screen shots for this book were saved in Corel PhotoPaint and the *TIFF Bitmap* format was chosen (Figure 3) as it allows 16.7 million colours. TIFF graphics are very flexible: they can be any resolution, and can be black and white, greyscale, or full colour. It is the preferred format for desktop publishing as it produces excellent printing results.

Assessment Hint

*Your e-portfolio must be saved by using the formats **.html**, **.pdf** or **.swf**, so that they are suitable for use on any computer.*

✓ TiP

Sometimes you may wish to rename a file – if you do, be sure to add the appropriate file extension to the new name, otherwise Windows might have trouble in opening it.

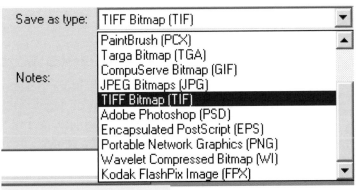

Figure 3 File formats

TiP

The JPEG format uses **lossy compression**, which means that you get very small files compared to TIFF format. However, they won't exactly match the original images, resulting in reduced quality.

TiP

The advantage of the PNG file format is that the compression of the file size is 'lossless' with full 24-bit colour, and can be read by a web browser.

Jargon buster

Files relating to one topic can be saved in a **folder** (Microsoft's name for a **directory**). This is an area on the computer's hard disk created in order to organise your computer's file system.

JPEG format is the most suitable format for full-colour photographs or greyscale images, such as scanned photographs, with large variations in the colour. It is not so effective for text, cartoons or black and white line drawings.

The maximum number of colours a *GIF format* image supports is 256, much less than the TIFF and JPEG formats. However, GIF format is significantly better for images with a just a few distinct colours, where the image has sharp contrasts – such as black next to white, as in cartoons.

PNG (Portable Network Graphics) is an alternative format for a variety of applications. PNG offers many of the advantages of both TIFF and GIF file formats, but the file size is smaller. This may be an important consideration, as your complete e-portfolio will be limited to a maximum file size.

Each project brief for your e-portfolio will specify acceptable file formats. These are likely to be PDF for paper-based publications, JPG or PNG for images, HTML for on-screen publications and SWF (Flash movie) for presentations, although may change depending on future developments. To convert files such as Word to PDF format you will require software such as Adobe Acrobat. Files that have not been created in HTML (or web format), can be converted from Word, Excel and PowerPoint by selecting **File, Save As** and choosing the **Web Page** format from the *Save as type* box. You can choose other alternative formats through this method and may need to experiment to find the most suitable one.

Figure 4 Saving a Word document as a web page

Setting up folders to organise files

If you save all your files in one place on a hard drive, it can be quite difficult to find the one you want. The solution is to create a main folder for a particular project, and then sub-folders to contain particular elements of the project. Figure 5 shows a main folder called 'Digital Applications', which contains a sub-folder called 'Standard Ways'. All the work for this book was saved in the main folder, and the material for this chapter was saved in the first-level sub-folder. As more and more chapters were written, more sub-folders were created to contain them. One sub-sub-folder is called 'Screen dumps', where all the screen shots were saved in TIFF format.

If you need to copy or delete files or folders, open Explorer as explained below, right-click on the relevant file or folder and select **Copy** or **Delete**. If you are copying the file or folder, move your mouse pointer to where you wish to place the copy, right-click the mouse and select **Paste**.

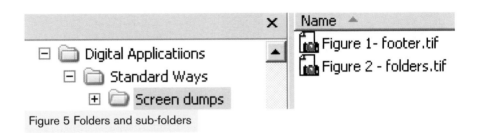

Figure 5 Folders and sub-folders

Go out and try!

1 To make sure you are organised right from the start, create the following folders and sub-folders to save the work you will produce for these chapters:

Standard Ways
ICT Skills
    Word-processing software
    Spreadsheet software
    Database software
    Presentation software
    Artwork and imaging software
    Digital sound
    Internet and intranets
    Email
    Website software
Creating an e-portfolio
Project Planning
Review and Evaluation

- From the **Start** menu, right-click the mouse and select **Explore**.
- In the left-hand pane, click on the drive where you want to create your folders.
- The contents of the drive are shown in the right-hand pane. Right-click in the white space of this section. The following menu appears.

✔ TiP

Organising your electronic files may vary, depending on the software available to you.

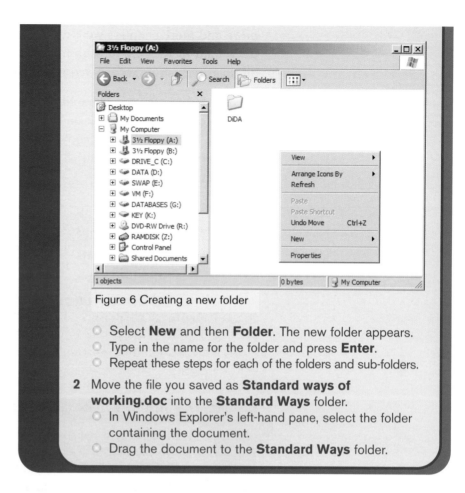

Figure 6 Creating a new folder

- Select **New** and then **Folder**. The new folder appears.
- Type in the name for the folder and press **Enter**.
- Repeat these steps for each of the folders and sub-folders.

2 Move the file you saved as **Standard ways of working.doc** into the **Standard Ways** folder.
- In Windows Explorer's left-hand pane, select the folder containing the document.
- Drag the document to the **Standard Ways** folder.

Open your file saved as 'Standard ways of working'. Create a new bold heading called '**SW Activity 2**' and write a short paragraph describing the skills you have demonstrated in this activity.
Save the file.

Limiting access to confidential or sensitive files

Most files saved on home computers are not particularly confidential or sensitive, but business data held on a computer can often be very confidential or sensitive. For example, medical records should not be accessible to the cleaning staff in a doctor's office or a hospital. Sometimes files in business may be confidential because the company is developing a new product and does not wish its competitors to know its plans.

There are several ways to protect confidentiality.

Using an ID and password to access the computer

Business systems are usually protected by passwords. Users should be prompted to change their passwords regularly. You will notice that when you enter the password, it is displayed as a series of asterisks (**************). This is to hide the characters and prevent anyone reading your password as it is shown on the screen.

Using a password to view data

Modern software systems also allow the use of passwords when saving files. You can set a password to open the file, or a password to modify it. Some people will be able to open the file to *read* it, but they will not be allowed to make any changes.

Many organisations *rank* data files according to their degree of confidentiality. Staff can be given different security levels or privileges which limit access to only *some files* or *some fields* within a file. This is a common method of protecting data and maintaining confidentiality.

Using additional security measures

Internet banking uses a series of security methods to ensure that customers' banking details are kept safe from unauthorised access. Apart from the usual login ID and password, the customer might have to choose another password or some memorable data. This time only certain characters are entered, changing each time the customer accesses the account. This helps to protect against *key loggers*.

For example, suppose the extra password is 'England'. You will see from Figure 7 that on this occasion only the first, fourth and fifth letters of the password are requested from the customer.

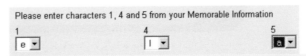

Please enter characters 1, 4 and 5 from your Memorable Information

1   4   5

| e ▼ | | l ▼ | | a ▼ |

Figure 7 Memorable data to protect confidentiality when using Internet banking

Another security measure is to limit the time that the file or web page can stay open for if it is not used. This ensures that the user's details are not left open on the computer if he or she forgets to close the file. A timeout message will appear (Figure 8).

Lloyds TSB online

Time out warning

You are not currently using Internet banking and for security reasons are about to be logged off.

Figure 8 A time-out warning

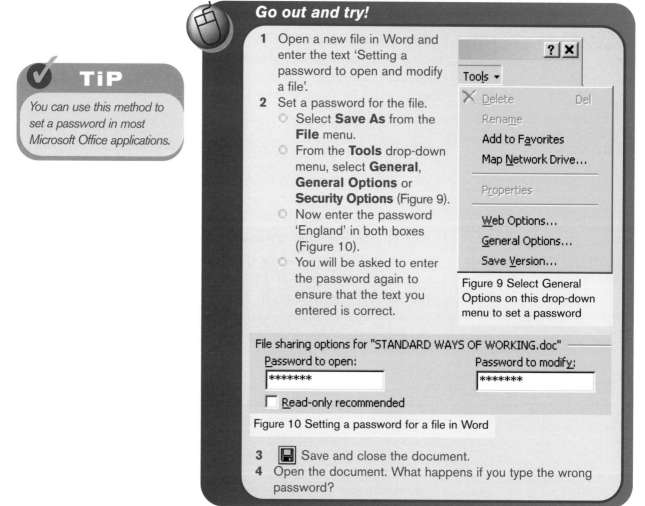

Go out and try!

1 Open a new file in Word and enter the text 'Setting a password to open and modify a file'.
2 Set a password for the file.
 ○ Select **Save As** from the **File** menu.
 ○ From the **Tools** drop-down menu, select **General**, **General Options** or **Security Options** (Figure 9).
 ○ Now enter the password 'England' in both boxes (Figure 10).
 ○ You will be asked to enter the password again to ensure that the text you entered is correct.

Figure 9 Select General Options on this drop-down menu to set a password

File sharing options for "STANDARD WAYS OF WORKING.doc"
Password to open: *******
Password to modify: *******
☐ Read-only recommended

Figure 10 Setting a password for a file in Word

3 Save and close the document.
4 Open the document. What happens if you type the wrong password?

Open your file saved as 'Standard ways of working'. Create a new bold heading called '**SW Activity 3**' and write a short paragraph describing the skills you have demonstrated in this activity. Save the file.

Using effective virus protection

A computer virus is a small program that has been developed by someone either for general mischief or to attack a particular organisation. The virus copies itself without the user intending it to, or even being aware of it happening until something goes wrong. Sometimes, in an attempt to prevent detection, the program will mutate (change) slightly each time it is copied.

Viruses can be spread by

- downloading software from the Internet
- opening an attachment to an email
- transferring files from one computer to another via a floppy disk
- using pirated software that is infected.

Your computer system is far less likely to be at risk if you

- use floppy disks only on one system
- delete emails from unknown sources, especially if they have an attachment
- regularly update your virus protection software.

Viruses can spread very quickly via email. A virus may cause problems such as clearing screens, deleting data or even making the whole computer unusable. Organisations treat the risk of infection very seriously, controlling emails and not allowing staff to take disks between work and home. Anti-virus software is therefore essential, both in business and for the home user.

Anti-virus software

Anti-virus software works by scanning files to discover and remove viruses, a process known as *disinfecting*. There are thousands of viruses waiting to attack your computer. More viruses are being written all the time, so it is essential to keep your anti-virus software up to date. As soon as a new virus appears, the anti-virus companies work to produce a *pattern* file, which tells the software how to discover and stop the virus. Symantec (Norton), McAfee, Dr Solomon's and Panda are some of the companies providing anti-virus software.

Using Readme files

Readme files are files on a CD that give an explanation about how to use the software on that CD. For example, the Readme file might

TiP

Make sure you run the anti-virus software at least once a week or set it to scan automatically.

TiP

It is essential to ensure that the virus definitions are kept up-to-date. Many anti-virus programs will remind you when this is necessary.

- explain how to install the software
- describe important points
- give specific information that might apply to your particular setup
- say how much hard disk space is needed to install and run the software effectively
- contain late-breaking information that reveals how reported problems with the software can be solved.
- link to additional resources.

Personal effectiveness

To ensure your own personal effectiveness in preparing your project, you must

- select appropriate tools and techniques
- customise settings
- create and use shortcuts
- use available sources of help
- use a plan to organise your work and meet deadlines.

We will look at each of these skills in turn.

Selecting appropriate tools and techniques

If you decide to use video editing in your project, but have access to a video camera and the video editing software for only one hour a week, you are not likely to be able to finish the project. Although it might be a very interesting, exciting project about which you are really enthusiastic, if you can't resolve the problem of access to the equipment it is better to think again and choose an alternative project or presentation style.

Once you have decided on the tools to use, you should then think about suitable, effective techniques that you could apply. For example, if you are fortunate enough to have a video camera and video editing software available, you may need advice on the best techniques to use when making the film. No matter how great your expertise in editing

TiP

Before you decide how to present the summative project for your e-portfolio, it is very important to think about the tools that are available to you.

Figure 11 Toolbars available in Word

the film, if the original material is poor because there has been too much zooming in and out, and the sweeps across the views were too fast, then the end product is unlikely to be successful.

Customising settings

You can use the Control Panel to personalise your computer in numerous ways, for example by

- changing the appearance and colour scheme of your screen
- choosing a screen saver
- selecting the date, time and language settings
- changing the mouse buttons for a left-handed person.

Software applications, such as Word, Excel and Access, come with default settings pre-installed during manufacture, but there are many ways to customise the settings to suit your needs. For example, you would probably find the *Standard*, *Formatting* and possibly *Drawing* toolbars to be visible. As you can see from Figure 11, in Word there are 16 toolbars in total – but if most or all of them were shown at once, the screen would be far too cluttered, with not much room left for the page you were working on! Instead, select the ones most useful to you. Word is often set with a default font of Times New Roman 10pt, which is too small for everyday use, so you might wish to set the default to a different size and style.

Go out and try!

Investigate the Control Panel on your PC to find out how to customise the settings.

- From the **Start** menu, select **Control Panel**.
- Investigate how to customise the **Date and Time**, **Display**, **Keyboard** and **Sound** settings.

(a)

Open your file saved as 'Standard ways of working'. Create a new bold heading called '**SW Activity 4**' and copy the table shown below. Include a screen shot of the item with an explanation of how to change the settings. Save the file.

Desktop setting	Screen shot	Explanation of how to change the settings
Mouse		
Volume control		
Icons		
Cursor		
Colour scheme		
Resolution		
Screen saver options		
Date and time		
Office Assistant		

Figure 12 Record of your customised settings

Creating and using shortcuts

Every time you click on an icon on a toolbar – such as save or print – you are using a *shortcut*. Using the print icon allows you to print the document in a single step. If you use **File**, **Print** and **OK** it is at least three steps – but you might want to choose this method if you want to print two or more copies, or only certain pages.

Each of the toolbars has a list of shortcut icons, but only those most frequently used are automatically visible. You can choose to add any others that you find useful. For example, if you frequently send documents as attachments to an email, you might wish to add the relevant icon to the toolbar.

(b)

Shortcuts can also be placed on the desktop. No doubt you are familiar with using shortcuts to software applications – see Figure 13(a). However, you can also choose to create shortcuts to files or folders that you use regularly. For example, a shortcut to the folder containing your work for this qualification might prove useful – see Figure 13(b).

Figure 13 (a) Shortcuts on the desktop to software installed on the computer. (b) A shortcut to files for this book

Go out and try!

1   Add icons and shortcuts to your toolbar.
- Open Word and from the **Tools** menu, select **Customise**.
- Select the **Commands** tab.
- From the **Categories** menu, select **File**.
- Scroll down to **Mail Recipient (as Attachment)** by highlighting the icon and dragging it onto the toolbar.
- Follow the same method to add a **Go To** button (under the **Edit** category) and **Full Screen** button (under the **View** category) to your toolbar.
2   Select three other icons of your own choice to add to the toolbar.
3   Customise your desktop by adding shortcut items to software applications that are not already available.
- From the **Start** menu, select **Programs, Microsoft Office** and then whatever program you wish to create a shortcut to.
- Hold down the **Ctrl** key and drag the icon onto the desktop.
- Release the **Ctrl** key and a shortcut is created.
4   Customise you desktop by adding shortcuts to files or folders you use frequently.
- In **My Computer**, find the file or folder for which you wish to create a shortcut.
- Right-click on the icon and select **Create Shortcut**.
- A shortcut will be created in the same folder.
- You can now move the shortcut to the desktop by dragging it from the folder onto your desktop.

Open your file saved as 'Standard ways of working'. Create a new bold heading called '**SW Activity 5**' and write a short paragraph describing the skills you have demonstrated in this activity. Save the file.

Assessment Hint

Don't be afraid to ask for help, but do remember that the project must be your own work. On the other hand, don't embark on a project that is too complex in case you can't find the help you need.

Getting help

There will be a variety of sources of help available to you, and it is a good idea to take advantage of them. You may find help through

- software help files
- textbooks
- your teacher
- specialist staff within your school or college

- your peers (who may be more knowledgeable about some aspects of the software, whereas you may know more about other aspects and can offer them help in return)
- family or friends who are experienced in the project you are undertaking.

Using a plan to organise work and meet deadlines

In order to complete your e-portfolio you will have to undertake a number of tasks, gradually building up the content. All the various sections of the e-portfolio will need to be completed to a deadline.

When the final deadline is a long time ahead, it is all too easy to keep thinking there is no rush, and then find you are trying to do ten things at once and cannot possibly finish everything in time! Therefore it is essential to think about all the various items that will go into the e-portfolio and then plan a schedule of your work.

Remember that *it always takes longer than you think*, so make sure you plan to finish well before the final deadline, to allow for all those unexpected delays!

Skills check ▶▶

Information on how to plan and organise your work is presented in more detail in the chapter on project planning (page 279).

Quality assurance

To ensure that your work is accurate and effective, you will need to
- use tools such as spelling and grammar checks, and Print Preview
- proofread your work
- seek the views of others
- check your research.

Using spelling and grammar checks and Print Preview

Spellcheckers

Spelling errors spoil your work, so always use a *spellchecker* to detect words spelt incorrectly and repeated words (for example, 'and and'). Spellcheckers are available not only in word processors, but also in most other applications such as spreadsheets and email programs. Spellcheckers compare the words you have written against a list in the computer's dictionary, then any words not matching are queried and possible alternatives are suggested.

TiP

Be aware that many computer programs use American spellings of words. These are often slightly different from the British spellings.

Figure 14 Adding a word to the spellchecker dictionary

But beware! Although the spellchecker is an excellent tool, it does not understand what you are trying to say and so it can be wrong. This means that *it is still important for the operator to have a reasonable level of spelling!* For example, it will not correct 'whether' for 'weather', or 'to', 'too' or 'two' used in the wrong place.

Sometimes a spellchecker will suggest that a word is incorrect when you know that it is correct. The dictionary will include common names such as 'Smith' but not unusual names such as 'Tenterden', which is a village in Kent. For this the dictionary suggested three alternatives (Figure 14), but the name was spelt correctly.

If you are likely to use a particular word frequently, then it is worth adding it to the dictionary. You can right-click on the word and select the **Add** option. In future the spelling checker will accept the word.

Sometimes words are indicated as incorrect because the language of the spellchecker is set to English (US) not English (UK), so it's worth checking. Select **Tools, Language, Set Language** and choose **English (UK)** and **Default** (Figure 15).

Figure 15 Setting the language that Word will use for its spellchecker

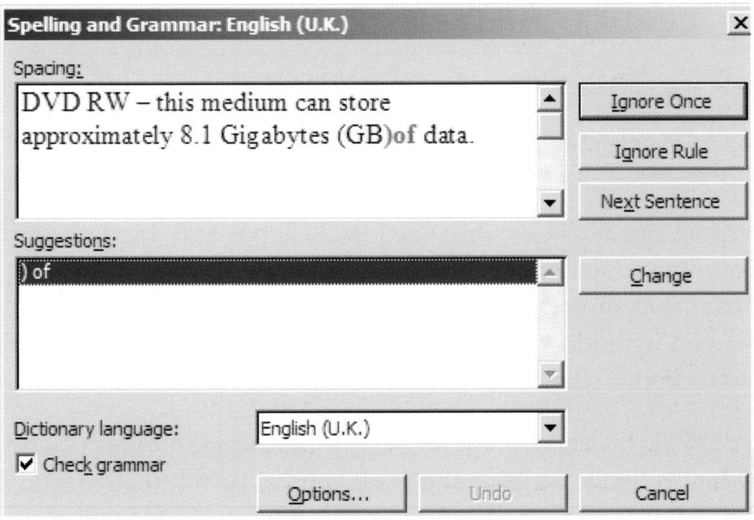

Grammar checker

The *grammar checker* can be more complicated and difficult to use than a spellchecker, and therefore tends to be rather less popular. As a starting point, the best way to use a basic grammar checker is as a tool to draw your attention to possible mistakes. It can be very useful for finding typing errors; such as the one shown in Figure 16, where

Figure 16 The grammar checker showing that there is no space after the bracket

there is no space after the closing bracket. At other times the suggestions may not be clear, so *think about* the suggestions made – the final decision is yours.

Print Preview

Before sending your work to the printer, it is a good idea to check it in Print Preview, which you will often identify poor layout that can be corrected before printing. This saves time and prevents you wasting paper.

When the author of this chapter used Print Preview at this point, it revealed a blank page that hadn't been noticed, which would have interfered with page numbering. It was an easy matter to delete the page before printing the file.

Proofreading your work

TiP

Proofreading isn't the most popular task, but it is important. You might discover quite silly errors, or an explanation that doesn't quite say what you intended. Correcting it before handing in your assignment or course-work might make all the difference to your final grade.

Even though you read your work on the monitor screen, it is surprising how often errors can be missed that the spelling or grammar checks have not shown up. In addition, you often find that although you were clear in your mind what you wanted to say, on re-reading the text you realise it is muddled, or you haven't fully explained the topic.

As authors of this book we received the proofs (the first copy of the book as it would look when finally printed) and we had to check that everything was correct, including the page layouts. At this stage we made some changes to our original work, not because it was necessarily wrong, but because it wasn't as clear as we wanted it, or it needed to be a little more detailed.

Seeking the views of others

TiP

Do ask someone else's opinion of the work you have produced for your e-portfolio – and do take note of the comments made. A critical evaluation of your project should be viewed as helpful advice to enable you to improve what you have done, not as a negative criticism.

Once you have an idea about the project you wish to undertake, it is excellent practice to ask other people what they think of the idea.

When writing this book, we discussed the syllabus and decided which of us was going to undertake which sections. We also brainstormed ideas about what should be included, and the presentation. Each one of us came up with ideas and suggestions, and together we produced (we hope!) a better result than if we had worked separately.

We also read each other's material and often asked colleagues to read what we had written. As an author you can be 'too close' to your own project to spot minor errors, whereas someone independent notices odd little mistakes, or a paragraph that is not clear. These can be edited to improve the final version. It is very important to keep draft versions of your work so you can show changes made as a result of comments from others.

Authenticating your work – checking your research

In general, textbooks are likely to contain reliable information because they will have been written to provide students with the information they need for a course they are studying, and are published by reputable companies. If it became obvious that an author or publisher was producing unreliable textbooks, they would soon go out of business: no one would buy their books.

Probably, by the time you read this book, information such as the amount of data a memory stick can hold will have changed. This does not mean that it contains deliberate misinformation – it's just that technology advances. If you do make use of that kind of data given in a book then it would be wise to check whether it is still accurate.

Figure 17 Discussing your work with other people

As you are well aware, the Internet is an amazing tool to use when researching almost any topic you could think of. It is, however, all too easy to drop into the trap of *believing everything on the Internet is accurate and reliable*. Unfortunately, that is not the case. Anyone can set up a website and put information on that site. Sometimes the author genuinely believes that the information posted is authentic or accurate, but sometimes the author wishes to deliberately mislead. Therefore, when using websites to obtain information, it is very important to use sites – such as those of the BBC or other well-known organisations – where it is likely that information given will be authentic.

Legislation and codes of practice

To ensure that you comply with legislation and codes of practice relating to the use of ICT, you will need to

- acknowledge your sources
- avoid plagiarism
- respect copyright
- protect confidentiality.

Acknowledging your sources and avoiding plagiarism

In order to complete your portfolio evidence you will need to undertake research. This may be from books, from newspapers or journals, from the Internet, or from people through surveys, questionnaires or face-to-face discussions. It is essential that you acknowledge where you obtained this information – your *sources*.

In some cases you may have to gain permission from the author, artist or relevant organisation to use the material. You should also include a *bibliography* of books, journals, articles and websites that you have found useful in your research.

People may copy original work and present it as their own. This is much easier to do from ICT systems (and especially from the Internet) than it is from a paper-based source such as a textbook. This is called *plagiarism* and, because it breaks copyright law (explained opposite), it is a serious offence.

It is quite acceptable to *quote* a reasonable amount of someone else's work, as long as you put inverted commas (" ") at the beginning of the text and at the end, and identify the original author, the book, web address or newspaper where you found the information.

Jargon buster

A **bibliography** is a list of sources of information that were useful when undertaking your research, and helped you to form your own opinions when writing an essay or producing the e-portfolio. For example, if you have a project to design a website, you might study other websites first to help you decide what makes an effective site and what doesn't.

The bibliography should include enough information for other people to be able to find the same source you used: the book, journal or newspaper, title of the article, author, date of publication, and web address.

Assessment Hint

*Note that your portfolio evidence will **not** be acceptable if it is a succession of quotes from other people, with very little original effort on your part.*

Think it over...

Check out the sources that we might have used when writing this textbook.

Open your file saved as 'Standard ways of working'. Create a new bold heading called '**SW Activity 6**' and write a short paragraph explaining what you have learned about plagiarism and acknowledging sources. 🖫 Save the file.

Respecting copyright

You are probably familiar with *copyright* warnings at the beginning of books, rental videos and DVDs, when there is a statement along the lines of *'All rights reserved. No part of this publication may be reproduced or transmitted, in any form or by any means, without the prior permission of the publisher.'* This is also true for most computer programs, published text and images.

Check for the symbol ©, followed by a date and sometimes a name, as shown at the beginning of this book. This indicates that the work is covered by copyright. It is very important to understand what copyright means and to respect copyright law (Figure 18).

- The Copyright Designs and Patents Act 1988 was originally set up in order to protect the work of authors, artists and composers from being reproduced or copied without permission.

- Current European copyright law extends for 70 years after the death of the author/creator. During this period, the work (book, work of art, software, photograph, music score, etc.) may not be reproduced without permission.

- This original Copyright Designs and Patents Act was in existence long before computers were invented. It has subsequently been extended to include computer software, making it illegal to copy applications without permission from the copyright holder.

Figure 18 Facts about the Copyright Designs and Patents Act

When you buy computer software it generally comes with a *licence* that allows you to install, use, access, display or run just one copy of the software on one computer and one notebook. Your school or college will have purchased a network licence in order to be granted permission to run the software on all of its machines.

Imagine a small business that started with just one computer. The owner bought the software for that computer and will have the necessary licence. As the business expands, he might decide to install a network and use the same software on the network, forgetting to buy a new licence. He has in fact broken the law, even though it was not intentional.

This law affects everyone who owns a computer. You must not let other people borrow your software to install on their computers. Similarly, you should not borrow software from a friend and install it on your computer. The software houses have, after all, invested a great deal of time and money in order to develop the software, so you are stealing from them by not paying for the software. It's no different from going into a shop and stealing a box of chocolates or a DVD.

In order to help protect software copyright, the Federation Against Software Theft (FAST) was set up in 1984 to investigate software piracy. The federation will prosecute when instances of illegal copying of software come to their attention. Be warned!

Go out and try!

In Word, click the **Help** menu and choose **About Microsoft Word**. Here you will find details of the licence holder and a product registration number. It also carries a strong warning. What does the warning say?

Open your file saved as 'Standard ways of working'. Create a new bold heading called '**SW Activity 7**' and write a short paragraph explaining what you have learned about copyright. Save the file.

Protecting confidentiality

The Data Protection Act of 1994, which was updated in 1998, was introduced to deal with the increasing amount of personal data being held on computers and the potential misuse of that personal data. Think of the many different organisations that hold computerised records containing details of our personal lives, school records, employment history, financial and medical records, criminal activities, etc. Under the Data Protection Act, these organisations must ensure that the data remains confidential. They must also allow people to access the data that is being held about them, in return for a small administration fee.

Both employers and employees have a responsibility under the Act to ensure that personal information is not disclosed, however

Skills check ▶▶

The information on confidential or sensitive files on page 68 is also relevant here.

- Passwords should be kept secret. A note stuck to the side of your computer is not a sensible way to remember your password!

- Personal information should not be passed on to third parties at any time. Imagine a situation where an insurance company employee had access to personal information. Think of the consequences if a list of addresses and details of valuable house contents fell into the wrong hands.

- Staff working with confidential data must be very careful not to disclose personal information during a conversation, however innocently.

- Computer screens in public places – such as a doctor's surgery – should not be visible to the general public. It could be very unfortunate if somebody waiting at the reception desk read personal and confidential information about another patient.

Figure 19 Facts about passwords

innocently. Staff must be aware of straightforward things they can do to protect the confidentiality of the data. Examples are described in Figure 19.

Apart from personal information, a commercial organisation will want to keep information about the company confidential. They do not want their competitors finding out how well or badly they are doing, and what new products or designs are being prepared.

Organisations have always been at risk from dishonest staff, but the main difference since the arrival of computers is that it is so much easier to obtain the information – you do not even need to be in the room or the building! Inevitably there has to be trust in and reliance on the users of ICT, especially in a business environment. In fact most people are honest and have no intention of defrauding their employer or disclosing confidential information.

It is essential to take security issues seriously, so that you do not *unintentionally* give someone else access to uncensored or private materials. Also, if you *accidentally* discover uncensored or private materials, you must not take advantage of the opportunity, and it may be appropriate to report that a breach of security has occurred.

Naturally we all chat about our jobs, but it is important to know which information should be kept to ourselves, and when it is OK to talk about something to a friend or relative. If in doubt then keep quiet.

Working safely

Employers are responsible for promoting health and safety in the workplace. However, each employee also has the duty to take sensible precautions. For example, if you spend a lot of time using a computer, you may tend to develop backache, eyestrain or repetitive strain injury, but good working practices will greatly reduce the risk of suffering from such problems. It is important to

- ensure that the positioning of hardware, cables and seating is correct
- check that the lighting is appropriate
- take regular breaks
- handle and store media correctly.

Positioning hardware, cables and seating

Desks should have a non-reflective surface and be at the correct height with sufficient space for a computer, mouse mat, telephone and supporting documents. There should be enough space around the desk for you to change position and vary your movements. It may be beneficial to use a wrist rest to support your wrists.

The ideal working position is to sit with your eyes level with the top of the screen, the small of your back against the chair, and your feet flat on the floor (Figure 20).

Figure 20 The fundamentals of good posture at a computer workstation

Since we all come in different shapes and sizes, it is important to use a chair that can be adjusted to suit the user. A good computer chair will have five feet with castors to increase stability and to allow freedom of movement. You will be able to adjust the height of the seat to suit your own height, as well as the position and tilt of the backrest in order to support your back. If you are short and your feet don't reach the floor, you can ask for a footrest to be provided so that you can support your feet and legs.

Cables should be correctly and safely positioned where no one can fall or trip over them. They should be securely fastened, usually inside trunking that is attached to the walls. They should *never* be trailing across the floor.

Using appropriate lighting

The ideal position for the computer monitor is at right-angles to a window. In order to keep sun off the screen and help reduce glare, blinds should be provided at the windows. If glare is a problem then an anti-glare shield can be fitted. The office should be well lit and the lighting should offer a contrast between the screen and surrounding area. If the light is too dim, documents will be hard to read, leading to eyestrain. If necessary, adjust the brightness of the screen in response to changes in light.

Taking regular breaks

Bad posture is the main cause of backache. If you work *continuously* at a computer monitor you should be allowed to take a short break (say 5–10 minutes) away from the screen after an hour's *uninterrupted* screen or keyboard work. Ideally your job will involve a variety of tasks so that this situation will not arise in the first place.

Handling and storing media correctly

Think it over ...

How safe is your working environment at home? What could you change to improve it?

It is important to know how to protect the media you are using, by handling and storing them correctly. Care should be taken when handling floppy disks, CDs and DVDs in order to protect the data. Store them in protective cases to keep them clean, away from dust and moisture. Avoid touching the surfaces, and keep them away from extremes of temperature.

Open your file saved as 'Standard ways of working'. Create a new bold heading called '**SW Activity 8**' and insert a table with three columns, headed 'Health and Safety', 'Good Practice' and 'Bad Practice'. In the first column, enter a checklist of the health and safety issues identified in this section of the chapter. Check out the computer lab at school or college and tick the relevant column where health and safety issues are good or need to be improved.

For any items that you have put in the bad-practice column, explain what the problem is and what needs to be done. You might like to work in pairs for this activity.

🖫 Save the file.

Section 2 | ICT skills

Word-processing software

If somebody asked you 'What is word-processing?' you would probably describe it as *the process of creating, storing and editing text-based documents*. While you would be quite right in saying this, in fact word-processing offers so much more.

Word-processing is one of the most effective ways of communicating information to other people through paper-based documents such as letters, reports, leaflets, newsletters, posters and flyers. In fact, effective word-processing skills also underlie successful communication through on-screen publications such as presentations or web pages.

Your word-processing skills are a valuable asset that you will make use of throughout your student and adult life. Word-processing is more than just sitting down at a computer and producing a document without a second thought. It is the skill of designing a document to convey specific information to different groups of people.

LEARNING OUTCOMES

You need to learn about

✓ entering, cutting, copying, pasting and moving text

✓ formatting text

✓ using paragraph formatting features

✓ using page formatting features

✓ using tables

✓ creating, selecting and inserting components

✓ using images/objects

✓ using spelling and grammar checkers

✓ using mail merge.

DiDA

Entering, cutting, copying, pasting and moving text

Entering text

Text is keyed in (or *entered*) via the keyboard. When a word will not fit on the end of a line, it is moved on to the next line. This feature is called *word wrap*, and the word processor automatically inserts *soft returns* at the end of each line. These soft returns are adjustable and will move within the document if necessary – such as when you insert an extra word or two in a paragraph or decide to delete some text.

You only need to use the **Enter** key when you want to start a new line, perhaps after a heading or at the start of a new paragraph. The returns that *you* put into a document are called *hard returns* and they are not adjustable by the software. If you display the formatting marks in a document by selecting the **Show/Hide** icon on the *Standard* toolbar, the ¶ character identifies all hard returns.

As you enter text, there are some basic steps you can take to improve the general presentation of the document:

- For most text-based documents, a font size of 11pt or 12pt will be appropriate.
- Remember to leave one clear line space (achieved by pressing the **Enter** key twice) after a heading and between each paragraph. Look at Figure 21, where the ¶ symbol shows that the **Enter** key has been used.
- Nowadays it is common practice when using a word processor to leave only one space following a sentence. However, in the days of the typewriter, it was standard practice to leave two spaces following any punctuation at the end of a sentence. There are many people today who feel that using two spaces between sentences makes your text easier to read because the sentences stand out clearly. You must make your own decision or follow the guidance from your teacher/tutor.
- Leave one space after all other punctuation.
- If possible, use a *fully blocked* style of presentation when producing letters, reports, etc. This means that everything starts at the left-hand margin. Figure 21 is an example of fully blocked working.

Jargon buster

A manual typewriter has a **carriage return key**, which the typist must press between lines to return the carriage to the left of the paper. Because of this the **Enter** key is sometimes called the **Return** key, and the hidden characters it inserts into documents are called **returns**.

Skills check ▸▸

Refer to page 91 for more detailed information on font sizes.

 TiP

If you study DiDA Unit 4 you will learn how to use styles to add space after headings and between paragraphs automatically.

88

```
Travelbug¶
¶
17·London·Road¶
Whychton¶
TO9·3WN¶
¶
Tel:··→543·2134·5678¶
Fax:·→543·2134·5679¶
Email:→travelbug@userve.co.uk¶
¶
¶
¶
There·is·so·much·to·see·and·do·in·Brussels·that·a·weekend·just·won't·be·long·enough!¶
¶
There·are·over·30·museums·to·visit,·fine·restaurants·and·bars,·shops·selling·anything·
from·high·fashion·to·antiques·to·sophisticated·chocolate·creations...Browse·the·open-air·
markets·or·stroll·around·the·magnificent·cobbled·Grand·Place.·¶
¶
A·visit·to·Brussels·isn't·complete·without·a·visit·to·the·famous·Manneken·Pis·which·can·
be·guaranteed·to·draw·a·crowd.¶
¶
Travel·by·Eurostar·from·Waterloo·and·arrive·in·Brussels·in·2·hours·20·minutes...Selected·
services·also·available·from·Ashford·International·Station·in·Kent.¶
¶
Prices·start·at·£125.00·for·2·nights.¶
```

Figure 21 An example of work presented in a 'fully blocked' style

Cut, copy, move and paste

A significant benefit of word processors is that they let you cut, copy, move and paste text. These features allow you to edit (change) the on-screen text without having to retype the whole document.

It is easy to get muddled over the meaning of the terms *cut*, *copy*, *move* and *paste*.

- **Cut** deletes the selected text and places a copy onto the *Clipboard* (a special part of the computer's memory) from where it can be retrieved.
- **Copy** copies the selected text onto the Clipboard, without deleting it. It can then be placed elsewhere in the document.
- **Move** means to cut selected text from one place and immediately paste that text elsewhere in the document.
- **Paste** inserts the text from the Clipboard elsewhere in the document, or even into a different document.

Go out and try!

1. Type out the text showing in Figure 21 in a new document.
   - Open Microsoft Word and key in the text.
   - Proofread what you have typed.
   - Position the cursor at the start of the document and click on the **Spelling and grammar** button.
   - The *Spelling and grammar* dialogue box appears.
   - If the word is incorrect, select the correct spelling from the suggestions and click on **Change** to accept it.

2. Locate the **Show/Hide** button on the *Standard* toolbar and click on it to display the formatting in the document. Notice how the spaces between words are shown as a small dot raised above the typing line. Have you got two dots at the end of each sentence to indicate that you have put in two spaces?

3. Copy the text and paste a second copy underneath.
   - Select all the text.
   - Click on the **Copy** button. The text will be saved onto the Clipboard.
   - Position the cursor at the end of the first piece of text and click on the **Paste** button.

4. Make the following changes to the second copy.
   - In the first paragraph add 'break' after 'weekend' and notice how the original text moves on to a new line to accommodate the additional word.
   - In the second paragraph, delete the words 'and bars' and notice how the original text moves up to close the gap.
   - Copy 'Travelbug' at the top of the document to the very end.
     - Select the word 'Travelbug'.
     - Click on the **Copy** button.
     - Position the cursor at the very end of the document and click on the **Paste** button.
   - Move the paragraph beginning 'Travel by Eurostar' so that it becomes the second paragraph.
     - Select the paragraph beginning 'Travel by Eurostar'.
     - Click on the **Cut** button.
     - Position the cursor immediately before the second paragraph, where you want the text to appear.
     - Click on the **Paste** button.

5. Save this document as 'WP Activity 1' in your 'Word-processing software' sub-folder.

Create a file called 'Word-processing software'. Insert a bold heading called '**WP Activity 1**' and write a short paragraph describing the skills you have demonstrated in this activity. Save this file in your 'Word-processing software' sub-folder.

Formatting text

Font type and font size

A *font* is the name given to describe the style of typeface you are using. Two popular styles frequently used in the preparation of business documents are Times New Roman and Arial.

○ This is an example of Times New Roman. It is referred to as a *serif* font because of the 'little feet' at the bottom of each letter.

○ This is an example of Arial. It is referred to as a *sans serif* font because it does not have the 'little feet'.

Your default font will generally be Times New Roman, and the size is likely to be somewhere between 10 and 12 points. *Point* refers to the size of the character – the higher the number, the larger the font. A point size of 72 would give you a letter approximately 2.54 centimetres (1 inch) tall.

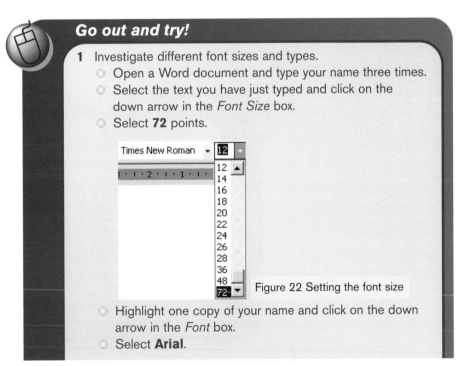

Go out and try!

1 Investigate different font sizes and types.
   ○ Open a Word document and type your name three times.
   ○ Select the text you have just typed and click on the down arrow in the *Font Size* box.
   ○ Select **72** points.

Figure 22 Setting the font size

   ○ Highlight one copy of your name and click on the down arrow in the *Font* box.
   ○ Select **Arial**.

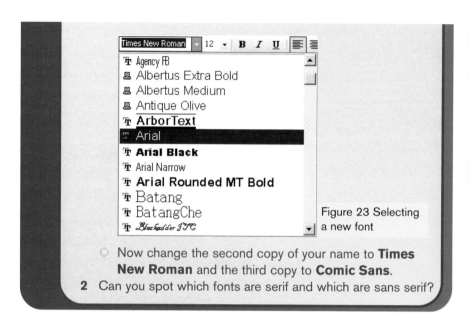

Figure 23 Selecting a new font

○ Now change the second copy of your name to **Times New Roman** and the third copy to **Comic Sans**.

2 Can you spot which fonts are serif and which are sans serif?

It is important that you choose a style and size of font to suit the task you are doing. Some font styles are rather elaborate and difficult to read, so you should use them with care. Similarly, choose a suitable font size.

For example, text contained in a poster will probably need to be quite large so that it is eye-catching and can be read from a distance. In contrast, a leaflet or newsletter might contain fairly large headings, with the body text printed in a smaller font.

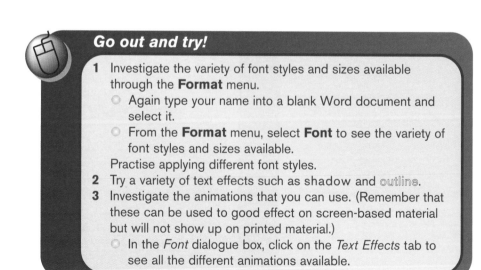

Go out and try!

1 Investigate the variety of font styles and sizes available through the **Format** menu.
   ○ Again type your name into a blank Word document and select it.
   ○ From the **Format** menu, select **Font** to see the variety of font styles and sizes available.
   Practise applying different font styles.
2 Try a variety of text effects such as shadow and outline.
3 Investigate the animations that you can use. (Remember that these can be used to good effect on screen-based material but will not show up on printed material.)
   ○ In the *Font* dialogue box, click on the *Text Effects* tab to see all the different animations available.

Bold, underline and italic

In addition to using different font styles and sizes, you can also use **bold**, underline or *italic* to emphasise text. ***<u>However, it is not generally a good idea to apply all three to the same text!</u>***

Go out and try!

Investigate the effect of making text bold, italic and underlined.

- Type your name three times into a document.
- Select the first name and click on the **Bold** B button.
- Select the second name and click on the **Italic** *I* button.
- Select the third name and click on the **Underline** U button.

Using colour

Colour is not generally applied to text in standard documents, such as letters or reports, but it can be very effective in leaflets, posters, flyers, etc. However, for it to be effective you should use it in moderation – otherwise your document will be messy, difficult to read and therefore may not be fit for the purpose intended.

Your word-processing software has a selection of standard colours (Figure 24(a)). It also has the facility to customise a colour, (Figure 24(b)), which can be useful if you need to match an existing colour. For example, some companies have 'corporate colours' that they replicate on their logo, advertising material, brochures, on-screen presentations, and so on.

DiDA

Jargon buster

The **custom colour** option makes it possible to create a colour of your own choosing. Figure 24(b) shows a white cross-hair shape that can be dragged around to find the colour match. Each colour is made up of a unique combination of red, green and blue (RGB) numbers. If you know the RGB numbers you can enter them to give you an exact colour match.

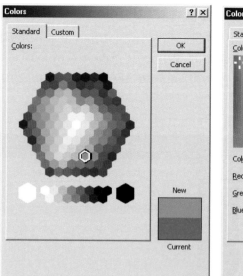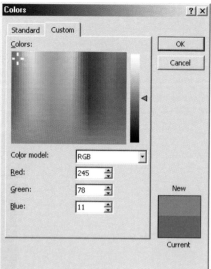

Figure 24 The standard colour palette and the custom colour option

Go out and try!

Apply different colours to fonts.

- Open a document and key in some text.
- Select the text that you wish to apply colour to.
- Click on the down arrow to the right of the **Font Color** button to show the choices (Figure 25).

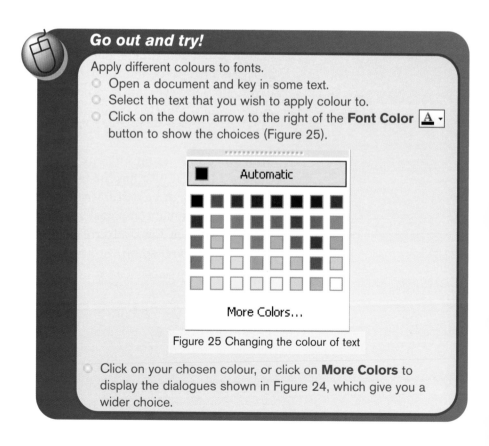

Figure 25 Changing the colour of text

- Click on your chosen colour, or click on **More Colors** to display the dialogues shown in Figure 24, which give you a wider choice.

Go out and try!

1 Start a new document in Word.
2 Look at Figure 26 and list the headings given on the left.
3 Under each heading give at least three examples.
4 Using the skills you have learned, format the example to match the style, colour etc.

One example of each has been given to start you off.

Headings	Examples
Serif font	Times New Roman
Sans serif font	Comic Sans MS
Font size	20 point
Font effect	SMALL CAPITALS
Animated text effects	Marching Red Ants
Colour	Dark blue
Emphasis	Underline

Figure 26 Examples of font options

5 Save this document as 'WP Activity 2' in your 'Word-processing software' sub-folder.

Open your 'Word-processing software' file. Create a new bold heading called 'WP Activity 2' and write a short paragraph describing the skills you have demonstrated in this activity. Save the file.

Using paragraph formatting features

Alignment

When you completed WP Activity 1, did you notice how your text automatically lined up against the left-hand margin, leaving the right-hand margin uneven (or *ragged*)? This is because the default style of paragraph alignment is *left aligned*. Word-processing software offers you alternative styles of paragraph format, such as *justified* or *centred*.

Here the text is **left-aligned** and the right-hand margin is uneven or *ragged*. This is the default setting. The spaces between words are equal.

Here the alignment is **justified** and both the left and right margins are straight. The program automatically adjusts the spaces between words to distribute the text evenly between the margins. The spaces between words are not equal.

Here the text is **centred** between the margins. This is generally used for presentation and display rather than letters or notes.

Figure 27 Text left-aligned, justified and centred

The default setting of left alignment is quite acceptable for most text-based documents and on-screen presentations. However, there are occasions when justified alignment may be more appropriate. For example, a newsletter produced in columns looks more professional with justified margins (Figure 28(a)). Lines of text in a poster may be centred between the margins; and, in order to balance the presentation, paragraphs in the same poster look neater if they are justified leaving an equal space against the left and the right margins (Figure 28(b)).

Figure 28 A newsletter and a poster

Go out and try!

Create a poster to demonstrate centred and justified paragraph alignment.

○ Open the file you saved as 'WP Activity 1'.

○ Copy the edited text and paste it into a new document.

○ Select the text that you want to centre.

○ Click on the **Center** ≣ button.

○ Select the text that you want to justify and click on the **Justify** ≣ button.

○ Apply suitable font styles and sizes to make the poster more interesting. Will 'white space' make the poster more effective?

○ 💾 Save this document as 'WP Activity 3' in your 'Word-processing software' sub-folder.

Open your 'Word-processing software' file. Create a new bold heading called '**WP Activity 3**' and write a short paragraph describing the skills you have demonstrated in this activity. 💾 Save the file.

Bullets and numbering

Bullet points are used to make items in a list stand out. The standard bullet point is represented by the character symbol ●, but you can choose different symbols. For example

⧫ a bullet point chosen from the standard selection in Bullets and Numbering (Figure 25)

💣 a bullet point customised from a selection in Wingdings

♪ a bullet point customised from a selection in Webdings

As you can see from these examples, the standard bullet point is the clearest and is the style most commonly used in the preparation of paper-based documents.

Sometimes different styles of bullet point are used to indicate different 'levels' in a list. For example:

- Fully-inclusive holidays
  - » Full-board
  - » Half-board
  - » Self-catering
- Activity holidays
  - » Skiing
  - » Water sports

The important thing to remember is that you should use a style of bullet that is fit for the purpose of the document. Use the decorative or picture bullets only for more informal documents, on-screen presentations or web pages.

Sometimes it is preferable to number a list rather than using bullets. The 'Numbered' tab illustrated in Figure 30 offers a variety of options – such as **1**, **2**, **3** or **a**), **b**), **c**). Figure 29 shows both bullets and numbering used in a document.

TRAVELBUG CRUISE CLUB

Our Cruise Club is totally independent and we can therefore offer a varied range of cruises from all leading cruise line operators. Our knowledgeable staff are on hand 7 days a week to help you plan the perfect trip.

Membership is free and Cruise Club members have the following advantages:

- 2 for 1 cruise offers
- Services of our specially trained staff
- Monthly newsletter with the latest information and offers
- Cabin upgrades and on-ship spending vouchers
- Exclusive visits to see the ships whilst docked in the UK
- Specially discounted rates

How to join

1. Call us for an application form or download from our web site
2. Complete the application form
3. Return to us in Whychton
4. Your application membership pack will be sent out by return post

Figure 29 The use of bullet points and numbering

Go out and try!

1 Copy the text shown in Figure 29 to a new document and apply bullets and numbering.
2 Insert a page break at the foot of the document.
   ○ Press **Ctrl** and **Enter** to insert a page break.
3 Make a copy of page 1 and paste it onto the second page.

4 Customise the bullets to a style of your choice.
- Select the bulleted text
- From the **Format** menu, select **Bullets and Numbering**. Select the new style of bulleted list and click on **OK**.

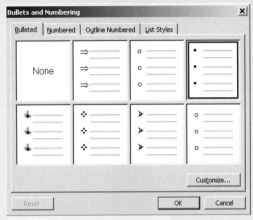

Figure 30 Different bullet styles

- Select the numbered list.
- Change the style of the numbered list by selecting **Bullets and Numbering** from the **Format** menu.
- Select the **Numbered** tab, click on the new style of numbered list and then press **OK**.

5 Insert a further page break at the end of the document.

6 On the third page enter the following text as a list against the left margin: France, Accommodation, Travel, Weather, Summer, Winter, Spain, Accommodation, Travel, Weather, Summer, Winter.

7 Apply a numbered list style to the text you have just entered and then indent it.
- Highlight the text you entered in Step 6.
- From the **Format** menu, select **Bullets and Numbering**.
- In the **Bullets and Numbering** dialogue box select the **Outline Numbered** tab and select the option shown in Figure 31.

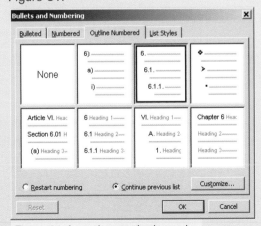

Figure 31 A section numbering style

Your list will now be numbered from 1 to 12.

○ Position the cursor to the right of the number 2 (to the left of the word 'Accommodation') and click the **Increase Indent** button on your *Formatting* toolbar. Number 2 should change to 1.1.

○ Position the cursor to the left of 'Travel' and then 'Weather' and in each case click the **Increase Indent** button once.

○ Now position the cursor to the left of 'Summer' and then 'Winter' and in each case click the **Increase Indent** button twice. The start of your list should look like this:

1. France
   1.1. Accommodation
   1.2. Travel
   1.3. Weather
      1.3.1. Summer
      1.3.2. Winter

○ Do the same again for the headings under Spain.

○ 🖫 Save your work as 'WP Activity 4' in your 'Word-processing software' sub-folder.

Open your 'Word-processing software' file. Create a new bold heading called '**WP Activity 4**' and write a short paragraph describing the skills you have demonstrated in this activity. 🖫 Save the file.

Tabs

The **Tab** key is located to the left of the letter Q on your keyboard. Every time you press the **Tab** key the cursor jumps across the page. The **Tab** key is used to place and align text on the page.

In the example in Figure 32, tabs have been used to position the three columns headed 'Coffee', 'Beer' and 'Meal for 2 people'.

Approximate costs

		Coffee		Beer		Meal for 2 people
→	→	*Coffee*	→	*Beer*→	→	*Meal for 2 people*
France→	→	£1.40→	→	£2.50→	→	£44.00
Italy→	→	£0.70→	→	£1.45→	→	£27.50
Spain→	→	£0.80→	→	£1.00→	→	£20.00

Figure 32 The use of tabs to form a simple table

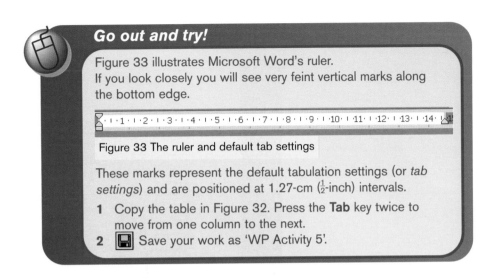

Tab styles

The default tab settings are known as *left tabs* because the text is left-aligned with the tab. There are three other useful tab settings illustrated in Figure 34:

- right – text is right-aligned with the tab
- centre – text extends either side of the tab setting
- decimal – text before the decimal point extends left and after the decimal point extends right.

4 STAR OFFERS

Date	Place	Hotel	No. of Nights	Cost
10 October	Derby	Broadmeadow	4	£210
16 November	Chester	Lodge Gate	6	£249.50
23 November	Edinburgh	Monterry	5	£265.99
6 December	Brighton	Hurlingham Park	1	£75
13 December	London	Stretford	2	£150
↑ Left		↑ Right	↑ Centred	↑ Decimal

Figure 34 Column alignments in a tabbed table

Go out and try!

1 Open a new document and set the following tabs:
   left tab setting = 3 cm
   right tab setting = 8.5 cm
   centre tab setting = 10.5 cm
   decimal tab setting = 13 cm.
   ○ From the **Format** menu, select **Tabs**.
   ○ In the *Tabs* dialogue box, key in the first tab stop position in the *Tab stop position* box. Ensure *Alignment* is set to **Left**. Click on **Set**.
   ○ Repeat for each tab, remembering to change the alignment and to press **Set** after each one.
2 Type the table in Figure 34 into this document.
3 💾 Save your work as 'WP Activity 6' in your 'Word-processing software' sub-folder.

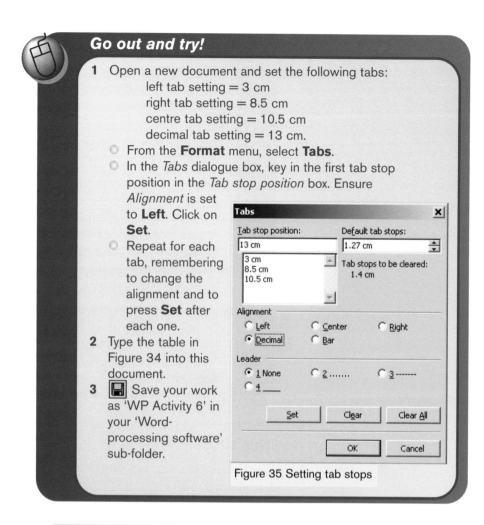

Figure 35 Setting tab stops

Open your 'Word-processing software' file. Create a new bold heading called '**WP Activity 6**' and write a short paragraph describing the skills you have demonstrated in this activity. 💾 Save the file.

Indents

Paragraph indents can be used to make paragraphs stand out. Indents can be applied by selecting **Format, Paragraph** from the menu, or by dragging the indent markers on the horizontal ruler (Figure 36). Figure 37 shows some examples of paragraph indents in a leaflet.

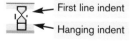
← First line indent
← Hanging indent   Figure 36 Indent markers on the horizontal ruler

Figure 37 Examples of indents on a newsletter

Go out and try!

1 Open the file you saved as 'WP Activity 1' and copy the four paragraphs that describe the trip to Brussels.
2 Paste these paragraphs into a new document.
3 Create hanging indents on the first two paragraphs.
  ○ Select the first two paragraphs.
  ○ From the **Format** menu, select **Paragraph**.
  ○ Ensure the *Indents and Spacing* tab is selected.
  ○ In the *Special* box, select **Hanging**.

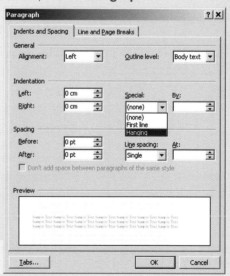

Figure 38 Setting a hanging indent

4 You are now going to indent the third paragraph by 2.54 cm from the left and right margins.
  ○ Select the third paragraph.
  ○ In the *Paragraph* dialogue box (Figure 34), click in the *Left* box and key in **2.54 cm**.
  ○ Repeat in the *Right* box.
  ○ In the *Special* box, ensure that **(none)** is selected.
  ○ Click on **OK**.
5 Create a first-line indent on the last paragraph.
  ○ Select the last paragraph and follow the instructions in Step 4, selecting **First line** in the *Special* box instead.
6 Save your work as 'WP Activity 7' in your 'Word-processing software' sub-folder.

Open your 'Word-processing software' file. Create a new bold heading called '**WP Activity 7**' and write a short paragraph describing the skills you have demonstrated in this activity. Save the file.

Using page formatting features

Margins

The *margin* is the area around the edge of the page that generally remains free of text. The default margins leave approximately 2.54 cm (1 inch) at the top and bottom of the page, and 3.17 cm (1.25 inches) on the left and right sides (Figure 39). For most everyday word-processing tasks these margins are quite appropriate.

Sometimes, however, it is sensible to change one or more of the margin settings. If you are producing a document that is to be bound, such as a report or brochure, then a *gutter* ensures that sufficient space is left so that the binding does not block out the text.

If you are creating a double-sided document, *mirror margins* ensure that the margins on the left page are a mirror image of those on the right page.

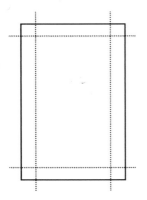
Figure 39 An A4 page showing the margin settings

Portrait

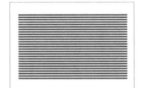

Landscape

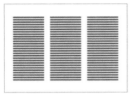

Landscape

Landscape

Figure 40 Page orientations: landscape can be very effective if you are working in columns or producing tables of data

Page orientation

Most documents containing text are produced using the default page orientation of *portrait*. However, there are times when you might want or need to turn the page the other way round, to *landscape* (Figure 40).

The margin settings and page orientation (sometimes called alignment) are generally changed through **File, Page Setup** (Figure 41). However, dragging the left and right margin markers on the ruler is an alternative way to change margins.

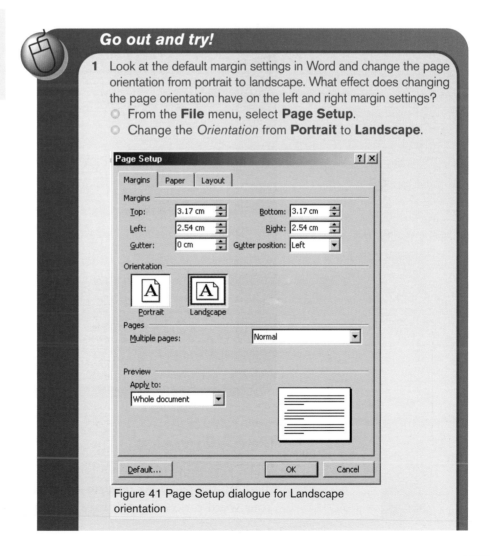

Go out and try!

1 Look at the default margin settings in Word and change the page orientation from portrait to landscape. What effect does changing the page orientation have on the left and right margin settings?
  ○ From the **File** menu, select **Page Setup**.
  ○ Change the *Orientation* from **Portrait** to **Landscape**.

Figure 41 Page Setup dialogue for Landscape orientation

2 What happens to the preview of the page when you increase or decrease the default settings of the left and right margins?
- In the *Page Setup* dialogue box, delete the measurements in the *Top*, *Bottom*, *Left* and *Right* margin boxes and increase and decrease the values.

3 Set the left and right margins to 3 cm (30 mm) and set the gutter to 1.5 cm (15 mm). What do you notice?
- In the *Page Setup* dialogue box, type in **3 cm** in the *Left* and *Right* boxes and **1.5 cm** in the *Gutter* box
- Reset the *Gutter* to **0**.

4 Set the left margin to 5 cm (50 mm) and the right margin at 3 cm (30 mm). What happens to the preview if you select mirror margins?
- With the *Page Setup* dialogue box open, type in **5 cm** in the *Left* box and **3 cm** in the *Right* box.
- Under *Multiple pages*, select **Mirror margins**.

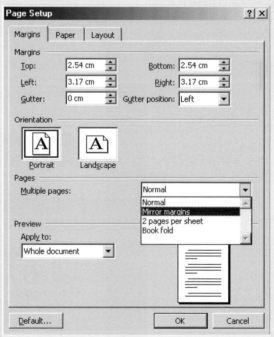

Figure 42 Page Setup dialogue for mirror margins

Page breaks

When you are working on a long document and you run out of space on the page, the text automatically runs onto the next page. Your word-processing software has inserted a *soft page break* and

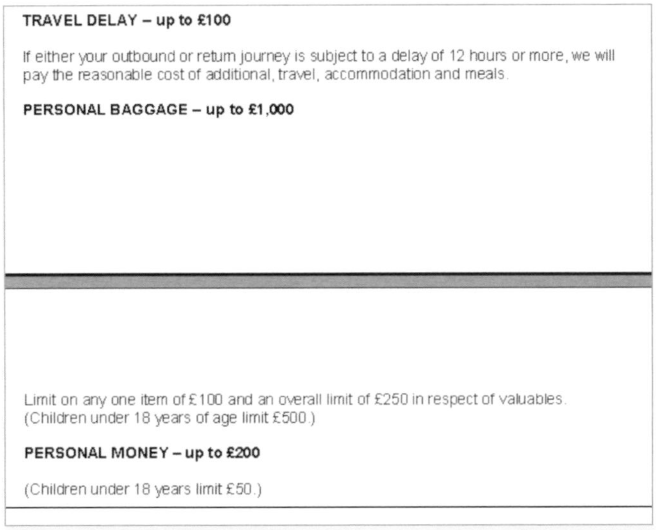

TRAVEL DELAY – up to £100

If either your outbound or return journey is subject to a delay of 12 hours or more, we will pay the reasonable cost of additional, travel, accommodation and meals.

PERSONAL BAGGAGE – up to £1,000

Limit on any one item of £100 and an overall limit of £250 in respect of valuables. (Children under 18 years of age limit £500.)

PERSONAL MONEY – up to £200

(Children under 18 years limit £50.)

Figure 43 A soft page break has been inserted by the program, but immediately under a heading

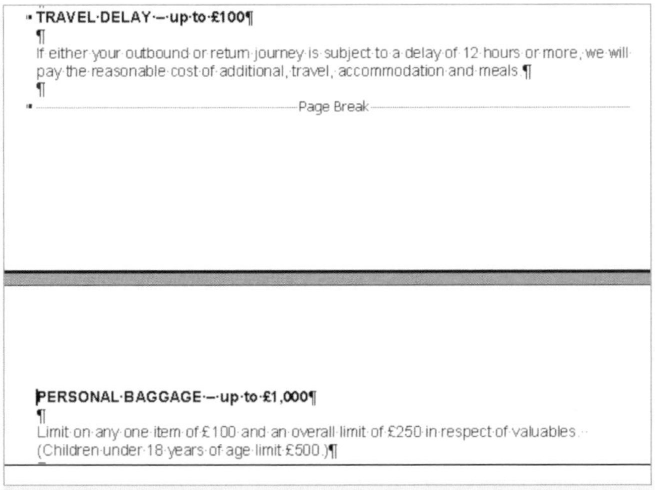

·TRAVEL·DELAY·—·up·to·£100¶
¶
If·either·your·outbound·or·return·journey·is·subject·to·a·delay·of·12·hours·or·more,·we·will·pay·the·reasonable·cost·of·additional,·travel,·accommodation·and·meals.¶
¶
————————————————Page Break————————————————

PERSONAL·BAGGAGE·—·up·to·£1,000¶
¶
Limit·on·any·one·item·of·£100·and·an·overall·limit·of·£250·in·respect·of·valuables. (Children·under·18·years·of·age·limit·£500.)¶

Figure 44 The user has inserted a hard page break to prevent the heading from being separated from the text beneath it (compare this with Figure 43)

forced the remaining text on to a new page. A soft page break is flexible – rather like the soft returns we looked at on page 88. If you delete a section of text in front of a soft page break, text on the following page moves up to fill the gap.

Usually when this occurs we don't have to worry about it. However, look at Figure 43. The soft page break has left the heading 'PERSONAL BAGGAGE' on one page and the paragraph that should be with it is on the following page. This is not acceptable.

In situations like this you can use a *hard* (or *manual*) *page break* to push the heading onto the next page (Figure 44). A hard page break is not flexible – it will always force a new page at the point you have inserted it, even if text is later inserted or deleted.

There are two ways to insert a hard page break. Whichever way you choose, position the cursor immediately in front of the text that is to move onto the next page. Either

- select **Insert, Break, Page break**; or
- use key strokes – hold down **Ctrl** and at the same time press **Enter**.

By using the **Show/Hide** ¶ option you can see where the hard page break has been inserted.

Headers and footers

Anything inserted as a *header* or *footer* will appear on every page of the document in the same position (Figure 45).

- The document *header* is the space in the top margin above the first line of text on a page. You might find a company name or the title of the document inserted in the header area.

Figure 45 The header and footer areas in a document

○ The document *footer* is the space at the bottom of the page after the last line of text. The date, page number and file reference are often inserted in the footer.

When you use the word processor to produce any work at school or college, it is a good idea to put your name in the header or footer. There is a selection of options available through **Insert AutoText** in the header and footer areas (Figure 47). From this selection you can choose to show in the header or footer a variety of information, such as filename and path. This will help you to locate a document easily at a later date. *Last printed* is also useful to check that you are looking at the most recent copy of a printed document.

Page numbers

When producing a multi-page document, it is very sensible to number the pages. Page numbers can be placed in the header or footer area of the page either through **View**, **Header and Footer** or through **Insert**, **Page Numbers**.

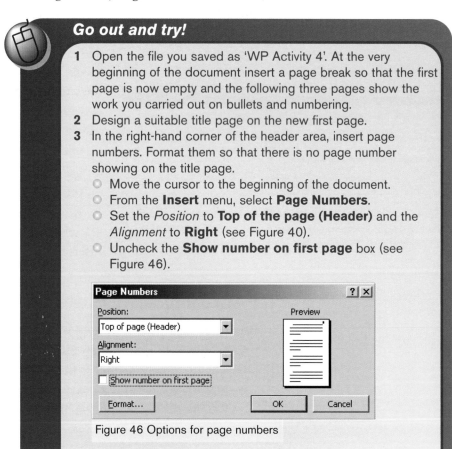

Go out and try!

1 Open the file you saved as 'WP Activity 4'. At the very beginning of the document insert a page break so that the first page is now empty and the following three pages show the work you carried out on bullets and numbering.
2 Design a suitable title page on the new first page.
3 In the right-hand corner of the header area, insert page numbers. Format them so that there is no page number showing on the title page.
   ○ Move the cursor to the beginning of the document.
   ○ From the **Insert** menu, select **Page Numbers**.
   ○ Set the *Position* to **Top of the page (Header)** and the *Alignment* to **Right** (see Figure 40).
   ○ Uncheck the **Show number on first page** box (see Figure 46).

Figure 46 Options for page numbers

4 In the footer of the document, insert the filename and path against the left-hand margin and the date against the right-hand margin.

- Move the cursor to the beginning of the document.
- From the **View** menu, select **Header and Footer**.
- In the *Header and Footer* box select 🗒 **Switch Between Header and Footer** to switch to the footer.
- Ensure the cursor is at the left of the *Footer* box and, from the **Insert AutoText** menu, select **Filename and path**.

Header and Footer

Insert AutoText ▾
- PAGE -
Author, Page #, Date
Confidential, Page #, Date
Created by
Created on
Filename
Filename and path
Last printed
Last saved by
Page X of Y

Close

Figure 47 Options for adding AutoText

- Tab the cursor to the right-hand margin of the *Footer* box and click on the 📅 **Insert Date** button.

5 💾 Save your work as 'WP Activity 8' in your 'Word-processing software' sub-folder.

Open your 'Word-processing software' file. Create a new bold heading called '**WP Activity 8**' and write a short paragraph describing the skills you have demonstrated in this activity. At the same time check the pagination in your 'Word-processing software' file and number the pages.
💾 Save the file.

Line spacing

The distance between each line of text in a paragraph is known as the *line spacing*. The default setting in your word-processor will produce text in single line spacing. However, there are occasions when it is useful to leave a larger space between the lines. For instance, you might want to make a section of text stand out, or to leave room between lines to make handwritten notes (Figure 48).

This example of text has been produced in **single line spacing**. This is the default setting and is probably the most commonly used.	This example shows text in **one and a half line spacing**. It is used to make sections of text stand out and therefore become easier to read.	This example shows text produced in **double line spacing**. It is particularly effective if you wish to write notes between the lines, as on a draft document.

Figure 48 Examples of single, 1.5 and double line spacings

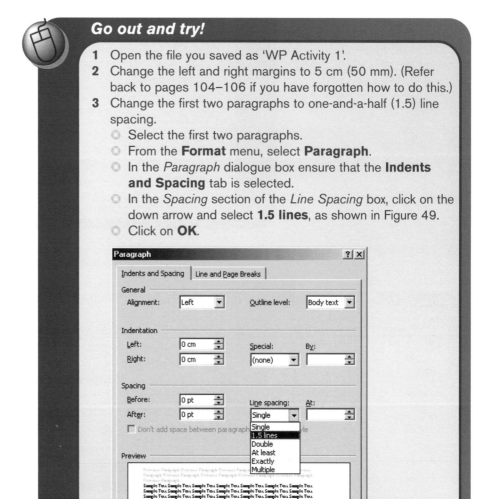

Go out and try!

1 Open the file you saved as 'WP Activity 1'.
2 Change the left and right margins to 5 cm (50 mm). (Refer back to pages 104–106 if you have forgotten how to do this.)
3 Change the first two paragraphs to one-and-a-half (1.5) line spacing.
   ○ Select the first two paragraphs.
   ○ From the **Format** menu, select **Paragraph**.
   ○ In the *Paragraph* dialogue box ensure that the **Indents and Spacing** tab is selected.
   ○ In the *Spacing* section of the *Line Spacing* box, click on the down arrow and select **1.5 lines**, as shown in Figure 49.
   ○ Click on **OK**.

Figure 49 Options for paragraph indents and spacing

4 Change the remaining paragraphs to double line spacing. Use the instructions in Step 3 but select **Double** in the *Line Spacing* box instead.

5 Save your work as 'WP Activity 9' in your 'Word-processing software' sub-folder.

Open your 'Word-processing software' file. Create a new bold heading called '**WP Activity 9**' and write a short paragraph describing the skills you have demonstrated in this activity. Suggest one occasion when you might use 1.5 line spacing and one occasion when you might use double line spacing. Save the file.

Using columns

Word makes it easy to set up multiple columns on the same page. This is particularly useful if you are writing a newsletter.

The easy way to set up columns is to use the **Columns** icon on the *Standard* toolbar. This pops up an area that lets you choose how many columns you want (see Figure 50).

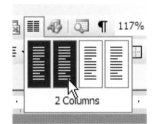

Figure 50 Setting two columns

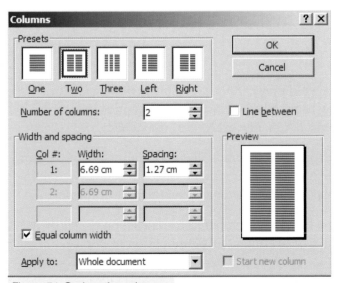

Figure 51 Options for columns

If you need to use more advanced features, such as uneven column widths, you can select **Format, Columns** from the menu. This displays the *Columns* dialogue box shown in Figure 51.

Go out and try!

1 Open the file you saved as 'WP Activity 1'. Make a copy of the text and paste it into a new document.

2 Select the five paragraphs at the foot of the page and display the text in two columns using the **Columns** button on the *Standard* toolbar. Justify the text.

3 Use the **Undo** button to remove the justification and columns.

4 Select the text again and use **Format**, **Columns** from the menu to display the text in three columns. Justify the text again.

5 Use the **Undo** button to remove the justification and columns.

6 Turn the page to landscape and repeat steps 2 to 5.

7 Decide which of the four versions you prefer and reformat the text to that style.

8 Save your work as 'WP Activity 10' in your 'Word-processing software' sub-folder.

Open your 'Word-processing software' file. Create a new bold heading called '**WP Activity 10**' and write a short paragraph describing the style of columns you preferred and justifying your reasons for choosing this style.

Save the file.

Tables

We have already seen on page 000 that columns of data can be presented tidily by using tabs. A more powerful option, which can help you to display information effectively, is to use *tables*.

Tables consist of rows and columns that form individual boxes (or *cells*) – rather like a spreadsheet. Each individual cell may contain any amount of text, a picture or even a mathematical formula.

Figure 52 shows a basic table prepared by Travelbug to tell their customers the price of overnight accommodation in France.

Hotel stopovers
Prices shown in £s per room

Category	Accommodation	Weekend	Extra Child
Room only	Twin/double	£35	N/A
	Family	£45	2 free
Bed and Breakfast	Twin/double	£55	1 free
	Family	£75	2 free

Figure 52 A basic table layout

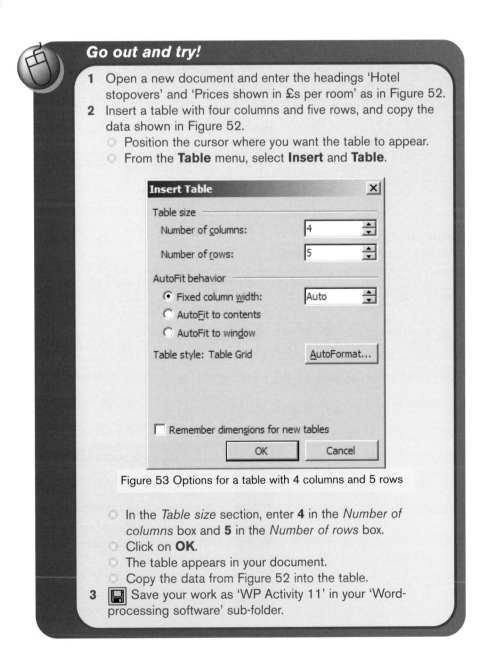

Go out and try!

1 Open a new document and enter the headings 'Hotel stopovers' and 'Prices shown in £s per room' as in Figure 52.
2 Insert a table with four columns and five rows, and copy the data shown in Figure 52.
   ○ Position the cursor where you want the table to appear.
   ○ From the **Table** menu, select **Insert** and **Table**.

Figure 53 Options for a table with 4 columns and 5 rows

   ○ In the *Table size* section, enter **4** in the *Number of columns* box and **5** in the *Number of rows* box.
   ○ Click on **OK**.
   ○ The table appears in your document.
   ○ Copy the data from Figure 52 into the table.
3 Save your work as 'WP Activity 11' in your 'Word-processing software' sub-folder.

Open your 'Word-processing software' file. Create a new bold heading called '**WP Activity 11**' and write a short paragraph describing the skills you have demonstrated in this activity. Save the file.

Borders and shading in tables

There are additional features in your word-processing software that give you the opportunity to enhance or improve the general appearance of a table. For example you can apply borders and shading, and introduce colour.

Figure 54 shows the table from Figure 52 with the addition of some features.

Hotel stopovers
Prices shown in £s per room

Category	Accommodation	Weekend	Extra Child
Room only	Twin/double	£35	N/A
	Family	£45	2 free
Bed and Breakfast	Twin/double	£55	1 free
	Family	£75	2 free

Figure 54 The table in Figure 52 with the addition of an outside border, shading and colour

Go out and try!

1 Open the file you saved as 'WP Activity 11'.
2 Change the outside border to a double line.
   ○ Click anywhere within the table.
   ○ From the **Table** menu, choose **Select** then **Table**.
   ○ From the **Format** menu, select **Borders and Shading**.
   ○ In the *Borders and Shading* dialogue box, select the **double line** option in the *Style* box and **Box** in the *Settings* box. Ensure **Table** is selected in the *Apply to* box.

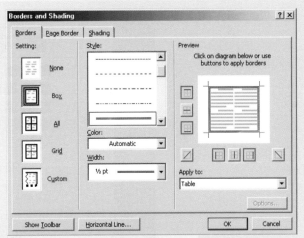

Figure 55 A double-line table border

3   Shade the cells containing the column headings.
   ○ Select the cells containing the column headings and right-click on them.
   ○ In the pop-up menu, select **Borders and Shading**.
   ○ With the *Shading* tab selected, choose a colour.
   ○ Click on **OK**.

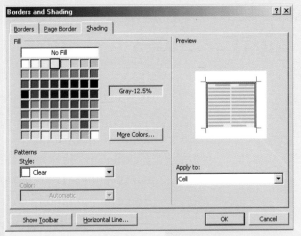

Figure 56 Options for shading

4   Add a coloured background to the cells showing the row headings, and apply a contrasting font colour.
   ○ Select the row headings and follow the instructions in Step 3 to apply shading to the cells.
   ○ With the row heading cells selected, click on the arrow next to the A ▾ **Font Color** button to show the colours available.

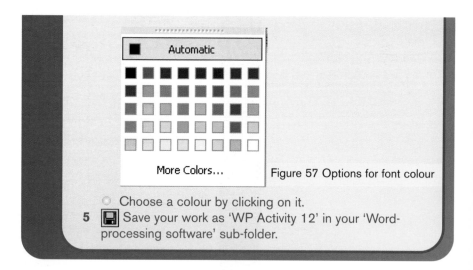

Figure 57 Options for font colour

○ Choose a colour by clicking on it.

5 💾 Save your work as 'WP Activity 12' in your 'Word-processing software' sub-folder.

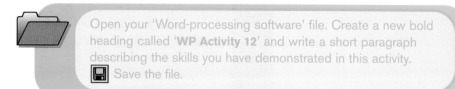

Open your 'Word-processing software' file. Create a new bold heading called '**WP Activity 12**' and write a short paragraph describing the skills you have demonstrated in this activity.
💾 Save the file.

Modifying row and column sizes

The columns showing prices for weekends and extra child details are wider than they need to be. The column width can be modified by picking up the arrow shape ◄╫► and dragging the column border to a new position. The effect of doing this is shown in Figure 58.

You can also modify the row height by picking up the arrow shape ╪ and dragging up or down.

Hotel stopovers
Prices shown in £s per room

Category	Accommodation	Weekend	Extra Child
Room only	Twin/double	£35	N/A
	Family	£45	2 free
Bed and Breakfast	Twin/double	£55	1 free
	Family	£75	2 free

Figure 58 Compare this with Figure 54: the column widths have been adjusted

Go out and try!

1 Open the file you saved as 'WP Activity 12'.
2 Carefully move your cursor across the rows and columns to see it change shape as it rests on row and column boundaries.
3 Reduce the column widths for 'Weekend' and 'Extra Child'.
  ○ Select the column showing 'Weekend'.
  ○ Place your cursor over the right column border and, when it changes to a double-headed arrow, drag it to the correct position.
  ○ Do the same for the 'Extra Child' column.
4 🖫 Save your work as 'WP Activity 13' in your 'Word-processing software' sub-folder. Leave the file open.
5 Apply Autofit to the 'Weekend' column.
  ○ Position the cursor on the column border between 'Weekend' and 'Extra Child'.
  ○ Double-click on the border to see what happens to the width of the 'Weekend' column. The column width should automatically reduce to fit the text within it.
  ○ Try it again on the outside column border.
  ○ Close the file without saving these changes.

Open your 'Word-processing software' file. Create a new bold heading called '**WP Activity 13**' and write a short paragraph describing the skills you have demonstrated in this activity.
🖫 Save the file.

Inserting and deleting columns and rows

In Figure 59 an extra column has been added to the table to show the midweek prices. Extra rows have also been added to enable the headings to become part of the table and to separate the two different categories of accommodation. Extra columns and rows can be inserted by selecting **Table, Insert**.

HOTEL STOPOVERS				
ALL OFFERS SUBJECT TO AVAILABILITY				
Category	**Accommodation**	**Weekend**	**Midweek**	**Extra Child**
Room only	Twin/double	£35	£35	N/A
	Family	£45	£45	2 free
Bed and Breakfast	Twin/double	£55	£60	1 free
	Family	£75	£80	2 free
Prices shown in £s per room				

Figure 59 Compare this with Figure 58: the table now has an extra column, and five additional rows have been inserted

Go out and try!

1 Open the table you saved as 'WP Activity 13'.

2 Insert a new column between Weekend and Extra Child and head the column 'Midweek'.
- Select the Extra Child column and right-click on it.
- From the pop-up menu, select **Insert Columns**.
- Type in **Midweek** as the column heading.

3 Insert two rows above the cell headed 'Category'.
- Select the row containing the heading category.
- From the **Table** menu, select **Insert**, then **Rows Above**.
- Repeat to add a second row.

4 Using the method described in Step 3, insert a new row above 'Bed and Breakfast'.

5 Add an extra row at the foot of the table.
- Click in the last cell in the table.
- Press the **Tab** key.
- An extra row should appear.

6 For each of the four new rows you are going to merge the cells.
- Select each of the new rows, one at a time.
- From the **Table** menu, select **Merge Cells**.
- The four rows should each appear as one cell running the width of the table.

7 Complete the table with the additional information (from Figure 59).

8 🖫 Save the file as 'WP Activity 14' in your 'Word-processing software' sub-folder.

Open your 'Word-processing software' file. Create a new bold heading called '**WP Activity 14**' and write a short paragraph describing the skills you have demonstrated in this activity.
🖫 Save the file.

Text boxes

A *text box* is a drawing object that contains text. You can format the text in a text box in the same way as any other text in your document, but because it is contained in a box you can resize it and move it. You can use a text box to realign text and can add shadow and 3-D styles.

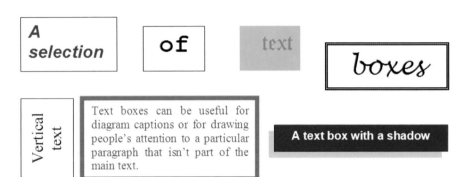

Figure 60 A selection of text boxes

You can add a text box by selecting **Insert, Text Box** from the menu, or by using the **Text Box** icon on the *Drawing* toolbar. You must then click and drag your mouse over the area in which you want the text box to appear.

Go out and try!

1 Create a new blank document.
2 Try creating some text boxes. Give them some text.
3 Practise moving and resizing them.
4 Experiment with changing the colours, fill effects and line styles of your text boxes.
   ○ Double-click the border to display the *Format Text Box* dialogue.
   ○ Use the options on the *Colors and Lines* tab.
5 Realign the text by highlighting it and choosing **Format, Text Direction** from the menu.
6 Add shadows and 3-D styles using the tools on the *Drawing* toolbar.
7 Save the file as 'WP Activity 15' in your 'Word-processing software' sub-folder.

Open your 'Word-processing software' file. Create a new bold heading called '**WP Activity 15**' and write a short paragraph describing the skills you have demonstrated in this activity. Save the file.

Creating, selecting and inserting components

Types of components

Many of the publications you produce may comprise more than one component, such as

- images
- lines and simple shapes
- tick boxes
- comments
- hyperlinks.

You must remember that whatever you include in a publication should be there because it improves the effectiveness of that publication and not just because you felt like putting something in.

Images

Images used to illustrate a topic can certainly help people to understand the topic and generally make a publication more interesting for the reader. However, you should only include images that are fully relevant to the topic and that serve a purpose by being included.

You may search through a picture library to find a relevant image, but you must be very careful to obtain permission to use the image if it is protected by copyright laws. Images taken with a digital camera can be inserted directly from the camera. Photographs and images in books and magazines or photographs you take with a traditional camera will need to be scanned into the document.

Remember to record full details of the sources of all images you include in your work.

Lines and simple shapes

You will find it very useful to investigate the *Drawing* toolbar and to experiment with the variety of lines and shapes that are available for you to use. Move your mouse pointer over the toolbar to see the names given to the various tools.

Figure 61 The Drawing toolbar

TiP

If you find it difficult to place one object in front of another use the **Order** option in the Draw menu to send an object in front or behind another.

TiP

If you hold down the **Ctrl** key whilst using the arrow directional keys you can 'nudge' the lines and shapes across the screen in very small steps. If you increase the zoom on the screen to 200% or 500% you can see very clearly when lines and shapes are in the right position.

The arrow tool is very helpful if you need to label a diagram. Other shapes can be built up to form a variety of objects.

The image of the train in Figure 62 is made up from approximately 30 lines and shapes. Some have been copied, some have been filled with colour and all lines have been made thicker.

Figure 62 A train constructed from simple shapes

Go out and try!

1. Open the *Drawing* toolbar on your screen and spend a few minutes investigating the selection of features it offers.
2. Draw some simple shapes and lines and experiment with the fill colour, line colour and line style options.
3. Move the shapes across the screen with the arrow directional keys.
4. Use a variety of lines and shapes and produce an image of your choice.
5. Save your work as 'WP Activity 16' in your 'Word-processing software' sub-folder.

Grouping and ungrouping

You have produced an image that is made up of many different lines and shapes. If you try to move the image, it will be impossible to keep all the shapes together unless you *group* them. Grouping allows you to treat a group of objects as a single object that can be rotated, resized or flipped. Any group of images can be *ungrouped* and treated as a number of separate objects again.

DiDA

Go out and try!

1 Use the **Select Objects** tool (the arrow) and drag a large rectangle around the complete image you have formed. You will see that every component of the image becomes selected.
2 From the *Draw* menu select **Group**. The image can now be treated as a single object.
3 Experiment with the **Rotate or Flip** options.
4 Try to resize the image by double-clicking it and choosing the Size tab. Ensure the **Lock aspect ratio** box is selected and re-size by changing the dimensions.
5 Save your work as 'WP Activity 17' in your 'Word-processing software' sub-folder.

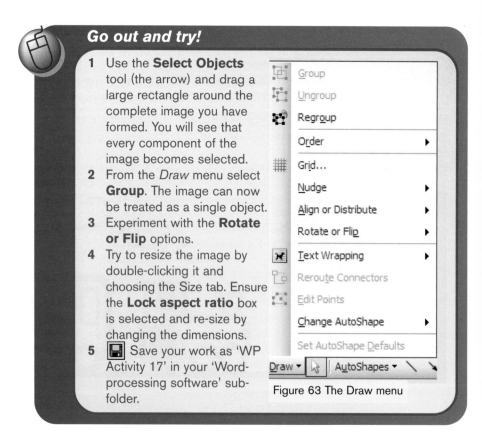

Figure 63 The Draw menu

Borders

You already know how to place a border round text (see page 114) but you may sometimes wish to place a border round a full page, for example on a poster. You will find a wide choice of artwork and line styles available in **Format, Borders and Shading, Page Border**.

You can use the *Rectangle* tool to place a border around an image or object. Draw the rectangle shape over the image with the **Rectangle** tool on the *Drawing* toolbar. The image will disappear under the rectangle but you can double-click the rectangle, remove the 'Fill' colour and choose a suitable line style and colour. You can resize the rectangle as necessary.

Go out and try!

1 Open the image you created in the previous activity.
2 Place a border round the image.
3 Choose a line style and colour to enhance the image.
4 Save your work as 'WP Activity 18' in your 'Word-processing software' sub-folder.

Tick boxes

Tick boxes are useful on questionnaires and surveys if you are supplying a set of choices and you want people to tick one or more boxes. You will find a selection of tick (or check) boxes through **Insert, Symbol, Wingdings**. To increase their size, treat them like any other character symbol.

Figure 64 Characters useful for tick boxes

Comments

You know it is essential that your work is reviewed regularly by a wide range of people and that you should consider carefully any comments your reviewers make. Sometimes it may be convenient to ask your reviewer to look at a printed version of your work. In that case your reviewer might write his or her comments down or talk them over with you.

However, there may be occasions when you send a copy of your work by email if the reviewer is not nearby, for example if he or she is a member of a specialist group or team. The reviewer can use the 'comments' feature of your word processor to insert his or her thoughts directly into the document file. The file can then be emailed back to you and the comments will be on-screen for you to consider. This can save a lot of time for a reviewer.

You will also find comments useful for you to use as your projects develop. If you have a change of mind about something, you can insert a comment into the document explaining and justifying your reasons. This can then be presented as evidence in your e-portfolio.

 Go out and try!

1 Open the file you saved as WP Activity 8. This is a multi-page file containing several features such as bullets and numbers, page breaks, and headers and footers.
2 Insert comments into the document describing the features contained within it.
3 Place the cursor against the first feature (or highlight a particular section of text if this is relevant) and select **Insert, Comment**.

4 Your comments can be entered into the comment boxes.
5 Look at the toolbars on display on your screen. Has the *Reviewing* toolbar appeared? If not, display it through **View, Toolbars**. Place your mouse pointer over the toolbar and investigate the options offered.
6 Save your work as 'WP Activity 19' in your 'Word-processing software' sub-folder.

TiP

*If you include a web site reference or email address, Microsoft Word automatically turns it into a hyperlink. If you position your mouse pointer over the link, a message pops up telling you to press **Ctrl + click** to follow the link. If you do not want the link to appear as a hyperlink you can point to it, right-click the mouse and then select **Remove hyperlink**.*

TiP

*If you want to set a link to another section of the same document you must bookmark the word (or words) that you wish to link to. Use **Insert, Bookmark**. You can then create the hyperlink to the bookmark.*

Hyperlinks

You have learnt how to insert and use hyperlinks in web pages. You can insert hyperlinks in word-processed documents too. For example in your e-portfolio you might have a series of versions of a document showing all of its development stages; you can use hyperlinks to take you from one version of the document to another. Imagine how effective it will be for your assessors to follow the progress and read your comments as each element of your project is considered.

Go out and try!

1 Open your Word-processing software file. Create a new bold heading '**WP Activities 167 to 19**'. Write short paragraphs explaining what you have learnt about lines and simple shapes, tick boxes, comments and hyperlinks. Resave the file in your 'Word-processing software' sub-folder.
2 Select the heading **WP Activity 1** and insert a hyperlink that will automatically open the file 'WP Activity 1', as follows.
   ○ Select the text that indicates the hyperlink position.
   ○ From the menu, select **Insert**, **Hyperlink** and browse your files.
   ○ Double-click on the file name you wish the hyperlink to open – in this example 'WP Activity 1'.
3 Insert a second hyperlink in that file that will return you to the 'Word-processing software' file.
4 Repeat this activity with several of the headings.
5 Resave the file.

Styles

When you open your word processor, you know that some things will always be the same. For example

   ○ the first letter is always positioned in the same place on the page
   ○ the font size and style always start the same

- the line spacing starts the same
- the margins start the same
- paragraph alignment starts the same.

This style of presentation is the default or *Normal* style, which always presents itself when you open a new document.

The current style is displayed through the *Style* button and if you click on the button you will be able to see the styles that are available.

A style can be any combination of formatting characteristics that you name and store as a set, such as font style, font size, margin settings and page orientation. When you apply a style, all the formatting instructions in that style are applied at one time. Any style can be created and saved to suit the requirements of a particular document. For example, if certain documents must always be set up in Comic Sans 14 pt, double line spacing with centre justification then it would be sensible to set a style so that you don't have to reformat the standard features every time you need to create such a document. You would just select the style from the stored list.

Use styles to improve the overall appearance of your documents, to help retain consistency of presentation throughout and to make them smarter.

Go out and try!

1 Open a new document and enter the following text:

What can I do in my school holidays?

Are you looking for some ideas to help fill the long, summer days? Travelbug are sponsoring a series of events in Whychton Park throughout the summer. Entrance is free to all children aged 5 to 12 years but you must be accompanied by an adult.

Treasure Hunt

Come and unscramble the clues to find the hidden treasure. Monday, 31 July at 10.00 am and 2.00 pm for children aged 7–12.

Bouncy Castles

Visit Whychton Park from Monday 7 August until Friday

11 August and have fun on the inflatables. Open from 10.00 am to 5.00 pm for children aged under 10.

Archery

Sign up for one of the following sessions according to your age and experience.

Beginners

We will run a series of introductory sessions for boys and girls on Tuesday, 1 August and Wednesday, 2 August.

Intermediates

If you have completed the beginners session, come along and improve your technique any time on Thursday 3 August and Friday 4 August.

2   Open the *Styles and Formatting* task pane through the *Format* menu and apply the following styles:
   ○ **Heading 1** to the main heading
   ○ **Heading 2** to Treasure Hunt, Bouncy Castles and Archery
   ○ **Heading 3** to Beginners and Intermediates.
3   Decide on a style of your own choice for the paragraphs in the document you have just produced. For example Comic Sans, Red, 14 pt font and one-and-a-half line spacing.
4   Create a new style based on your choice through the *Styles and Formatting* task pane and call the style 'My Style'. Position the cursor in each paragraph and click on 'My Style'.

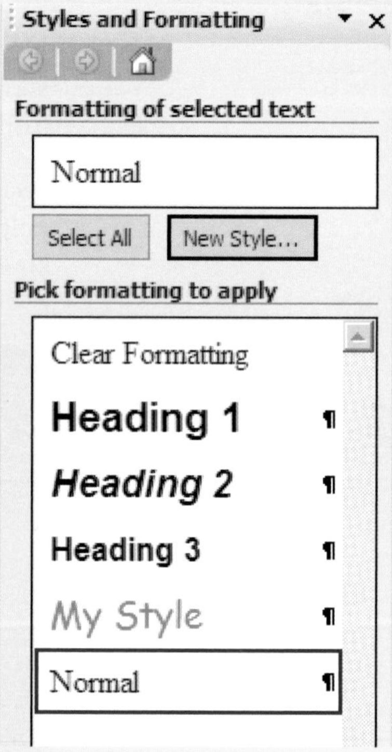

Save the file as 'WP Activity 20' in your 'Word-processing software' sub-folder.

Styles and Formatting   ▼ ✕

Formatting of selected text

Normal

Select All   New Style...

Pick formatting to apply

Clear Formatting

Heading 1   ¶

Heading 2   ¶

Heading 3   ¶

My Style   ¶

Normal   ¶

Figure 65 The Styles and Formatting task pane

Open your Word-processing software file. Create a new bold heading called 'WP Activity 20' and write a short paragraph describing the skills you have demonstrated in this activity. Suggest 3 occasions when this feature may be useful to you. Save the file.

Using images and objects

Many documents and on-screen presentations contain illustrations. These are included to help simplify the information contained in the text, or simply to provide decoration. In this book many types of illustrations have been used: pictures, photographs, charts, graphs, screen prints, text boxes, clip art, WordArt, etc. Collectively these are referred to as *objects*.

Sensible use of images will greatly improve a document and make it more appealing to the target audience. Figure 66 is an example.

An image or object can be inserted by selecting the **Insert** drop-down menu.

TRAVELBUG WATER SPORTS

Departing 20 June
Travel by luxury coach from Whychton
14 nights half-board accommodation in 3-star hotel

A fantastic opportunity to experience a variety of water sports including:

Windsurfing

Learn the basics of windsurfing, including rigging, equipment care, sailing across the wind and self-rescue. Advanced skills include instruction on topics such as water starts, harness use, and shortboards. Wetsuits and windsurfing gear are provided.

Snorkelling

For many people the water's edge is the limit of their activity and knowledge. Learn to snorkel and enjoy the world that lurks beneath the surface of the water. You will be introduced to snorkelling equipment including the mask, flippers and snorkel and will learn how to move safely in the water.

Water skiing

If you are a complete beginner you will start on land and learn the fundamentals of body position, technique and safety. Once you and your instructor are confident in understanding the basics on land, you move to the water. First-time skiers will use the static boom on the side of the boat to offer stability. When you have mastered the boom, then it is off to the long line! Who knows, you may be able to Slalom, Trick or Jump before the end of your holiday!

£585 per person
(based on two people sharing a room and fully inclusive of all equipment and tuition)

17 London Road   Whychton   TO9 3WN
Tel: 543 2134 5678   www.travelbug.co.uk
Fax: 543 2134 5679   Email: info@travelbug.co.uk

Figure 66 Sensible use of images will greatly improve a document and make it more appealing to the target audience

Positioning images and objects

Any image in a document should be there to serve a specific purpose, and its positioning is therefore very important. The position of the cursor when the image is inserted into the document will determine where it appears. Figure 67 shows an example. After the image was inserted, the text was pushed down the page.

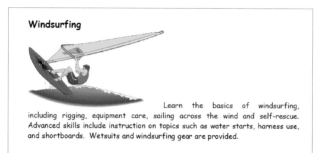

Figure 67 An example of text before the insertion of an image, and the same text with an image: notice how the text has been pushed down the page

Wrapping text around an image

As you can see from Figure 67, although an image has been placed in the document, its inclusion does not really improve the document because it is positioned on the left with empty space at the side. In order to make the document more interesting and the image more manageable, you can format the image and select a *wrapping style* to improve the layout. Figure 68 shows two examples.

 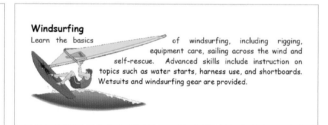

Figure 68 A 'square' wrapping style, and a 'tight' wrapping style in which the text hugs the edges of the image

Wrapping of an image can be achieved by selecting the **Format, Picture** (or **Object**), **Layout** drop-down menu.

Images and objects that are formatted to wrap text can also be moved more easily within the document by clicking and dragging them to a new position.

TiP

Take care when resizing an image. If you select a corner handle the image will be resized while retaining its true proportions. However, if you select a centre top, bottom or side handle you could end up with images looking like Figure 69.

Sizing an image

Sometimes the size of an image or object should be restricted because of the amount of available space on the page. Any object can be resized by selecting the object to show the selection handles and dragging one of the handles with the mouse.

Figure 69 Images that have been resized without retaining the original proportions: inclusion of these images would not improve a document!

Cropping an image

From time to time an image we require might be part of a larger image. We can 'crop' the unwanted area from the image by using the **Crop** tool in the *Picture* toolbar.

(a)

(b)

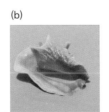

(c)

Figure 70 (a) A clip art image of a sea shell on the beach. (b) The sea shell has been 'cropped', removing the surrounding area. (c) The cropped image can then be resized if necessary.

Go out and try!

1 Write four paragraphs describing different activities you like to do in your spare time. Each paragraph should cover about six lines on the page.

2 Find four clip art images that relate to the activities you have described.
- Place your cursor where you want your image to appear.
- From the **Insert** menu, select **Picture** then **Clip Art**.
- In the *Insert Clip Art* task pane, type in to the *Search For* box words that describe your activities.
- Click on **Search**.

Figure 71 Clip art search options

- Click on your selection to insert the clip art into your document.
- Repeat to insert the other three images.

3 Resize the images to fit into the paragraphs.
- Click on the image to select it. It will have handles on the corners and at the sides.
- Hover over a handle until a double-sided arrow appears. Drag a corner handle to resize the image.

4 Find one more image that you can crop to leave only part of the image on display. Insert the image at the end of the document and crop as required.

5 Save the file as 'WP Activity 21' in your 'Word-processing software' sub-folder.

Go out and try!

1 Incorporate the images within the paragraphs by selecting different text wrapping styles.
  ○ Double-click on one of the images you have inserted to access the *Format Picture* dialogue box.
  ○ Select the *Layout* tab and choose the *Wrapping style* you want to use.

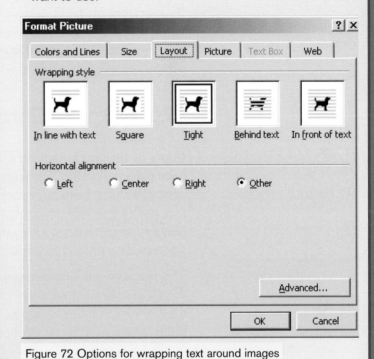

Figure 72 Options for wrapping text around images

  ○ Click **OK** to apply it to your document.
2 Resave your file.

Open your 'Word-processing software' file. Create a new bold heading called '**WP Activity 21**' and write a short paragraph describing the skills you have demonstrated in this activity.
Save the file.

Using spelling and grammar checkers

The importance of using spelling and grammar checkers has been stressed in Standard Ways of Working (on page 76) and in Unit 1 (on page 35).

As a student on an IT course, you have no excuse for submitting work which contains spelling and grammar errors – the tools to help you check the accuracy of your work are at your fingertips. Make sure nothing is left unchecked!

Using mail merge

Jargon buster

Mail merge is used when an organisation wishes to send the same letter to a large number of people.

Many of the letters that arrive in the post at your home will have been prepared using a process called *mail merge*. The letters will appear to have been addressed personally to their recipients, but in fact each letter will probably have been produced as part of a large batch of many letters, all containing exactly the same message but addressed to different people.

This is a very quick and easy way of contacting customers, whose details may be held on a company database. These letters are often sent from banks, building societies, insurance companies, large retail stores, utility companies, credit card companies and other financial businesses.

(?) Think it over ...

Think of five occasions your family might have received letters produced using mail merge.

How are the letters produced?

The letters are produced in two stages.

- First, a *data file* which contains the personal information of the recipients is required. This may be an existing database, or it might be produced in a word-processing or spreadsheet file for a one-off mail merge operation. It will contain details such as name, address, telephone number and account number.

- Second, a *standard letter* is produced. This will contain the text of the message. Instead of being addressed in the usual way, it will contain what are called *merge fields*.

Jargon buster

Merge fields are the points at which the individual personalised details will be inserted in each letter.

Go out and try!

Step 1

○ From the **Tools** menu, select **Letters and Mailings**, **Mail Merge Wizard**.

○ In the task pane's *Select document type* section, select **Letters**.

Figure 73 Mail merge: select the document type

○ Click on **Next: Starting document**.

Step 2

This gives you a choice of preparing the letter from a document (or blank document) on the screen, a letter saved in a file, or a template.

○ In the *Select starting document* section, select **Use the current document**.

Figure 74 Mail merge: select the starting document

○ Click on **Next: Select recipients**.

Step 3

○ In the *Select recipients* section, select **Type a new list**.

Figure 75 Mail merge: the address list can be customised to suit you needs

○ Click on **Create**.
○ A *New Address List* dialogue box appears.

TiP

If you have the names and addresses in an existing data file, you can link that file to the letter by browsing through your files and opening the file that contains the data. It may be in a word-processing, spreadsheet, database or email application.

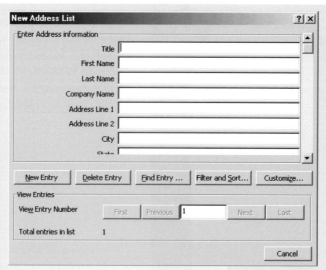

Figure 76 Entry screen for an address list

You can customise your address list to suit your needs and delete any unwanted information.

○ Click on the **Customize** button.

○ Delete any unwanted fields (e.g. company name).

○ Make your list the same as in Figure 77.

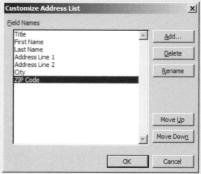

Figure 77 Mail merge: this address list has been customised

Create three entries in the revised list.

○ Enter your own details in the appropriate boxes as the first entry.

○ Click on **New Entry** and enter the two records shown in Figure 80 on page 136.

○ Click on **Close**.

Save your address list with a suitable filename.

○ In the **Save As** dialogue box, save your address list with a suitable filename, such as 'Mail merge addresses', in your 'Word-processing software' sub-folder.

○ Click on **Next: Write your letter**. The *Write your letter* task pane appears.

Figure 78 Mail merge: write your letter

Step 4

You are now ready to write your letter

○ Copy the letter shown in Figure 79.

○ Where you see merge fields such as <<Title>>, <<First_Name>> and <<Last_Name>>

   ● click on the **More items** link.

   ● select the merge field from the list and click on **Insert**.

○ When you have inserted all the merge fields, click on **Close**.

NB Remember to insert spaces between <<Title>>, <<First_Name>> and <<Last_Name>> and to press **Enter** at the end of each line of the address.

Insert the current date

«Title» «First_Name» «Last_Name»
«Address_Line_1»
«Address_Line_2»
«City»
«ZIP_Code»

Dear «Title» «Last_Name»

Thank you for your interest in the forthcoming weekend visit to northern France.

I enclose your tickets and confirm the coach will pick you up at «City» station at the time indicated on the ticket.

I hope you have an enjoyable visit to France.

Yours sincerely

Figure 79 Mail merge: the skeleton letter template with fields highlighted

○ 🖫 Save your letter as you go along in your 'Word-processing software' sub-folder, with a suitable filename such as 'Mail merge letter'.

○ Click on **Next: Preview your letters**.

○ Click on **Next: Complete the merge**.

You will now have three letters, each personally addressed – and you only had to type the letter once! The merged letters should be similar to those in Figure 80.

Insert the current date

Mr John Gray
23 Deepfield House
Deepfield Way
Linfield
TO6 5DC

Dear Mr Gray

Thank you for your interest in the forthcoming weekend visit to northern France.

I enclose your tickets and confirm the coach will pick you up at Linfield station at the time indicated on the ticket.

I hope you have an enjoyable visit to France.

Yours sincerely

Insert the current date

Miss Jean Smith
4 Glebe Gardens
Whychton
TO7 3FD

Dear Miss Smith

Thank you for your interest in the forthcoming weekend visit to northern France.

I enclose your tickets and confirm the coach will pick you up at Whychton station at the time indicated on the ticket.

I hope you have an enjoyable visit to France.

Yours sincerely

Figure 80 Examples of two letters produced by mail merge

? Think it over ...

Remember that in business the data file will probably have hundreds of entries. Imagine the time it will save to produce hundreds of letters in this way.

Open your 'Word-processing software' file. Create a new bold heading called '**WP Activity 22**' and write a short paragraph describing the skills you have demonstrated in this activity. Save the file.

Spreadsheet software

You will almost certainly have used a spreadsheet for your schoolwork. You will know that the main purpose of a spreadsheet is to enter, edit and manipulate *numerical* data, and to *make calculations* using this data. As part of your e-portfolio evidence for your coursework, you will need to gather and analyse data to produce meaningful information, some of which will be in the form of spreadsheets and graphs or charts.

Spreadsheet programs make it much easier to perform financial tasks such as calculating staff wages, profit made on goods sold, VAT (value-added tax) returns for the government, and bank accounts. A spreadsheet program is an invaluable tool to all kinds of organisations, from small ones such as a neighbourhood card shop, to your own school or college, or huge companies such as Top Shop, Microsoft or government organisations such as the National Health Service.

On a personal level you might use a spreadsheet to keep track of how much income you receive, what expenses you have and how much is left to save.

LEARNING OUTCOMES

You need to learn about

✓ entering, cutting, copying, pasting and moving data

✓ formatting cells to match data types

✓ using operators

✓ replicating formulas using relative cell references

✓ replicating formulas using absolute cell references

✓ inserting or deleting rows and columns

✓ using simple functions

✓ sorting data

✓ producing fully customised charts and graphs

✓ using headers and footers

✓ printing selected areas.

Entering, cutting, copying, pasting and moving data

Let's look at the structure of spreadsheets in more detail, beginning with a very basic example.

The spreadsheet worksheet is divided into *rows* and *columns*, creating a *grid of cells*. Each row and column in a spreadsheet is given a unique number or letter, so each cell can be identified rather like a map reference – A1, B6, C12 etc.

Jargon buster

Spreadsheet files are known as **workbooks**. Each workbook may include several **worksheets** (pages) all related to the main purpose of that file.

	A	B	C	D
1				
2				
3				
4				

Figure 81 Spreadsheet cell references

Cell C2

Jargon buster

The **default size** of a spreadsheet cell is the width and height already set by the software.

The data – a row or column heading, text or number – is entered into a cell. However, the default size of a cell is quite small. If the data entered into the cell is too wide it will overlap into the next cell; but as soon as data is entered into the adjacent cell, some of the original data becomes hidden (not lost). You will then need to decide the best method of overcoming the problem, and this is discussed later.

After you start using a spreadsheet you may need to make changes because

- you have identified some improvements you could introduce
- you have learned more about the spreadsheet program's facilities
- the needs of the business have altered.

You can cut, copy, paste and move data between cells, rows and columns. Look back at page 89 – you will see that the icons and keystrokes work in exactly the same way in Excel.

Formatting cells to match their data types

Unless formatting techniques (use of bold, colour, borders, fill or shading) have been used, the spreadsheet can be very difficult to read – especially if it is very large, covering many rows and columns. So it is very important to consider the *appearance* of the spreadsheet as well as the data and the formulas.

Just as in word-processing software, you can enhance the text in a spreadsheet by

- using bold, italic or underlined text
- varying the font size for main headings or sub-headings
- using different font styles.

In addition you can improve the appearance of the spreadsheet by

- formatting a heading at an angle or vertically within cells
- centring a heading horizontally within a cell or across two or more columns
- centring a heading vertically within a cell (i.e. centred from top to bottom)
- wrapping text within a cell to avoid having an extremely wide column
- adjusting the cell width or height
- highlighting significant cells (e.g. ones with totals) with borders or colours.

You should also pay attention to the following when formatting numerical data:

- How many decimal places do you need, if any? For example, if you have a column for the number of students in different tutor groups, you would not have $\frac{1}{2}$ or 0.5 of a student! However, if you are listing the sales of fruit or vegetables, you might well have $\frac{1}{2}$ or 0.5 of a kilo. In the first case you do not need any decimal places, but in the second you might well want to show two decimal places.
- If the data is the cost of the item, do you wish to show the currency symbol, or is it enough to format the money to two decimal places? What would be suitable for house prices?
- If the currency symbol is used, is it too cluttered to show the £ sign everywhere, or might it be better to use it just for the totals?
- Do you wish to show negative numbers in red? If so, this can be set automatically.

Figure 82 Angled headings

Columns marked A, B, C etc.

Rows marked 1,2, 3 etc.

Notice text that is partially hidden by data in the next cell

Data entered into the cells

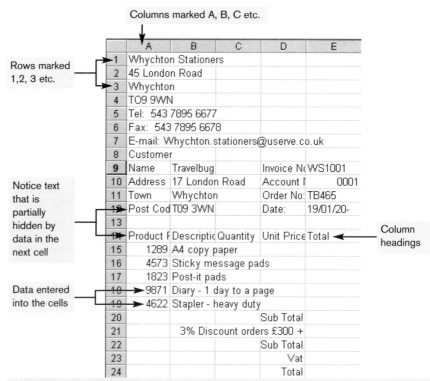

Column headings

	A	B	C	D	E
1	Whychton Stationers				
2	45 London Road				
3	Whychton				
4	TO9 9WN				
5	Tel: 543 7895 6677				
6	Fax: 543 7895 6678				
7	E-mail: Whychton.stationers@userve.co.uk				
8	Customer				
9	Name	Travelbug		Invoice No	WS1001
10	Address	17 London Road		Account I	0001
11	Town	Whychton		Order No:	TB465
12	Post Cod	TO9 3WN		Date:	19/01/20-
13					
14	Product F	Descriptic	Quantity	Unit Price	Total
15	1289	A4 copy paper			
16	4573	Sticky message pads			
17	1823	Post-it pads			
18	9871	Diary - 1 day to a page			
19	4622	Stapler - heavy duty			
20				Sub Total	
21		3% Discount orders £300 +			
22				Sub Total	
23				Vat	
24				Total	

Figure 83 Whychton Stationers invoice to Travelbug: a very basic spreadsheet layout before quantity, unit price and formulas have been entered

Go out and try!

Thomas Tripp of Travelbug likes to give business to the local shops and has placed an order with Whychton Stationers, which has recently opened. When businesses place orders with each other, they do not usually pay for the goods immediately, but are sent an invoice – the bill – at a later stage.

Figure 83 shows the invoice to Travelbug from Whychton Stationers, but as you can see the invoice form is badly laid out and there has been no attempt to format the spreadsheet. Peter Paperly, the manager of Whychton Stationers, realises that the invoice template needs to be improved before it can be used for customers.

1 Study the spreadsheet shown in Figure 83. Look back at the tips on formatting spreadsheets and list any improvements you could make. Think about the formatting techniques described and whether the company address should be set out like a letterhead.

2 Enter the data into your spreadsheet program. The words you can't quite read because of overlapping cells should be

cell D9 – Invoice No:
cell D10 – Account No:
cell A12 – Post Code
cell A14 – Product Ref:

3   Format the layout, including the improvements you have identified.
   ○ To make columns wider, move the mouse pointer to the line between the column header on the right side of the column, click and drag it to the required width.

	A	B	C	D
1		**Whychton Stationers**		
2		45 London Road		
3		Whychton		

Figure 84 Resizing a column

4   Add in the quantities and prices as follows:

A4 copy paper	40	5.99
Sticky message pads	12	3.99
Post-it pads	24	2.99
Diary – 1 day to a page	2	12.99
Stapler – heavy duty	1	24.99

5   Think about
   ○ how to format the numerical data
   ○ the calculations (formulas) you will need for column E.
   See if your formulas match those in Figure 85.
6   ▣ Save the file as 'Travelbug invoice' in your 'Spreadsheet software' folder. Make sure you save all your work for this chapter in the same folder.

Start a new word-processing file called 'Spreadsheet software'. Create a new bold heading called '**SS Activity 1**' and write a short paragraph describing the skills you have demonstrated in this activity. ▣ Save the file.

Entering and using formulas

Jargon buster

In a spreadsheet, a **formula** always starts with an equals sign (=). It is the **method** to make a calculation, but it is not the answer. The **result** of using the formula is the answer.

If you go into a sweetshop and buy three bars of chocolate at 50p each, you know that the total cost will be £1.50, but how would you work that out? You multiplied 3 by 50, and that was your *formula*.

Using operators

The important point to remember is that in Excel *a formula always starts with an equals sign*. This tells Excel that it needs to perform a calculation. In order to tell the spreadsheet what kind of calculation you need, you use the following *arithemetic operators*:

- adding +
- subtracting −
- multiplying *
- dividing /

The spreadsheet will calculate formulas using *values*, such as

	Formula	Result
Formula using values	=40*5.99	239.60

More typically, *cell references* are used in formulas. For example, in cell E15 in Figure 67 you would use the formula '=C15*D15' to calculate the cost of the A4 copy paper

	Formula	Result
Formula using cell references	=C15*D15	239.60

The big advantage with using cell references in formulas, rather than the actual numbers, is that the spreadsheet will automatically do a recalculation if any changes are made in the data. For example, if the price of the paper changes to £6.50, you enter the new price in cell D15 and the total cost will be automatically recalculated (£260).

Go out and try!

Figure 85 shows the Travelbug invoice from Figure 83 (page 140) with the formulas inserted in column E.

	A	B	C	D	E
1	Whychton St:				
2	45 London Rc				
3	Whychton				
4	TO9 9WN				
5	Tel: 543 789!				
6	Fax: 543 789				
7	E-mail: Whyc				
8	Customer				
9	Name	Travelbug		Invoice No:	WS1001
10	Address	17 London Road		Account Nc	0001
11	Town	Whychton		Order No:	TB465
12	Post Code	T09 3WN		Date:	19/01/20-
13					
14	Product Ref	Description	Quantity	Unit Price	Total
15	1289	A4 copy paper	40	5.99	=C15*D15
16	4573	Sticky message pa	12	3.99	=C16*D16
17	1823	Post-it pads	24	2.99	=C17*D17
18	9871	Diary - 1 day to a p	2	12.99	=C18*D18
19	4622	Stapler - heavy duty	1	24.99	=C19*D19
20				Sub Total	=SUM(E15:E19)
21				lers £300 +	=E20*3%
22				Sub Total	=E20-E21
23				Vat	=E22*17.5%
24				Total	=E22+E23

Figure 85 Travelbug invoice showing the formulas

1 Open the file you saved as 'Travelbug invoice' and enter the formulas into column E as shown in Figure 85.
   ○ Click into cell E15 and type **=C15*D15**. Press the **Enter** key or click the green tick on the toolbar to accept the formula.
   ○ Enter the rest of the formulas in the same way.
2 It is very easy to assume that because the computer has worked something out for you *it must be right*, so check the results of these formulas by using a calculator. Do they match? If not, why not? It might be a simple error such as entering a minus sign (–) when you should have entered a plus sign (+).
3 💾 Save the file 'Travelbug invoice'.

Open your file 'Spreadsheet software'. Create a new bold heading called '**SS Activity 2**' and write a short paragraph describing the skills you have demonstrated in this activity.
💾 Save the file.

Replicating formulas

Using relative cell references

The spreadsheet designed for Whychton Stationers had only a few formulas, so it did not take long to enter them into the cells. However, as already mentioned, spreadsheets used by business organisations can be huge, and it would be very tedious to enter the same formula across 100 rows or down 100 columns:

```
=SUM(C5:E5)
=SUM(C6:E6)
...
...
=SUM(C105:E105)!
```

One of the advantages of using a spreadsheet is the facility to *replicate* (i.e. copy) a formula across columns or down rows, rather than having to keep entering it again and again. If you need to have totals down several rows or across several columns, you can enter the formula into the first cell and then replicate the formula across to the last column or down to the last row. The spreadsheet will automatically change the formula to give the correct cell references.

Look back at Figure 85, where you can see the formula in cell E15 to calculate the total is '=C15*D15'. You could then enter the formula on the next row by keying in '=C16*D16', and so on down each row. However, once the formula is entered into cell E15, as it is copied down the rows the software automatically changes the cell references to '=C16*D16', '=C17*D17' and so on.

Using absolute cell references

Sometimes you wish to refer to a particular cell address many times. Therefore when you replicate the formula, the *cell address needs to remain the same*. The technical term for this is *absolute reference*.

Figure 86 illustrates this point. Travelbug have a number of villas for holiday rentals in different parts of Europe. As more and more customers are making enquiries via the Internet, Travelbug realised that it was important to quote prices in both pounds and euros. The price in euros is calculated by multiplying the price in pounds by the rate of exchange. The rate of exchange is entered in one cell: D2. In this case, as the formula is copied down the rows, the cell reference for the price in sterling needs to change from row to row, *but the cell reference for the rate of exchange – D2 – needs to remain the same.*

You will notice that the formulas in column E show $ signs before the D and 2 (note $D$2 in Figure 86). These signs are used in Excel to instruct the program that, when copying the formula, this cell reference must *not* be changed. Although in the small example shown it would be easy to key in the formula on each new line, as mentioned already, in a commercial spreadsheet you might replicate

	A	B	C	D	E
1			**Travelbug Villas**		
2			of Exchange £ to €	1.4	
3	**Destination**	**Resort**	**Name of Villa**	**Price per week Sterling**	**Price per week Euros**
4	Algarve	Bordeira	Casa Luz	799	=D4*$D$2
5	Algarve	Lagos	Casa Limoa	849	=D5*$D$2
6	Algarve	Estol	Casa Marco	719	=D6*$D$2
7	Algarve	Carvoeiro	Sete Estrelo	899	=D7*$D$2
8	Cyprus	Latchi	Irene	859	=D8*$D$2
9	Cyprus	Coral Bay	Villa Olivia	809	=D9*$D$2
10	Cyprus	Polis	The Vines	909	=D10*$D$2
11	Costa Blanca	Denia	Casa Moura	779	=D11*$D$2
12	Costa Blanca	Javea	Las Palmmares	829	=D12*$D$2
13	Costa Blanca	Calpe	Casa Alana	779	=D13*$D$2
14	Costa Blanca	Albir	Villa Marlene	649	=D14*$D$2
15	France	Dordogne	Eva	2225	=D15*$D$2
16	France	Dordogne	Chateau Alexa	1490	=D16*$D$2
17	France	Cote D'Azur	La Marina	2720	=D17*$D$2
18	France	South West Coast	Villa Zivia	1660	=D18*$D$2
19	France	West Coast - Charentes	La Belle Vacance	965	=D19*$D$2

Figure 86 The formula view of the price list for renting Travelbug villas: notice that the cell reference D4 changes to D5, etc., but the cell reference $D$2 does not

the formula down hundreds of rows. The other benefit is that, when the rate of exchange alters, it is a simple matter to enter the new rate in cell D2 and all prices in column E will change automatically.

Figure 87 shows the spreadsheet after the calculations have been done by the software.

	A	B	C	D	E
1			**Travelbug Villas**		
2			**Rate of Exchange £ to €**	**€ 1.40**	
3	**Destination**	**Resort**	**Name of Villa**	**Price per week Sterling**	**Price per week Euros**
4	Algarve	Bordeira	Casa Luz	£799	€ 1,119
5	Algarve	Lagos	Casa Limoa	£849	€ 1,189
6	Algarve	Estol	Casa Marco	£719	€ 1,007
7	Algarve	Carvoeiro	Sete Estrelo	£899	€ 1,259
8	Cyprus	Latchi	Irene	£859	€ 1,203
9	Cyprus	Coral Bay	Villa Olivia	£809	€ 1,133
10	Cyprus	Polis	The Vines	£909	€ 1,273
11	Costa Blanca	Denia	Casa Moura	£779	€ 1,091
12	Costa Blanca	Javea	Las Palmmares	£829	€ 1,161
13	Costa Blanca	Calpe	Casa Alana	£779	€ 1,091
14	Costa Blanca	Albir	Villa Marlene	£649	€ 909
15	France	Dordogne	Eva	£2,225	€ 3,115
16	France	Dordogne	Chateau Alexa	£1,490	€ 2,086
17	France	Cote D'Azur	La Marina	£2,720	€ 3,808
18	France	South West Coast	Villa Zivia	£1,660	€ 2,324
19	France	West Coast - Charentes	La Belle Vacance	£965	€ 1,351

Figure 87 The data view of the price list for renting Travelbug villas

Go out and try!

1 Key in the spreadsheet shown in Figure 86.

2 Format cells D4 to D19 to currency with the £ symbol and 0 decimal places and cells E4 to E19 with the € symbol with 0 decimal places.

3 Make sure you use a formula for the price in euros as shown in the next step.
   At first do not include the dollar signs.
   ○ In cell E4 enter the formula '=D4*D2'.

4 Copy the formula down to row 19.
   ○ Position the mouse pointer over the bottom right-hand corner of the cell and, when the white cross turns to a black cross, press the left mouse button and drag down the column.
   You will notice that there are errors in the results. Why is this? Look at the cell references to see whether you can find the problem.

Price per week Euros
=D4*D2
=D5*D3
=D6*D4
=D7*D5
=D8*D6
=D9*D7

5 Go back to cell E4 and change the formula to '=D4*$D$2'.

6 Copy the formula down to row 19. This time you should find the prices in euros do match those in Figure 87.

7 Make sure the prices in columns D and E are formatted to 0 decimal places.
- Click and drag over the prices in columns D and E to select them.
- From the menu, select **Format**, **Cells**.
- The *Format Cells* dialogue appears. Make sure the *Number* tab is displayed.
- Choose the **Currency** option and set the decimal places to **0** for column D.
- For column E choose the **Euro** from the *Symbol* drop down list.

Price per week Euros
=D4*$D$2
=D5*$D$2
=D6*$D$2
=D7*$D$2
=D8*$D$2
=D9*$D$2

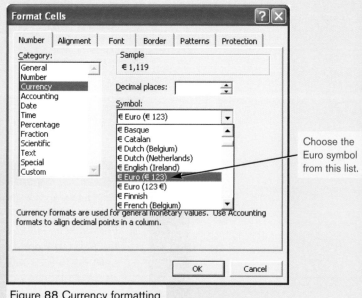

Choose the Euro symbol from this list.

Figure 88 Currency formatting

8 💾 Save the file as 'Villas' in your 'Spreadsheet software' sub-folder.

Open your 'Spreadsheet software' file. Create a new bold heading called '**SS Activity 3**' and write a short paragraph describing the skills you have demonstrated in this activity.
💾 Save the file.

Inserting or deleting rows and columns

Spreadsheet software makes it easy to add or delete rows or columns. To delete cells, select them and then use the **Delete** command on the right-click menu. To insert cells, select the location where you want to add them and use the options on the **Insert** menu.

Go out and try!

1 Open the file saved as 'Villas'.
2 The villa Eva has been sold, so delete row 15.
   - Right-click in the row number box.
   - Choose **Delete** from the shortcut menu that appears.

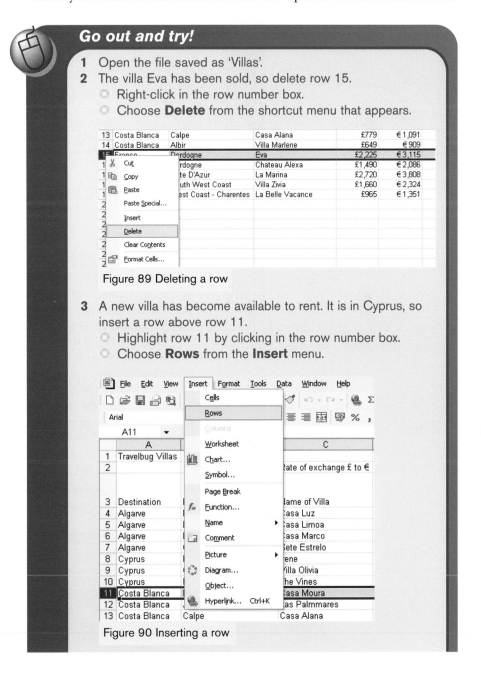

Figure 89 Deleting a row

3 A new villa has become available to rent. It is in Cyprus, so insert a row above row 11.
   - Highlight row 11 by clicking in the row number box.
   - Choose **Rows** from the **Insert** menu.

Figure 90 Inserting a row

The villa is in the resort of Angaka, is called Agathi and costs £859. Check that the price in euros has been calculated – if not, copy the formula.

4   Thomas Tripp has realised that the spreadsheet is showing only the prices for the high season and this is putting people off renting the villas in the low season. Insert two new columns before column D.

○ Highlight the two columns D and E

○ Choose **Columns** from the **Insert** menu.

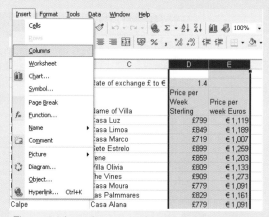

Figure 91 Inserting two columns

5   This should insert two columns, since you had selected two columns. If you only selected one then repeat the process so that there are two new columns.

6   The rate of exchange – €1.40 – is no longer next to the words, but has moved from cell D2 to cell F2.

○ Place the cursor in cell F2 and cut the data (**Edit**, **Cut**).

○ Place the cursor in cell D2 and paste the data (**Edit**, **Paste**) back in the right place.

7   Highlight row 3 (containing the headings 'Destination', etc.) and insert a row above it (**Insert**, **Rows**).

8   In cell D3, enter the heading 'Low Season' and centre it across columns D and E.

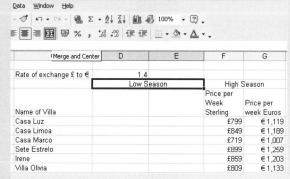

Figure 92 Two cells that have been merged and centred

- Highlight D3 and E3
- Click on the **Merge and Center** icon on the toolbar.
- In cell F3, enter the heading 'High Season' and centre it across columns F and G in the same way as before.

10 Highlight cells F4 and G4 and copy the data to the clipboard in the usual way. Place the cursor in cell D4 and paste the selection.

11 Key in the prices for the low season – see Figure 93.

12 In cell E5, enter the formula to convert the prices to euros and replicate it down the rows. Check your results with Figure 93.

	A	B	C	D	E	F	G
1			Travelbug Villas				
2		Rate of Exchange £ to €		€ 1.40			
3				Low Season		High Season	
4	Destination	Resort	Name of Villa	Price per week Sterling	Price per week Euros	Price per week Sterling	Price per week Euros
5	Algarve	Bordeira	Casa Luz	£559	€ 783	£799	€ 1,119
6	Algarve	Lagos	Casa Limoa	£594	€ 832	£849	€ 1,189
7	Algarve	Estol	Casa Marco	£503	€ 704	£719	€ 1,007
8	Algarve	Carvoeiro	Sete Estrelo	£629	€ 881	£899	€ 1,259
9	Cyprus	Latchi	Irene	£601	€ 841	£859	€ 1,203
10	Cyprus	Coral Bay	Villa Olivia	£566	€ 792	£809	€ 1,133
11	Cyprus	Polis	The Vines	£636	€ 890	£909	€ 1,273
12	Cyprus	Argaka	Agathi	£629	€ 881	£859	€ 1,203
13	Costa Blanca	Denia	Casa Moura	£545	€ 763	£779	€ 1,091
14	Costa Blanca	Javea	Las Palmmares	£580	€ 812	£829	€ 1,161
15	Costa Blanca	Calpe	Casa Alana	£545	€ 763	£779	€ 1,091
16	Costa Blanca	Albir	Villa Marlene	£454	€ 636	£649	€ 909
17	France	Dordogne	Chateau Alexa	£1,043	€ 1,460	£1,490	€ 2,086
18	France	Cote D'Azur	La Marina	£1,904	€ 2,666	£2,720	€ 3,808
19	France	South West Coast	Villa Zivia	£1,162	€ 1,627	£1,660	€ 2,324
20	France	West Coast - Charentes	La Belle Vacance	£675	€ 945	£965	€ 1,351

Figure 93 Low- and high-season prices for Travelbug villas

TiP

When you move a cell using cut and paste, any references to the original cell are automatically updated.

13 The rate of exchange has changed to €1.45. Change the rate in cell D2 and check that the prices in euros are automatically recalculated.

14 No, there is a mistake – the rate of exchange is still €1.40. Change it back again. Once again the prices in euros are automatically recalculated.

15 Customers need to know the number of bedrooms and the number of people the villa can sleep. Insert two columns before column D in the same way as before. The rate of exchange is now in cell F2, so move it back to cell D2 using cut and paste.

16 Add the data in Figure 94 to show the number of bedrooms and the number of people the villa can accommodate for sleeping.

Name of villa	No. of bedrooms	Sleeps up to
Casa Luz	3	6
Casa Limoa	3	6
Casa Marco	2	4
Sete Estrelo	4	8
Irene	4	8
Villa Olivia	3	6
The Vines	5	10
Agathi	4	8
Casa Moura	4	8
Las Palmmares	4	8
Casa Alana	3	6
Villa Marlene	2	4
Chateau Alexa	4	8
La Marina	5	10
Villa Zivia	4	8
La Belle Vacance	2	4

Figure 94 Data for your *Go out and try!* task

17 Save the file.

Open your 'Spreadsheet software' file. Create a new bold heading called '**SS Activity 4**' and write short paragraphs describing the skills you have demonstrated in this activity, under the following headings:

○ *Insert and delete rows or columns*
○ *Cut, copy and paste*
○ *Replicate formulas*
○ *Change the rate in the absolute cell reference.*

 Save the file.

Using simple functions

When you open an Excel worksheet and click on the function icon f_x, you will see that there are very many functions available. We shall look here at two frequently used functions – SUM and AVERAGE.

The SUM function

Look back at Figure 85 on page 142 and the formula in cell E20. Remember that the formula could have been written as

TiP

If you wish to find the total
of a column or row of cells,
select the cell at the bottom
of the column or to the right
of the row, click on the
AutoSum icon, and the
formula will be written for
you.

'=E15+E16+E17+E18+E19'. That becomes very tedious if you have
to add up 100 rows or columns, and it is easy to make mistakes, but
by using the SUM function you can add up the range of cells without
having to enter each cell reference.

You can use the SUM function by keying in a formula – in this case
'=SUM(E15:E19)'. The colon (:) tells the program to add up all the
cells in the range from E15 to E19.

It can be quicker to use the **Autosum** icon $\boxed{\Sigma}$ on the *Standard* toolbar.

Usually the correct range of cells will be selected, but do be careful
when using **AutoSum**: sometimes cells are included that are not
required.

Look at Figure 95, where the **AutoSum** command was used in cell F5
to calculate the total value of bookings. The range selected was
'B5:E5', but *this includes the individual weeks booked as well as the
total weeks booked*. To calculate the total number of weeks, only the
range 'C5:E5' is necessary. To correct the error you can either enter
'=SUM(C5:E5)' yourself, or select cells C5 to E5 by dragging with
the mouse. You can then copy the formulas down the rows using
relative cell references, as you learned earlier.

AutoSum command

	A	B	C	D	E	F	G
1			Travelbug Villas				
2	Quarterly Rentals						
3	Low Season		Number of weeks reserved				
4	Name of Villa	Cost of weekly rental	Jan	Feb	Mar	Total No Weeks Reserved	Total Value of Bookings
5	Casa Luz	£559	2	0	3	=SUM(B5:E5)	
6	Casa Limoa	£594	1	2	3	SUM(number1, [number2], ...)	
7	Casa Marco	£503	1	1	4	6	£3,018
8	Sete Estrelo	£629	3	1	2	6	£3,774
9	Irene	£601	3	2	4	9	£5,409
10	Villa Olivia	£566	4	4	3	11	£6,226
11	The Vines	£636	2	2	3	7	£4,452
12	Agathi	£629	1	2	2	5	£3,145
13	Casa Moura	£545	3	0	2	5	£2,725
14	Las Palmmares	£580	2	1	3	6	£3,480
15	Casa Alana	£545	2	2	1	5	£2,725
16	Villa Marlene	£454	3	1	3	7	£3,178
17	Chateau Alexa	£1,043	1	0	0	1	£1,043
18	La Marina	£1,904	0	0	1	1	£1,904
19	Villa Zivia	£1,162	0	1	2	3	£3,486
20	La Belle Vacance	£675	1	2	3	6	£4,050

1st Quarter / 2nd Quarter / 3rd Quarter / 4th Quarter /

Figure 95 The AutoSum command and four worksheets in the workbook: the status line near
the top shows the incorrect formula '=SUM(B5:E5)' selected by the AutoSum command

TiP

The only time it is necessary
to include the word SUM in
a formula is when you are
adding a range of cells
without keying in all the cell
references.

Quite often, students enter '=SUM' as part of a formula when it is not necessary. Look back at Figure 85 (page 142). The formula in cell E24 is '=E22+E23', but students sometimes enter '=SUM(E22:E23)'. This will work, but it is *not* required in this case.

Go out and try!

1. Create a new spreadsheet file as shown in Figure 95. Enter the headings given in rows 1 to 4.
2. Instead of entering the names of all the villas again, reopen the file you saved as 'Villas'. Highlight cells C5 to D20 and copy the names of the villas and the low-season costs of rental. Switch back to the new spreadsheet, click in cell A5 and paste the data into the new file.
3. Copy the data for the number of weeks reserved for January, February and March from Figure 95.
4. Add a formula into column F to add up the number of weeks.
   - Click in cell F5.
   - Click on the **AutoSum** button.
   - Highlight the correct cells (to exclude the cost cell) and press **Enter**.
   - Copy down to the other rows.
5. Calculate the total value of bookings.
   - Click in cell G5.
   - Key in '=B5*F5'.
   - Copy down to the other rows.

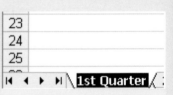

Figure 96 Renamed worksheet

6. Save the file as 'Villa Rentals' in the 'Spreadsheet software' sub-folder.
7. Name the worksheet '1st Quarter'.
   - Double-click on the 'Sheet 1' worksheet tab and enter the name '1st Quarter'.
   - Press **Enter**.
8. Make a copy of your worksheet.
   - Right-click with the mouse on the worksheet tab.
   - Choose **Move or copy**.
   - Select (**move to end**) and click in the **Create a copy** checkbox.
9. Repeat twice more so that you have three new worksheets. Rename them

Figure 97 Creating a copy of a worksheet

'2nd Quarter', '3rd Quarter' and '4th Quarter'. 💾 Save your work.

10 Select the 2nd Quarter sheet and change the months to 'April', 'May' and 'June'. This is the high season so change the heading in cell A3 to 'High Season'.

11 The rental costs need to be changed to the high season rates.
    ○ Open the file saved as 'Villas'.
    ○ Copy the high season rates from H5 to H20.
    ○ Switch back to the 'Villa Rentals' file and its '2nd Quarter' worksheet.
    ○ Place the cursor in cell B5 and use **Paste** 📋.
    The high season rates will replace the low season rates and the value of bookings will automatically be recalculated.

12 Highlight cells C5 to E20 and press the **Delete** key to remove the data.

13 Select the '3rd Quarter' worksheet, which is also high season, and change the months to 'July', 'August' and 'September'. Also change the heading in A3 to 'High Season'. Repeat steps 11 and 12 for the '3rd Quarter' worksheet.

14 Select the '4th Quarter' worksheet, which is low season, and change the months to 'October', 'November' and 'December'. Because this is low season the rates do not need to be changed. 💾 Save your work.

15 Enter the data in Figure 98 into the 2nd, 3rd and 4th Quarter worksheets. Notice that the total number of weeks reserved and the total value of bookings automatically recalculate as you enter the new data. 💾 Save the file.

Name of villa	April	May	June	July	Aug	Sept	Oct	Nov	Dec
Casa Luz	2	3	4	4	4	3	2	2	2
Casa Limoa	3	2	3	4	4	3	3	3	4
Casa Marco	2	3	4	4	4	4	4	2	3
Sete Estrelo	1	2	3	4	4	2	3	2	3
Irene	3	3	3	4	4	4	3	3	4
Villa Olivia	4	3	4	4	4	3	4	3	4
The Vines	3	3	4	4	4	3	3	4	4
Agathi	4	2	4	4	4	4	3	2	3
Casa Moura	4	2	4	4	4	4	3	2	3
Las Palmmares	3	3	3	4	4	3	4	2	2
Casa Alana	1	3	3	4	4	3	4	3	3
Villa Marlene	3	2	4	4	4	3	4	3	0
Chateau Alexa	2	2	3	4	4	3	3	1	0
La Marina	1	2	3	4	4	3	2	0	4
Villa Zivia	1	3	2	4	4	4	2	0	3
La Belle Vacance	2	3	4	4	4	4	4	3	2

Figure 98 Data for your *Go out and try!* task

Open your 'Spreadsheet software' file. Create a new bold heading called '**SS Activity 5**' and write a short paragraph describing the skills you have demonstrated in this activity, under the following headings:

- Copying data from another spreadsheet file
- Using AutoSum
- Renaming worksheets
- Copying worksheets.

💾 Save the file.

The AVERAGE function

When you calculate the average, you are trying to establish the typical value of a group or situation. You do this by adding up all the relevant items and dividing by the number of items. For example, if you wanted to find out the average rental price of the villas, you would add up all the prices and divide by the number of villas in the list.

Look at Figure 99. The formula '=AVERAGE(F5:F20)' is entered into cell F21, and this calculates the average cost to rent a villa for a

	A	B	C	D	E	F	G	H	I
1			Travelbug Villas						
2			Rate of Exchange £ to €		€ 1.40				
3						Low Season		High Season	
4	Destination	Resort	Name of Villa	No of bedrooms	Sleeps up to	Price per week Sterling	Price per week Euros	Price per week Sterling	Price per week Euros
5	Algarve	Bordeira	Casa Luz	3	6	£559	€ 783	£799	€ 1,119
6	Algarve	Lagos	Casa Limoa	3	6	£594	€ 832	£849	€ 1,189
7	Algarve	Estol	Casa Marco	2	4	£503	€ 704	£719	€ 1,007
8	Algarve	Carvoeiro	Sete Estrelo	4	8	£629	€ 881	£899	€ 1,259
9	Cyprus	Latchi	Irene	4	8	£601	€ 841	£859	€ 1,203
10	Cyprus	Coral Bay	Villa Olivia	3	6	£566	€ 792	£809	€ 1,133
11	Cyprus	Polis	The Vines	5	10	£636	€ 890	£909	€ 1,273
12	Cyprus	Argaka	Agathi	4	8	£629	€ 881	£859	€ 1,203
13	Costa Blanca	Denia	Casa Moura	4	8	£545	€ 763	£779	€ 1,091
14	Costa Blanca	Javea	Las Palmmares	4	8	£580	€ 812	£829	€ 1,161
15	Costa Blanca	Calpe	Casa Alana	3	6	£545	€ 763	£779	€ 1,091
16	Costa Blanca	Albir	Villa Marlene	2	4	£454	€ 636	£649	€ 909
17	France	Dordogne	Chateau Alexa	4	8	£1,043	€ 1,460	£1,490	€ 2,086
18	France	Cote D'Azur	La Marina	5	10	£1,904	€ 2,666	£2,720	€ 3,808
19	France	South West Coast	Villa Zivia	4	8	£1,162	€ 1,627	£1,660	€ 2,324
20	France	West Coast - Charentes	La Belle Vacance	2	4	£675	€ 945	£965	€ 1,351
21			Average price of weekly rental			£727	€ 1,017	£1,036	€ 1,450

Figure 99 The formula for AVERAGE is shown in the status line near the top, and the average weekly rental is in bold and boxed

week. You will notice that none of the villas costs £727 to rent, but this was the *average* or typical cost in the low season.

If you were working out the average cost of rental yourself, you would need to add up the cost to rent all the villas (£11 629), and divide by the number of villas in the list (16) to find the average (£727). The advantage of using the AVERAGE function is that these various stages are all worked out automatically for you.

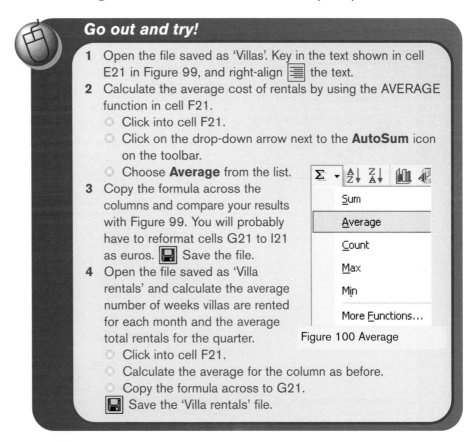

Go out and try!

1   Open the file saved as 'Villas'. Key in the text shown in cell E21 in Figure 99, and right-align ▤ the text.
2   Calculate the average cost of rentals by using the AVERAGE function in cell F21.
    ○ Click into cell F21.
    ○ Click on the drop-down arrow next to the **AutoSum** icon on the toolbar.
    ○ Choose **Average** from the list.
3   Copy the formula across the columns and compare your results with Figure 99. You will probably have to reformat cells G21 to I21 as euros. 💾 Save the file.
4   Open the file saved as 'Villa rentals' and calculate the average number of weeks villas are rented for each month and the average total rentals for the quarter.
    ○ Click into cell F21.
    ○ Calculate the average for the column as before.
    ○ Copy the formula across to G21.
    💾 Save the 'Villa rentals' file.

Figure 100 Average

Open your 'Spreadsheet software' file. Create a new bold heading called '**SS Activity 6**' and write a short paragraph describing the skills you have demonstrated in this activity, under the heading Average. 💾 Save the file.

Sorting data

It can often be useful to sort the data in the spreadsheet *alphabetically* (from A to Z or from Z to A), or *numerically* (from lowest to highest or from highest to lowest).

DiDA

Go out and try!

1 Open the file saved as 'Villas'. Try sorting the data by the Low Season price.
- Highlight cells A4 to I20.

It is essential to highlight the whole section. Otherwise you risk sorting only one column, which jumbles the data.

- Click on the A–Z icon .

Notice that Excel assumes you want to sort by the first column – 'Destination' – so highlight cells A4 to I20 again.

Figure 101 The Sort dialogue box

- Choose **Sort** from the **Data** menu.
- Select **(1) Price per week Sterling**, as in Figure 101.
- 💾 Save your file.

2 Now practise sorting the data
- highest to lowest – select **Descending**
- by the number of bedrooms.

3 Save the 'Villas' file.

4 Open the file saved as 'Villa rentals' and sort the data as follows:
- 1st Quarter – Total no weeks reserved, descending
- 2nd Quarter – Total value of bookings, descending
- 3rd Quarter – Total no weeks reserved, ascending
- 4th Quarter – Total value of bookings, ascending

5 💾 Save the file.

	A	B	C	D	E	F	G	H	I
1			Travelbug Villas						
2		Rate of Exchange £ to €		€ 1.40					
3						Low Season		High Season	
4	Destination	Resort	Name of Villa	No of bedrooms	Sleeps up to	Price per week Sterling	Price per week Euros	Price per week Sterling	Price per week Euros
5	Costa Blanca	Albir	Villa Marlene	2	4	£454	€ 636	£649	€ 909
6	Algarve	Estol	Casa Marco	2	4	£503	€ 704	£719	€ 1,007
7	Costa Blanca	Denia	Casa Moura	4	8	£545	€ 763	£779	€ 1,091
8	Costa Blanca	Calpe	Casa Alana	3	6	£545	€ 763	£779	€ 1,091
9	Algarve	Bordeira	Casa Luz	3	6	£559	€ 783	£799	€ 1,119
10	Cyprus	Coral Bay	Villa Olivia	3	6	£566	€ 792	£809	€ 1,133
11	Costa Blanca	Javea	Las Palmmares	4	8	£580	€ 812	£829	€ 1,161
12	Algarve	Lagos	Casa Limoa	3	6	£594	€ 832	£849	€ 1,189
13	Cyprus	Latchi	Irene	4	8	£601	€ 841	£859	€ 1,203
14	Cyprus	Argaka	Agathi	4	8	£629	€ 881	£859	€ 1,203
15	Algarve	Carvoeiro	Sete Estrelo	4	8	£629	€ 881	£899	€ 1,259
16	Cyprus	Polis	The Vines	5	10	£636	€ 890	£909	€ 1,273
17	France	West Coast - Charentes	La Belle Vacance	2	4	£675	€ 945	£965	€ 1,351
18	France	Dordogne	Chateau Alexa	4	8	£1,043	€ 1,460	£1,490	€ 2,086
19	France	South West Coast	Villa Zivia	4	8	£1,162	€ 1,627	£1,660	€ 2,324
20	France	Cote D'Azur	La Marina	5	10	£1,904	€ 2,666	£2,720	€ 3,808
21				Average price of weekly rental		£727	€ 1,017	£1,036	€ 1,450

Figure 102 Spreadsheet sorted by price per week sterling

Open your 'Spreadsheet software' file. Create a new bold heading called '**SS Activity 7**' and write a short paragraph describing the skills you have demonstrated in this activity, under the heading 'Sort data'. 💾 Save the file.

Producing graphs and charts

TiP

*It is important to check that the type of graph or chart chosen is appropriate for the data and that it is clearly labelled. The reader must be able to understand it easily **and** must find it useful to have the information presented in this way, otherwise it is a waste of time producing it!*

Graphs and charts can be very helpful tools to illustrate numerical data in a visual format, and spreadsheet programs provide easy-to-use facilities to create the graphs and charts.

Probably the most frequently used examples are

- column charts
- bar charts
- pie charts.

A well-presented graph or chart might include

- a *main title*
- *axis titles* – used on bar and column charts to show what the axes represent
- *data labels* – which can show the actual value or a percentage figure
- a *legend* (sometimes referred to as a *key*) to explain the segments of a pie chart or two or more sets of data in a column or bar chart.

You can see quite clearly in Figure 103 that the 3rd Quarter has the highest number of weeks reserved. However, do you think that Figure 104 might be more useful because it shows the actual values at the end of the bars? Figure 105 shows the value of bookings as a percentage, which indicates that the income in the 3rd Quarter is nearly half of the income for the year. These three charts provide useful graphical representation of different aspects of the data relating to the bookings and income of the villas.

Axis label →

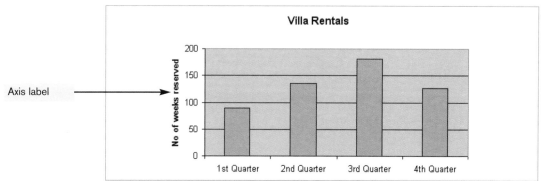

Figure 103 Column chart showing the total number of weeks for which villas were reserved each quarter

Data label →

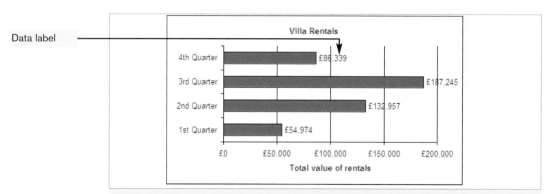

Figure 104 Bar chart showing the total value of bookings for each quarter

Legend or key →

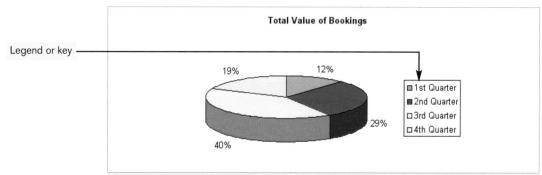

Figure 105 Pie chart showing the total value of bookings for the year, as percentages per quarter

When creating graphs or charts, it is essential to be absolutely clear about what data you wish to illustrate. When you have completed the graph or chart, ask yourself these questions:

- Is the chart style effective?
- Are the titles suitable?
- Do you need axis titles?
- Do you need a legend?

Go out and try!

1 Open the file saved as 'Villa rentals'.
2 Insert a new worksheet and rename it 'Totals'.
- From the menu, select **Insert**, **Worksheet**.
- Drag the worksheet tab after the '4th Quarter' worksheet.
- Double-click the **Sheet1** tab to rename it 'Totals'.
3 Key in the totals for each quarter, as shown in Figure 106.
4 Create a column chart from cells A2 to B6 similar to the one in Figure 103.
- Highlight cells A2 to B6.
- Click on the Chart wizard 📊.
- Select **Column** from the *Chart type* list and click **Next**.

	A	B	C
1	**Travelbug Villas**		
2		**Total No weeks reserved**	**Total Value of Bookings**
3	1st Quarter	89	£54,974
4	2nd Quarter	136	£132,957
5	3rd Quarter	181	£187,245
6	4th Quarter	127	£86,339

Figure 106 Data for your *Go out and try!* task

	A	B	C
1	**Travelbug Villas**		
2		**Total No weeks reserved**	**Total Value of Bookings**
3	1st Quarter	89	£54,974
4	2nd Quarter	136	£132,957
5	3rd Quarter	181	£187,245
6	4th Quarter	127	£86,339

Figure 107 Selected cells

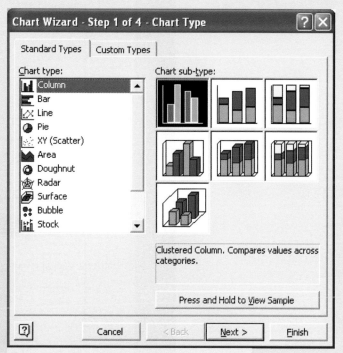

Figure 108 Chart Wizard: setting the chart type

- Click **Next** – Step 2 should be OK if the correct cells were highlighted.
- Type in the *Chart title* 'Villa Rentals'.
- Type in the *Value (Y) axis* title 'No of weeks reserved'.

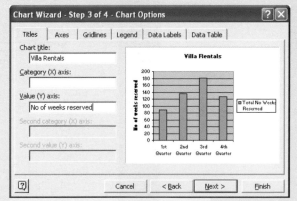

Figure 109 Chart Wizard: setting titles

- Click on the **Legend** tab and remove the tick from the **Show legend** checkbox – the legend needs to be removed as it serves no useful purpose when there is only one set of data.

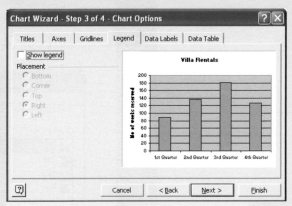

Figure 110 Chart Wizard: removing the legend

- Click **Next**.
- Click in the **As new sheet** option and then click **Finish**.

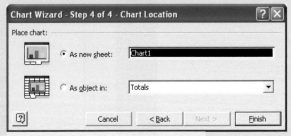

Figure 111 Location for the new chart

Go out and try!

1 Create a bar chart similar to the one in Figure 104 (page 158) from cells A2 to A6 and C2 to C6.
   ○ Highlight cells A2 to A6.
   ○ Hold the **Ctrl** key down and highlight cells C2 to C6.
   ○ Click on the **Chart Wizard** icon on the toolbar.
   ○ Select **Bar** from the *Chart type* list and click **Next** twice.
   ○ Key in a title and a y-axis title.
   ○ Remove the legend as before and click **Next**.
   ○ Click in the **As new sheet** option and click **Finish**.
2 Create a pie chart from cells A2 to A6 and C2 to C6 similar to Figure 105 (page 158).
   ○ Highlight cells A2 to A6.
   ○ Hold the **Ctrl** key down and highlight cells C2 to C6.
   ○ Click on the **Chart Wizard** icon on the toolbar.
   ○ Select the **Pie** option from the *Chart type* list.
   ○ Choose the *Chart sub-type* at the top of the second column (**Pie with a 3-D visual effect**).
   ○ Click **Next** twice.
   ○ Leave the title as it is.
   ○ Click on the **Data labels** tab.
   ○ Click in **Percentage** and then click **Next**.
   ○ Click in **As new sheet** and then click **Finish**.

TiP

*Holding down the **Ctrl** key allows you to highlight non-adjacent cells (cells that are not next to each other).*

Open your 'Spreadsheet software' file. Create a new bold heading called '**SS Activity 8**' and write a short paragraph describing the skills you have demonstrated in this activity, under the following headings:

   ○ *Creating a column chart*
   ○ *Adding a chart title*
   ○ *Adding an axis label*
   ○ *Creating a bar chart*
   ○ *Adding data labels*
   ○ *Creating a pie chart showing percentages.*

 Save the file.

TiP

When you create spread-sheets for your e-portfolio, it will be an excellent plan to include your own name, the filename and date in the footer. You might want to include other information as well.

Headers and footers

Just as in a word processor, you can include a header or footer in your spreadsheet. In Excel you can choose to have the page number, the sheet name, filename and date inserted automatically.

If the worksheet covers more than one page, the header or footer will automatically appear on all the pages. However, if you have more than one worksheet in your workbook, then you will need to put the footer on all the worksheets.

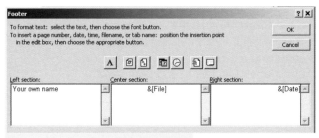

Figure 112 Creating a footer in Excel

To insert a footer into a worksheet, select **View**, **Header and Footer** and then **Custom Footer**. The dialogue box shown in Figure 112 will appear. The filename was automatically inserted in the centre section by clicking on the Excel icon 🗐, and the date in the right section by clicking on the date icon 🗓. The date will be updated each time you make changes to the file. When the spreadsheet is printed, the actual filename and date will be shown.

Printing a spreadsheet

To print from Excel you can either click on the familiar **Print** icon (🖨) or you can select **File**, **Print** and press **OK**.

However, it is well worth checking **Print Preview** before sending the file to print, to make sure the printout will *look* as you want it. Do remember that with spreadsheets the layout is usually wide, so landscape orientation is more common than portrait.

As with Microsoft Word, through the *Page Setup* dialogue box you can
- change margins
- select portrait or landscape
- include a header or footer.

You can also print the spreadsheet
- with or without gridlines
- with or without row and column headings
- showing the values or the formulas.

Businesses rarely print the row and column headings, but your teacher or tutor may want them included in your coursework, since it makes it easier to check your formulas.

Spreadsheets used in business are often very large – one worksheet in Excel allows you to use hundreds of columns and more than 10,000 rows! We have never used a worksheet that large, and you probably won't either, but even with much smaller worksheets you are likely to want to print just a part of it. Excel allows you to do this very easily.

Jargon buster

The **print area** is the actual part of the worksheet that you want to print. This may mean selecting all the data without any surrounding blank cells. Alternatively it might involve selecting just a part of the worksheet that you wish to print.

Go out and try!

1 Open the file you saved as 'Travelbug invoice'.
2 Set the print area.
   ○ Highlight from cell A1 to the last cell used in column E – probably around row 27 or 28.
   ○ From the menu, select **File**, **Print Area**, **Set Print Area**.

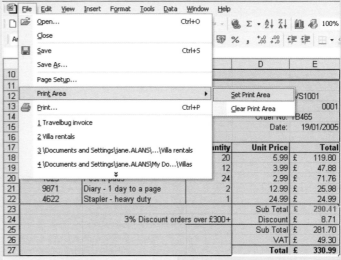

Figure 113 Setting the Print Area

   ○ From the menu, select **File**, **Print Preview**. Check that it shows the correct area, then close it.
3 Open the *Page Setup* dialogue box (**File**, **Page Setup**) and study each of the tabs in turn. Find out how to do the following:
   ○ *Add gridlines.* Are they helpful in your printout? In some cases it is better to omit them, perhaps because borders are used to divide the cells.
   ○ *Adjust the margins.* You can drag the margin markers or give an exact width or height. In this case set the left and right hand margins to 1.5 cm.
   ○ *Centre the spreadsheet.* Try this vertically and horizontally on the page.
   ○ *Change from portrait to landscape.* Decide whether you need to change to landscape, perhaps because the spreadsheet is wide.
   ○ *Create the header or footer.* Create a footer as shown earlier in Figure 112, putting your name in the left-hand box.
   ○ *Fit the spreadsheet to the page.*
   ○ *Show row and column headings.*
4 Print the spreadsheet.
5 Print the spreadsheet showing the formula view.
   ○ Hold down the **Ctrl** key and press the backwards quote key (`), which is above the **Tab** key and left of the **1** key.
   ○ Repeat to return to normal view.

TiP

*A quick way to show the formulas in Excel is to press the **Ctrl** key with the key to the left of the **1** key.*

Open your 'Spreadsheet software' file. Create a new bold heading called '**SS Activity 9**' and write short paragraphs describing the skills you have demonstrated in this activity, under the following headings:

- *Page setup*
- *Margins setup*
- *Headers and footers.*

Save the file.

Database software

If you were asked to explain what a database is, you might say that it is a way of keeping names, addresses and telephone numbers on a computer. That is true, but a database is a file of any set of *related* data. Other examples of databases are

- records of stock held in a shop or warehouse
- school or college examination results
- attendance and punctuality records
- records of customers and suppliers.

Every business, large or small, needs to store and access databases of information. For example, the publisher of this book (Heinemann) will have information on its authors, customers (such as your own school or college), staff who work for the company, and printers who produce the books, as well as details of the stock held in the warehouse.

In today's world, more databases than we are even aware of will hold information about us, because it is so much easier to store and transfer data held on a computer than it was when all databases were handwritten. Your school or college will have a database of student records, and each record will contain the same *fields*, such as ID *number, last name, first name, address, telephone number* and *date of birth*. Heinemann's stock records will include *book title, author(s), ISBN number* and *price*.

LEARNING OUTCOMES

You need to learn about:
- ✓ creating simple flat-file database structures
- ✓ setting and modifying field characteristics
- ✓ creating validation rules
- ✓ entering, editing and deleting records
- ✓ importing data sets
- ✓ designing data entry forms that facilitate data entry
- ✓ creating data entry forms
- ✓ sorting on one field
- ✓ sorting on two fields
- ✓ creating and using searches to extract relevant information
- ✓ producing customised reports
- ✓ exporting information from a database into other applications.

So what are the benefits of storing the data in a computerised database, compared with using a paper-based system such as an address book? Figure 114 provides some answers to that question.

Advantages of a computerised database	Disadvantages of a paper-based database
A vast amount of data can be stored on one disk.	You would need many, many files to store the same quantity of data.
Records are entered only once, but can be searched in all kinds of ways (e.g. alphabetically, numerically, selectively, by date).	If student details are stored alphabetically, but you also wanted to store them in order of date of birth, you would have to photocopy all the forms and file them again in date order. You would then have the problem of making sure both sets were kept up to date.
Searching for information is fast, even in a huge database.	Searching for information can be very slow.
Although data can be lost, you should be able to get it back if you keep backups.	When a paper form is removed from the file, it is easily mislaid, filed in the wrong place, lost or damaged.
It is easy to update details (e.g. a change of address).	It is easy to write a new address in an address book, but eventually the book wears out and you have to rewrite all the data in a new book.
It can perform calculations. You could search the database to check the dates of birth of all students and provide a list of those aged over 18. The report will be produced almost immediately.	To search the paper-based system, each form must be checked and then the relevant names copied on to a separate sheet. If the school or college has hundreds or even thousands of students this would be very slow and tedious.

Figure 114 Highlighting the advantages of using a computerised database

You will notice that Figure 114 refers to both *data* and *information*; so what is the difference?

- The details such as the students' names and dates of birth form the *data*.
- A list of all those students aged over 18 is an example of *information* obtained from the data.

Creating simple flat-file database structures

A *database* consists of a file, containing many records. Each record will include the *fields*, into which will be entered the appropriate data. Each record will contain the same fields, but sometimes a field is left empty in a particular record (for example, if there is no email address the field for 'email' will be left blank). A flat-file database is a fairly simple one consisting of only one table.

Tables and forms

Jargon buster

A database **table** is a grid with one row for each record (see Figure 115).

A database **form** shows only one record on the screen at once (see Figure 116).

A database is usually designed through a *table*. Once the table design is complete, a form is usually created. The data entry clerk will use the form to enter new data or to look at existing data on the screen.

The on-screen layout can be designed in a variety of styles, just as paper forms for different purposes are laid out differently. You may wish to view one record at a time on screen, or you might want to see all records listed under the different field names. A computerised database provides great flexibility in the way you look at the data, and it is easy to switch between viewing a list of all records in a table or one record on a form.

This is illustrated in Figures 115 and 116, which show the records of Travelbug's database of Cruise Club members.

Member's ID	Title	First Name	Last Name	Street	Town	Post/Zip Code	Country	E-mail	Phone No	Date joined
1	Miss	Sharon	Weeks	16 Glebe Way	Whychton	TO7 3GH	UK	S.Weeks@userve.co.uk	543 1111 2222	26/09/2005
2	Mr	Otto	Mortensen	Grasvej 9	Helsinge	3489	Denmark	Otto.M@danebank.de	300 4555 3456	29/09/2005
3	Mrs	Kristelle	Mortensen	Grasvej 9	Helsinge	3489	Denmark	Otto.M@danebank.de	300 4555 3456	04/10/2005
4	Mr	Jason	Jarrett	28 Rue Moliere	Margon	34276	France	J.Jarrett@servez.fr	400 3377 3727	05/10/2005
5	Mrs	Naomi	Harrison	28 Rue Moliere	Margon	34276	France	J.Jarrett@servez.fr	400 3377 3727	06/10/2005
6	Mrs	Elizabeth	Cambridge	3108 Crown Walk	Santa Barbara	Ca 92373	USA	Liz.Cam@service.com	600 6789 6789	07/10/2005
7	Mr	James	Cambridge	3108 Crown Walk	Santa Barbara	Ca 92373	USA	Jim.Cam@service.com	600 6789 6789	07/10/2005
8	Mr	Paul	Cambridge	3108 Crown Walk	Santa Barbara	Ca 92373	USA	Paul.Cam@service.com	600 6789 6789	07/10/2005
(AutoNumber)										

Figure 115 A table in Microsoft Access showing the data relating to the Cruise Club members

Figure 116 Form showing one record from the Cruise Club members database

Setting and modifying field characteristics

Before you design a database, it is important to think about the characteristics that will be most useful and suitable for the fields. It would be perfectly possible to create every field as text, because text allows you to enter letters, numbers and symbols into the field. However, if you did use all text fields, you would not be able to

- make calculations, such as finding out the value added tax (VAT) on the price of an item
- search for orders placed in a specific month, or before or after a particular date, or students in a certain age range
- search easily for a particular category, such as male or female, or a particular item of stock (e.g. skirts, blouses, trousers, T-shirts).

In order to do these things

- the field design for the price of the item must be *numerical*
- the field design for the date an order is placed or a date of birth must be in *date format*.

Also, it will be much easier to find a category if the categories are specified in a choice field. Let's look at this in more detail.

Setting up a computerised database

Once you know the purpose of your database, you have to decide several things.

The fields you need

You must decide the names of the fields (e.g. Student ID, First Name). The name of each field indicates which data should be entered into it.

The primary key

This field provides a unique reference for each record. No doubt when you enrolled at school or college you were given a student ID number, which is different for every student. It is essential that the primary key be unique; for example, a *surname* field would not make a good primary key. Records are automatically sorted in order of the primary key.

The data type for each field

You could just use text for everything, because text will accept letters, numbers and symbols. However, as we have just seen, your database would be much less effective when it comes to searching, and it would not be possible to make any calculations.

The size of the fields

How many characters do you need in a particular field? With fields such as names and addresses, obviously you need to allow enough space to enter a long name or long street reference, although it is possible to increase the length of the field later if necessary.

For numerical data you must decide whether the field can be an *integer* (whole number) or whether you need decimal places, and if so how many. You would not design a field with decimal places for the price of a house, as house prices are not quoted as £100,789.58. However, the price of grocery items ranges from less than a £1 upwards, so two decimal places would be necessary. Similarly, you might fix the length of the field for a house price at seven digits, which would allow a price up to £9,999,999. For items sold by a supermarket, you would probably fix the length at three digits to the left and two to the right of the decimal point, which would allow prices up to £999.99.

The format of the field

As with word-processing, you can format the font type, size and colour. It is tempting to select fancy fonts, which may look attractive, but are not necessarily easy to read.

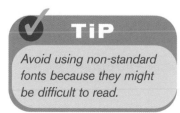

TiP

Avoid using non-standard fonts because they might be difficult to read.

Field data types

Figure 117 lists some typical fields, which are useful in a database. Note, however, that you may not find all these data types available in the database program you are using.

Type of field	Purpose	Advantages/possible uses
Text/character: Sometimes called *alphanumeric*	Any data – letters, numbers or symbols on the keyboard – can be entered into a text field.	• Names/addresses • Where you might include extra detail/description
Numerical – **integer**	A whole number	• Restricts data entry to whole numbers • Can restrict the number of digits • Reduces the risk of errors • Can be sorted in numerical order • Can also ask for list of items above/below/equal to a specific number • Reduces space for storage and display
Numerical – **decimal**	A number with decimal places	• Suitable for money where prices include pence – £13.67 • Measurements – 4.25 km
Numerical – **currency**	Can be set as an integer or with decimal places	• Suitable for money and would show the currency specified; e.g. £3.67, $287, €18
Numerical – **counter** or **AutoNumber**	A numeric value. As each new record is entered the counter automatically selects the next number in the sequence.	• Suitable for a member ID, student ID, account number etc. • The operator does not have to enter the number, and if a number has already been used, the computer will not allow you to use it again • Ensures that each member ID, account number etc. remains unique

Date	Storing dates	• Restricts data entry to 1–31 for the day, and 1–12 for the month
		• Reduces the risk of errors
		• Can be used to calculate a person's age, which will automatically update once his/her birth date has passed
		• Can search for
		  – birthdays in a given month
		  – those older or younger than a given age
		  – birthdays between particular dates
		  – orders placed before, after or on a given date

Time	Storing times	Might be used where employees are paid by the hour: • Hours worked can be calculated from time clocked on and off • Wages can be calculated as length of time worked multiplied by the hourly rate
Choice: male/female true/false red/blue/green/yellow	Data entry is limited to the selection that has been pre-determined. Choice fields can also be encoded; e.g. M for male, F for female, R for red	• Speeds up data entry • Can search for specific entries, such as 'male', 'true', or 'green' • Reduces space for storage and display

Figure 117 Typical database fields and their characteristics

List/combo boxes and check boxes

List/combo boxes and check boxes are facilities provided by the database program to make data entry easier and more accurate.

List boxes or *combo boxes* are used where the data is limited to a particular selection – for example

- male/female
- child/adult
- red/blue/yellow/green
- part-time/full-time
- Mr, Mrs, Miss, Ms.

Figure 118 Examples of combo boxes

Figure 118 gives examples of combo boxes from the Cruise Club members database, showing the drop-down lists. The data entry clerk can either key in the words or simply click on the correct choice, which speeds up data entry and reduces the risk of error.

When designing a combo box it is usually important to select 'Limit to List', as in Figure 119. This prevents the data entry clerk keying in any data not in the list.

General	Lookup	
Display Control	Combo Box	
Row Source Type	Value List	
Row Source	Austria;Denmark;France;	← Possible values
Bound Column	1	
Column Count	1	
Column Heads	No	
Column Widths		
List Rows	8	
List Width	Auto	
Limit To List	Yes ←	Do not allow any other values

Figure 119 Design of a combo box to limit data entry

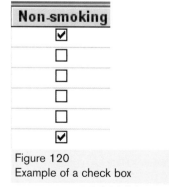

Figure 120
Example of a check box

Check boxes are used where there is a yes/no option. The data entry clerk clicks in the box to indicate 'Yes' and a ✓ appears. The clerk leaves the box blank to indicate 'No'. For example, the Cruise Club members are asked if they require a smoking or non-smoking cabin, and the tick indicates those who want non-smoking (Figure 120).

? Think it over ...

When planning the design of the database for Cruise Club members, think carefully about the different field types. Taking trouble at the design stage will make data entry easier and quicker, and searching more effective. You may wish to work in pairs to plan your design.

Go out and try!

1 Create a table in Word (or on paper) in two columns. List the column headings shown in Figure 115 on page 167 – Member's ID, Title, etc. – and, next to the field names, decide
   ○ the most suitable data type – look back at Figure 117 on page 170
   ○ field size
   ○ field format – font size, style – which will usually be the same for all the fields.
2 Compare your design with other students' designs and discuss it with your teacher.
3 Did you modify your design after you compared your work with other people's? If so, explain your changes.

Create a new word-processing file called 'Database software'. Create a new bold heading called '**DB Activity 1**' and write a short paragraph explaining field types – including the *primary key*, *text*, *number* and *combo box*. 💾 Save the file.

Go out and try!

Once you are confident that your field design is suitable, you are ready to create the database file.
1 Design the database table for Cruise Club members using the field types you have chosen. Save the database as 'Cruise Club Members'.
   ○ Start Access and choose **New**, **Blank Database** from the *New File* task pane.

← → New File	▼ ×

Open a file
📂 Files...

New
▣ Blank Database
▣ Blank Data Access Page
▣ Project (Existing Data)
▣ Project (New Data)

New from existing file
▣ Choose file...

New from template
▣ General Templates...
🌐 Templates on Microsoft.com

Click here ——→

🗔 Add Network Place...

Figure 121 New Blank Database command

2 Name the database 'Cruise Club Members'.

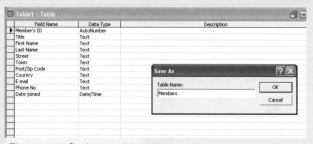

Figure 122 Naming a new database

3 Create a table for the members' details. Double-click on **Create table in Design view**. Enter the field names and data types you have chosen. Don't forget the primary key.

Figure 123 Saving a table

4 To set up a combo box for the *title* field, do the following steps.
   ○ Click into the *Title* field.
   ○ Click the *Lookup* tab in the properties section of the window.
   ○ Change the *Display Control* to read **Combo Box**.
   ○ Change the *Row Source Type* to **Value List**.

	Field Properties
General　Lookup	
Display Control	Combo Box
Row Source Type	Value List
Row Source	Mr;Mrs;Miss;Ms
Bound Column	1
Column Count	1
Column Heads	No
Column Widths	
List Rows	8
List Width	Auto
Limit To List	Yes

Figure 124 Properties for the Title field

○ In the *Row Source* box key in 'Mr,Mrs,Miss,Ms' (separated by commas).
○ Change *Limit To List* to **Yes**.
○ Save the design.

To set up a short date, do the following steps.

○ For the *Date joined* field select *Date/Time* as the data type.
○ Click into the *Format* property and change it to *Short Date* from the drop-down list.
○ Save the design.

5 Save the table as 'Members'. Close the table.
6 Open the table by double-clicking on the name in the database window view.
7 Enter the data given in Figure 115 on page 167.
○ Click into the cell for Member's ID.
○ Tab to the next field cell and key in 'Miss'.
○ Tab across the row and enter the details.
○ At the end of the row press **Tab** again to go to the beginning of the next row.
○ Continue until you have entered all eight records.

Open your word-processing file called 'Database software'. Create a new bold heading called '**DB Activity 2**' and write a short paragraph explaining the skills you have learned in designing a table and entering records. Did you have any problems, and if so how did you overcome them? Save the file.

Designing data entry forms

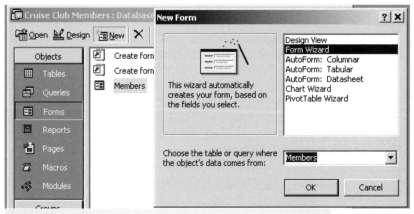

Figure 125 The Form Wizard to create a new form for members

As already explained (see page 167), the data in the database can be presented in table view or form view. Once you have created the table you can then create the form from the table. The easiest way to do this is to use the *Form Wizard* (Figure 125).

It is very convenient to use the wizard so that all the fields are transferred from the table into the form, but do customise it afterwards. You may wish to rearrange the fields into a more appropriate layout, change the font style and size, and add text boxes or navigation buttons.

Jargon buster

A **wizard** is a guide available in the software to take you step-by-step through the process of a specific task.

Go out and try!

1 Using the *Form Wizard*, create a form for the 'Members' table.
- Choose **Forms** from the *Objects* list.
- Double-click on **Create form by using wizard**.
- Ensure your table is selected in the *Tables/Queries* list.
- Click on the double chevron (**>>**) to transfer all the records to the *Selected fields* box.

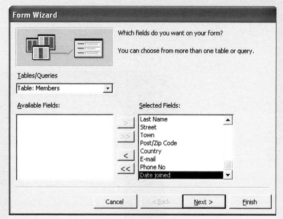

Figure 126 Form Wizard showing all fields selected

- Click **Next**.
- Select **Columnar** and click **Next**.
- Choose a style for your form and click **Next**.
- Enter a name for your form and click **Finish**.

Once the form is created, you will find that all the records are automatically available in the form view.

2 While in form view, add in your own details as if you were a new member.
- Click on the new record navigation button (**▶＊**) at the bottom of the form.
- Enter your details, pressing the **Tab** key to move from one field to the next.

3 Check whether your record is shown in the table.
- Close the form.
- Choose **Tables** from the **Objects** list.
- Open the table to view all the records.

Open your word-processing file called 'Database software'. Create a new bold heading called '**DB Activity 3**' and write a short paragraph explaining the skills you have learned in designing a form and entering a record using form view. Did you prefer to use the table or the form to enter records? 💾 Save the file.

Although the *Form Wizard* makes it very easy to create a form from the table, the result will probably be in columns, where all fields are listed one under the other (as shown in Figure 116 on page 168). All the right-hand side of the window is wasted, and the form may not fit in the screen window. Another common ready-prepared format is tabular, where all the field names are listed across the screen with the data in rows underneath. This is not much different from table view.

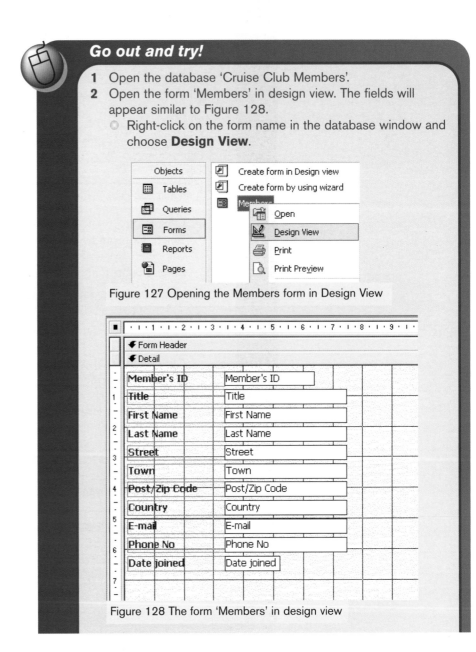

Go out and try!

1 Open the database 'Cruise Club Members'.
2 Open the form 'Members' in design view. The fields will appear similar to Figure 128.
  ○ Right-click on the form name in the database window and choose **Design View**.

Figure 127 Opening the Members form in Design View

Figure 128 The form 'Members' in design view

4   Experiment with moving the fields to see if it improves the layout.
  ○ Select a control (the field) and position the mouse pointer until it becomes a hand () and then drag the control to a new position.

5   Experiment with the font style and colour, or place a border around the fields.
  ○ Select the control to change.
  ○ Right-click and choose **Properties** from the menu that appears.
  ○ There are properties for font, font size, font colour, border, alignment, etc. Options are available on drop-down lists in each property.

6   Add the heading 'Cruise Club Members' using the **Label** tool from the *Toolbox* (Figure 129).

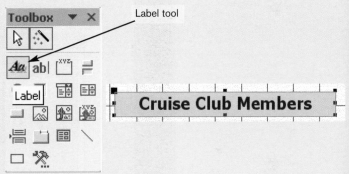

Figure 129 Adding a heading using the Toolbox

  ○ Switch to design view for the form.
  ○ Click on the **Label** tool.
  ○ Drag a heading box to the size you want in a space at the top of your form.
  ○ Type in the heading.
  ○ Press **Enter**.
  ○ With the control still selected, you can format the font, size, alignment, colour, etc. from the *Formatting* toolbar.

7   Add buttons for navigating to the previous and next records.
  ○ Click on the **Command Button** tool from the *Toolbox* (Figure 130).
  ○ Drag out a shape for the button on your form. The *Command Button Wizard* should start.

Figure 130 The Toolbox

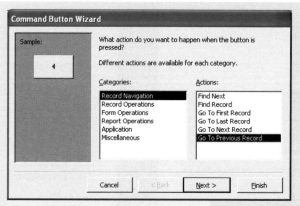

Figure 131 Choice of navigation action

○ Select **Record Navigation** from the *Categories* list and **Go To Previous Record** from the *Actions* list. Click **Next**.

○ Click in the option button for **Text** and click **Next**.

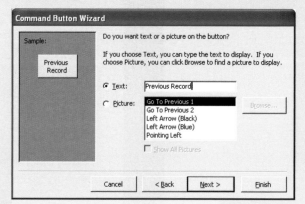

Figure 132 Setting a title for the button

○ Give the button a name and click **Finish**.

○ Repeat this process for 'Next Record'. In design view,

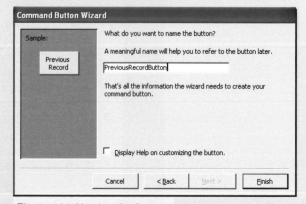

Figure 133 Naming the button

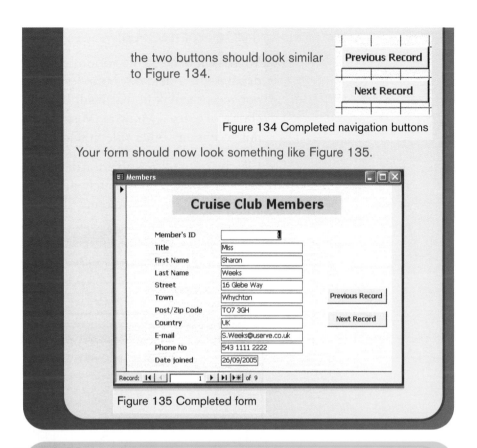

the two buttons should look similar to Figure 134.

Figure 134 Completed navigation buttons

Your form should now look something like Figure 135.

Figure 135 Completed form

Open your word-processing file called 'Database software'. Create a new bold heading called '**DB Activity 4**' and write a short paragraph explaining the skills you have learned in improving the form layout. Save the file.

Creating validation rules

The word 'valid' means *suitable*. Planes, boats and cars are all forms of transport, but if you want to cross a lake it is no use trying to drive across – you need a boat! That is a silly example, but in this case the car is not suitable – not valid.

Two very important validation checks used in computerised databases are

- type checks
- range checks.

If invalid or unsuitable data is entered into the field, the database program will indicate an error – such as the ones shown in Figure 136.

Type checks

We have looked at the various data types that may be used in a database. If a field has been designed for numbers, the computer will not accept letters in that field. If a field has been designed to accept a choice of titles – Mr, Mrs, Miss, Ms – by using a combo box, it will not accept any other title in that field.

Clearly, it is still possible for the data entry clerk to make errors, but some errors will immediately be apparent – often by a beep and an error message on the screen.

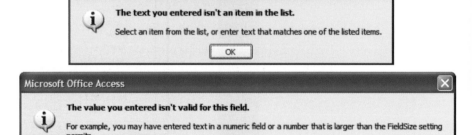

Figure 136 An error message when text not listed in the combo box was entered, and one when the date entered was 29/13/2005 – because there are only 12 months in a year

Figure 137 shows the effect of using a type check.

Data to be entered	Data actually entered	Data valid	Data correct
25	25	✓	✓
25	52	✓	✗ – but it is accepted because it is of the *correct type*
25	q5	✗	✗ – because 'q' is not a number – i.e. the *wrong type*
Mr	Mr	✓	✓
Mr	Mrs	✓	✗ – but it is accepted because Mrs is one of the titles listed in the combo box – i.e. the *correct type*
Mr	Doctor	✗	✗ – because Doctor is not one of the titles listed in the combo box – i.e. the *wrong type*

Figure 137 The effect of using a type check

Range checks

A number field may include a further check as well as the type check. The field can be limited within a set *range,* by giving a minimum or maximum figure or both.

For example, a date field will include an automatic range so that 13 will not be accepted as a month, and 31 will not be accepted as a day for the months of February, April, June, September and November. The effect of using a range check is demonstrated in Figure 138.

Data to be entered	Data actually entered	Data valid	Data correct
29/09/2005	29/09/2005	✓	✓
29/09/2005	29/08/2005	✓	✗ – but it is accepted because it is within the correct *range*
29/09/2005	29/13/2005	✗	✗ – computer immediately signals an error, because there are only 12 months in the year – 13 is outside the *range*

Figure 138 The effect of using a range check

Go out and try!

1 Open the database 'Cruise Club Members'. Test out the range and type checks given in Figures 137 and 138. If invalid data is accepted then check the field design.
2 Try entering the following. If the data is accepted, check your field design again.
   ○ **Senor** in the field for *Title.*
   ○ **Mongolia** for the field for *Country.*
   ○ **five43 1111 2222** in the field for *Phone no.*
   ○ **31/02/05** in the field for *Date joined.*

Think it over ...

Why might a number field **not** be appropriate for telephone numbers?

Open the word-processing file called 'Database software'. Create a new bold heading called '**DB Activity 5**' and write a short paragraph explaining what happens when invalid data is entered into the fields. 💾 Save the file.

Entering, editing and deleting records

As you have already discovered, it is usually much easier to edit a computerised database than a manual system. From time to time you may need to

- add a new record – e.g. a new customer
- delete a record – e.g. a product item that is discontinued
- edit a record – e.g. if an address changes
- add new fields or change existing ones.

To add a new record to the database, you either click on the next row in the table, or select a blank form and add in the new details. If the primary key is an AutoNumber, the next number available will be chosen and the new record will automatically be filed in correct order of the primary key.

With the small sample of records available in the 'Cruise Club Members' database, it does not take long to look at each one in turn if you need to find a particular record. However, this would be very time-consuming if the database had hundreds of records. You can 'ask' the computer to search the database by selecting **Edit, Find**, clicking on a specific field and entering what you are looking for into the *Find What* box. Click on **Find Next** and, if the data matches one of the records in the database, the record will be located.

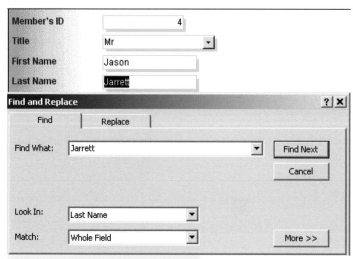

Figure 139 Finding a specific record

In Figure 139 the cursor was placed in the *Last Name* field, **Jarrett** was entered into the *Find What* box and, when **Find Next** was selected, the correct record was found.

When you have found a record, you can then either delete the record, change the data, or simply look up the information you need.

Go out and try!

1 Using the *Find and Replace* facility, find the record for Jarrett.
   - Open the table in either form view or datasheet view.
   - Click into the *Last Name* field.
   - From the menu, select **Edit**, **Find**.
   - Enter 'Jarrett' in the *Find What* box and click **Find Next**.
2 Select the 'Members' table and add a new field for Non-smoking, designed as a check box.
   - Open the table in Design view.
   - Click into the first empty *Field Name* box and key in 'Non-smoking'.
   - Tab into the *Data Type* column and set the type to **Yes/No**.
   - Save the design (the default setting is for a check box).
3 Select non-smoking for Sharon Weeks and the Cambridge family.
   - Switch the table to Datasheet view.
   - Click into the check boxes for Sharon Weeks and the three members of the Cambridge family.
4 You now need to add the field to your 'Members' form.
   - Open the form in Design view.
   - Select **View**, **Field List**.
   - Drag the field for *Non-smoking* on to the form (you may need to make room by dragging the bottom boundary of the design area).

Change to Form view to see that the records have been updated.

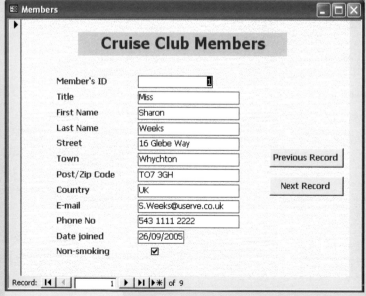

Figure 140 Form view

Sorting a database and using searches

As you saw earlier, records in the database are automatically saved *in the order of the primary key field*. However, you may wish to present the data in a particular order – e.g. alphabetical, numerical, chronological (order of date).

⊞ Cruise details : Table				
Cruise Ref	**Destination**	**Rating**	**Duration in days**	**Price**
AI01	Atlantic Islands	Budget	8	£875
ME04	Mediterranean	Budget	10	£950
NO12	Norway	Luxury	7	£1,100
GI10	Greek Islands	Standard	8	£1,150
FA07	Falklands	Budget	7	£1,500
TE03	Tenerife	Luxury	7	£1,999
BA11	Bahamas	Standard	12	£2,050
SP05	South Pacific	Standard	11	£2,100
AU06	Australia	Standard	14	£2,975
CA09	Caribbean	Luxury	12	£3,400
NZ02	New Zealand	Luxury	14	£3,750

Figure 141 A sorted Travelbug database

In Figure 141, Travelbug have created another database with details of the cruises, shown here sorted in order of price.

The order can be *ascending* (lowest to highest – A to Z or 1 to 100), or *descending* (highest to lowest – Z to A or 100 to 1).

If you wish to sort the database on one field only, then highlight the field name and click either the A–Z button (⧯) or the Z–A button (⧯) on the toolbar. However, if you wish to sort on one field and then on a secondary field, you will need to design a *query*, as explained in the next section.

Creating and using searches to extract relevant information

Searching the database to find specific information is known as a *query*. The query defines the *parameters*: what you want to find out. The result of your query may be presented on the monitor screen or printed on paper. You will need to know how to design a variety of different queries:

- sorting on one field with a secondary sort on another field
- using a single criterion or multiple criteria
- using relational operators
- using logical operators.

We shall now look at some examples.

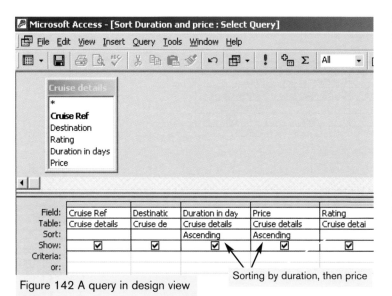

Figure 142 A query in design view

Sorting by duration, then price

Sorting on one field with a secondary sort on another field

A Travelbug customer would like to have a list of cruises sorted by duration and then by price. To design the query, Thomas Tripp first selects the table and then the fields he wishes to include. The field *Duration in days* must be listed before the field *Price* and both must be set to sort in ascending order. This is shown in Figure 142. The result of the search will then be sorted in the right order, as in Figure 143.

	Cruise Ref	Destination	Duration in days	Price	Rating
	NO12	Norway	7	£1,100	Luxury
▶	FA07	Falklands	7	£1,500	Budget
	TE03	Tenerife	7	£1,999	Luxury
	AI01	Atlantic Islands	8	£875	Budget
	GI10	Greek Islands	8	£1,150	Standard
	ME04	Mediterranean	10	£950	Budget
	SP05	South Pacific	11	£2,100	Standard
	BA11	Bahamas	12	£2,050	Standard
	CA09	Caribbean	12	£3,400	Luxury
	AU06	Australia	14	£2,975	Standard
	NZ02	New Zealand	14	£3,750	Luxury

Figure 143 Result of running a query to sort the database on two fields

TiP

If you tend to confuse the signs for greater than and less than, try to remember that less than (<) points to the left.

Relational operators

If you search a database using relational operators, you will be looking for a number *greater than*, *less than* or *equal to some value*. There are signs that are used to represent these relationships:

- < less than
- > greater than

185

- ⊙ = equal to
- ⊙ <> not equal to
- ⊙ <= less than or equal to
- ⊙ >= greater than or equal to.

Another Travelbug customer wishes to find cruises costing less than £2000. Figure 144 shows the design for this query, and Figure 145 shows the result.

Field:	Cruise Ref	Destination	Rating	Duration in day	Price
Table:	Cruise details	Cruise details	Cruise detail:	Cruise details	Cruise detail
Sort:					Ascending
Show:	☑	☑	☑	☑	☑
Criteria:					<2000
or:					

Figure 144 Search for a single criterion

Cruise Ref	Destination	Rating	Duration in days	Price
AI01	Atlantic Islands	Budget	8	£875
ME04	Mediterranean	Budget	10	£950
NO12	Norway	Luxury	7	£1,100
GI10	Greek Islands	Standard	8	£1,150
FA07	Falklands	Budget	7	£1,500
TE03	Tenerife	Luxury	7	£1,999

Figure 145 Result of running a query to find cruises costing less than £2000

Logical operators

The logical operators – *and*, *or*, and *not* – let you chain together multiple conditions in the same query.

Suppose a Travelbug customer enquires about luxury cruises under £2000. To get the list you need to query the records where *Price < 2000* **and** *Rating = 'luxury'*. In Access you do this by adding both criteria, as shown in Figure 146. There are just two cruises suitable, as revealed in Figure 147.

Field:	Cruise Ref	Destination	Price	Rating
Table:	Cruise deta	Cruise details	Cruise details	Cruise details
Sort:				
Show:	☑	☑	☑	☑
Criteria:			<2000	="luxury"
or:				

Figure 146 Search for multiple criteria – 'less than £2000' and 'luxury'

Cruise Ref	Destination	Price	Rating	Duration in days
TE03	Tenerife	£1,999	Luxury	7
NO12	Norway	£1,100	Luxury	7

Figure 147 Result of running the query in Figure 146

A Travelbug customer would like to go on a cruise for seven or eight days. Figure 148 shows the query criteria, and Figure 149 shows the result.

✔ TiP

To do a **not** search, use the **< >** operator in one or more of your criteria.

Field:	Cruise Ref	Destination	Duration in day	Price	Rating
Table:	Cruise details	Cruise details	Cruise details	Cruise details	Cruise detail
Sort:				Descending	
Show:	☑	☑	☑	☑	☑
Criteria:			=7		
or:			=8		

Figure 148 Design of a query to select cruises for seven or eight days

Cruise Ref	Destination	Duration in days	Price	Rating
TE03	Tenerife	7	£1,999	Luxury
FA07	Falklands	7	£1,500	Budget
GI10	Greek Islands	8	£1,150	Standard
NO12	Norway	7	£1,100	Luxury
AI01	Atlantic Islands	8	£875	Budget

Figure 149 Result of running the query in Figure 148

Go out and try!

1 Set up a new database with details of the cruises as shown in Figure 141 (page 184). Take care when deciding on the field types.
2 Enter the data.
3 Practise designing queries as shown in Figures 142 to 149
   ○ Close the table.
   ○ Choose **Queries** from the *Objects* list.
   ○ Double-click on **Create query in design view**.
   ○ Click **Add** to add the table and then close the *Show table* box.
   ○ Click into the first field cell in the design grid and, using the drop-down list, choose **Cruise Ref**.
   ○ Tab into the next field cell and set it to **Destination**.
   ○ Continue until you have entered all the required fields for the query shown in Figure 142.
   ○ Click into the *Sort* cell for the field you want to sort (in this case) and choose *Duration in days* **Ascending** .
   ○ Repeat for the *Price* field.
   ○ Click on the **Run** icon ( ) on the toolbar and compare your results with Figure 143.
   ○ Repeat these steps for the other queries, changing the criteria as appropriate.

Open your word-processing file called 'Database software'.
Create a new bold heading called '**DB Activity 7**' and write a short paragraph explaining what is meant by

- *a query*
- *relational operators*
- *logical operators.*

💾 Save the file.

Producing customised reports

Less 2000 and luxury

Cruise Ref	TE03
Destination	Tenerife
Price	£1,999
Rating	Luxury
Duration in days	7
Cruise Ref	NO12
Destination	Norway
Price	£1,100
Rating	Luxury
Duration in days	7

The result of a query is presented in table format, but you may wish to present your query more professionally. To do this you need to design a *report*.

Figure 147 (page 187) showed the query result for 'luxury' cruises 'less than £2000' in table format, whereas Figure 150 shows the same result in report format. You can choose various options in the report design, and wizards are available to help you design the report layout quickly and easily.

Figure 150 The report view of the same query shown in Figures 146 and 147

Go out and try!

Create reports for all the queries you have made in the Cruise database.
- Click on **Reports** in the *Objects* list
- Double-click on **Create report by using wizard**.
- From the *Tables/Queries* drop-down list, choose the query to use for the report.
- Click on the **>>** button to move all the fields to the *Selected Fields* box.

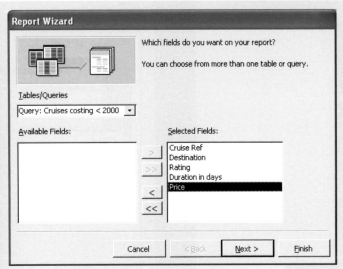

Figure 151 Report Wizard showing all fields selected

○ Click **Next**.
○ Don't add any grouping. Click **Next**.
○ Add any sorting required and click **Next**.
○ Click in the option for **Columnar** and select **Portrait**.

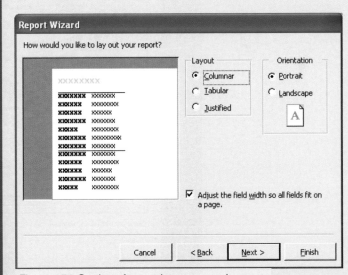

Figure 152 Settings for a columnar portrait report

○ Click **Next**.
○ Choose a style and click **Next**.

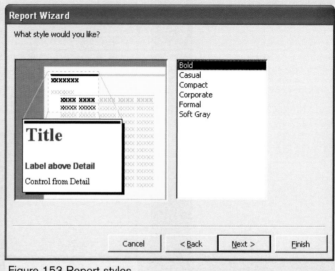

Figure 153 Report styles

○ Enter a title for your report and click **Finish**.

Figure 154 Entering a report title

○ Your report should look something like the one in Figure 150 (page 188).

Open your word-processing file called 'Database software'. Create a new bold heading called '**DB Activity 8**' and write a short paragraph describing the difference between a query and a database report. 💾 Save the file.

Exporting data for use in other applications

It is possible to export data held in the database for use in other software applications, and a particularly good example is exporting names and addresses for mail merge (see page 132).

One of the advantages of a computer is the facility to write one letter but send it out to a large number of people using mail merge. Instead of creating a data file in Word, if the names and addresses are already held in a database file then they can be exported to the word processor.

Go out and try!

1 Open the file saved as 'Members' and select the 'Members' table. Select **File**, **Export** and select the 'Members' table (Figure 155).

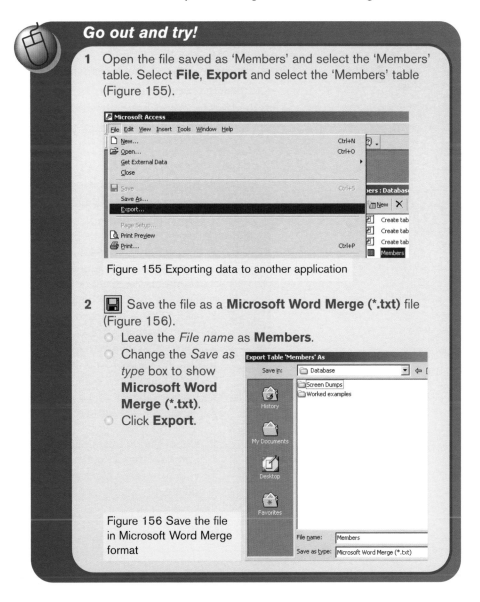

Figure 155 Exporting data to another application

2 Save the file as a **Microsoft Word Merge (*.txt)** file (Figure 156).
○ Leave the *File name* as **Members**.
○ Change the *Save as type* box to show **Microsoft Word Merge (*.txt)**.
○ Click **Export**.

Figure 156 Save the file in Microsoft Word Merge format

Importing data sets

As well as being able to export data, Access can import data from
other applications in a variety of common formats, such as text or
spreadsheet files. When a suitable set of data that is already available
is imported into Access, the field names and field types are
automatically assigned by the software.

If you have created the spreadsheet file saved as 'Villa Rentals', you
can practice importing data from the spreadsheet into the database.
If at this stage you have not created this file, but have a different
spreadsheet file available, then you could use that one instead.

Go out and try!

1 Open the file saved as 'Villa Rentals' and resave it as 'Villas to export'.

2 You will need to delete rows 1–3 on all four worksheets, but make sure you keep row 4 containing the column headings – Name of Villa, Cost of Weekly Rentals etc. Access will use this row for the field names. Close the file.

3 Open a new database file in Access and call it 'Villas'.

4 From the menu, select **File**, **Get External Data**, **Import**. The *Import* dialogue box appears.

5 Set the *Files of type* drop-down list to **Microsoft Excel (*.xls)** and find the file 'Villas to export.xls'.

6 Click on the file and then press **Import**.

7 Select the **1st Quarter** worksheet and then click **Finish** (Figure 157).

8 Press **OK** on the confirmation dialogue, and open the new *1st Quarter* table to check that the contents are OK. You may find you have some blank rows or columns, which you should delete.

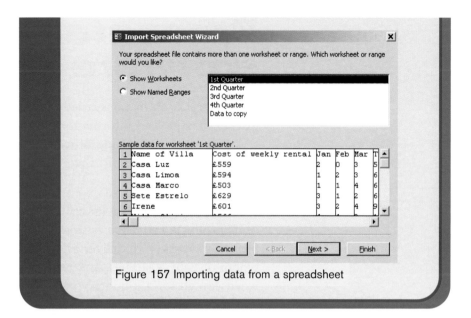

Figure 157 Importing data from a spreadsheet

Open your word-processing file called 'Database software'.
Create a new bold heading called '**DB Activity 10**' and write a
short paragraph explaining what is meant by importing data.
Save the file.

Presentation software

Presentations can be in a variety of forms. At school or college your teacher may present information using an overhead projector and slides. A cinema's booking office could use a computer to show a series of pictures about forthcoming films; this would also be a presentation.

Travelbug could use Microsoft PowerPoint to create a presentation of its products and services to show prospective clients. You will probably be asked to deliver a PowerPoint presentation during your school or college studies, and you may even be asked to deliver one when you go for a job interview. Learning to use PowerPoint effectively will therefore provide you with a skill that you will find useful both now and in the future.

LEARNING OUTCOMES

You need to learn about

✓ designing and creating the structure and navigation route of a presentation

✓ selecting and creating colour schemes

✓ creating and using a corporate style

✓ creating and selecting components – text, graphics and sound

✓ using master slides and templates

✓ using frames

✓ editing text – fonts, aligning, bullets, line spacing

✓ editing graphics – aligning, rotating, flipping, cropping and resizing, changing colour and resolution

✓ adding lines and simple shapes

✓ using text wrap

✓ inserting animation

✓ creating slide transitions

✓ producing speaker's notes and handouts to accompany slide shows.

Designing and creating the structure of a presentation

A PowerPoint presentation is made up of individual parts, called *slides*. You can build up a series of slides to create a presentation. Often you will see a PowerPoint presentation displayed through a digital projector on to a screen. You may have experienced your teachers doing this in lessons. Alternatively the presentation could be shown on a computer screen as an on-screen display – for example the presentation about forthcoming films.

It is essential to plan a presentation before creating it. This includes creating a *storyboard* that shows the layout and content of each individual slide. You should also plan the structure of the presentation, making sure you show the *navigation route*. There is an opportunity to learn more about storyboards and structures in Unit 2 of the qualification.

Jargon buster

A **storyboard** is a series of pictures that is used by multimedia developers to illustrate the proposed content, structure and navigation of the end product. For example, storyboards can be used to plan presentations, websites, films or videos.

Go out and try!

Plan a PowerPoint presentation about yourself and your friends. Create a storyboard to show the structure. You should plan a presentation that will allow you to practise all the skills you will learn about in this chapter.

Create a new word-processed file called 'Presentation software' and save it in your Presentation sub-folder. Create a bold heading '**PS Activity 1**' and write a short paragraph describing the skills you have demonstrated in this activity. Save the file.

Using wizards, templates and master slides

Wizards

You may already be familiar with the wizards used in applications such as Microsoft Access. PowerPoint also provides a wizard to simplify the creation of a presentation. In PowerPoint this is called the *AutoContent Wizard* (Figure 158). If you want to create a

Figure 158 The AutoContent Wizard

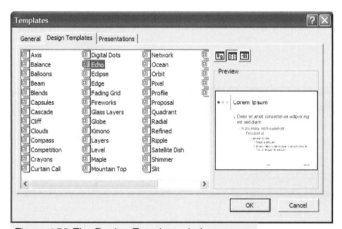

Figure 159 The Design Template window

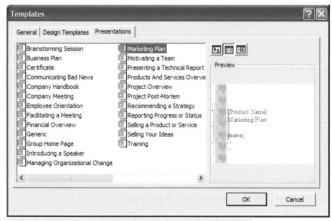

Figure 160 The Presentation Templates window

presentation quickly and be guided step by step, this is an ideal feature.

Templates

PowerPoint also makes creating a presentation easier by providing a wide range of design and presentation *templates* (Figure 159).

A design template is a file that has been designed with special backgrounds and layouts ready to use. It includes styles for the type and size of bullets and fonts. Using a design template is another timesaving feature, and, if you are not particularly artistic, can be invaluable.

The design template always has two slide designs – one used for the title slide (the first slide in a presentation) and one used for the remaining slides. This means that the title slide will have a slightly different design from the remaining slides in a presentation.

Presentation templates are pre-structured presentations that you can choose to suit a specific purpose (Figure 160). For example, Thomas Tripp from Travelbug could use the marketing plan template to create a presentation to market holidays to prospective clients.

If you don't want to use one of the templates supplied with PowerPoint, you can find different themes and design templates on the Internet, many of which you can download without charge.

The slide master

Each design template comes with a *slide master* on which you can put any graphics or text that you want to appear on every slide, and an optional *title master* where you can make changes to slides in your presentation that use the title slide layout. For example, Travelbug can put their logo on the slide master so that it will appear on every slide (Figure 161).

Figure 161 The slide master

If you wish to divide your presentation into several sections, each starting with a title slide, you can create a separate title master. You edit the slide masters and title masters to set the default text formats and styles for all slides in your presentation. You can also number each slide, include a footer, and show the date a presentation was created.

Selecting and creating colour schemes

Colours are used for the background, text and lines, shadows, title text, fills, accents, and hyperlinks on a slide. Together they are called the presentation's *colour scheme*.

If you choose to use an existing template for your presentation, one useful feature is that if you do not like the colour scheme then you can change it easily (Figure 162). A design template will include a default colour scheme for the presentation, together with additional alternative schemes to chose from.

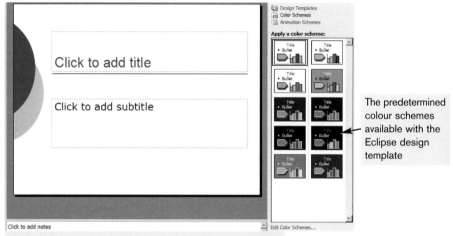

Figure 162 Changing the colours of a design template

You can even change certain aspects of a default colour scheme. For example, suppose Thomas Tripp of Travelbug wants to create a PowerPoint presentation to be shown at a travel exhibition. Because he wishes to ensure that the colour scheme uses the Travelbug house style, he can choose to modify the design template to reflect this. As PowerPoint allows you to change the colour for all or only certain elements of a colour scheme, Thomas Tripp could change the colour for text and lines, but leave the other elements unchanged (Figure 163).

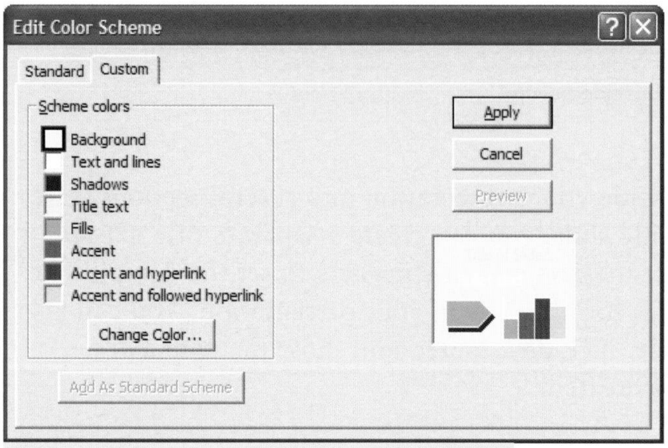

Figure 163 Dialogue box to edit a colour scheme

Colour schemes can be applied to one slide, selected slides or the entire presentation. If you are creating the template yourself for a presentation, you can apply colour schemes in the same way you would if you were using an existing design template.

Go out and try!

1 Choose a template that is appropriate the presentation you planned in Activity 1.
- Start PowerPoint.
- Click on **From Design Template** in the *New Presentation* task pane.
- Choose a design from *Apply a design template*.

2 Choose a colour scheme.
- Click on **Color Schemes** at the top of the task pane.
- Select a colour scheme for your design layout.

3 Modify the colour scheme.
- Click on **Edit Colour Schemes** at the bottom of the task pane.
- Click on an item in the *Scheme colors* list (Figure 163), then use the **Change Color** button to change the colour of that item.
- Repeat the previous step for any other items you want to change.

4 🖫 Save your presentation.

Skills check ▶▶

Create and use corporate styles

Unit 4 (ICT in Enterprise) covers the topic of creating a corporate identity. If you study that unit you will learn the importance of a company having a brand image which customers or potential customers can recognise. For example, the Travelbug logo is used on all publicity materials, including their website, the presentation Thomas Tripp has been creating, letterheads and so on. You can use the skills you have learnt earlier in this chapter to create and use a corporate style.

Open your 'Presentation software's file. Create a new bold heading '**PS Activity 2**' and write a short paragraph describing the skills you have demonstrated in this activity when selecting and creating colour schemes for a PowerPoint presentation. 🖫 Save the file.

Viewing your slides

There are three main ways of viewing slides.

- *Normal view*. This is the main view used for editing. It displays three areas. On the left-hand side there are tabs which alternate between slide and outline view, the slide pane and the notes pane. You can adjust the pane sizes by dragging the pane borders. Slides are displayed individually and you can work on the slides in this view. The notes pane allows you to enter notes that you want to make about a slide, which will assist you when making a presentation.

- *Slide sorter*. This allows you to view all the slides in miniature form. Not only can you delete slides, change the order of slides or insert new slides in slide sorter view, you can also copy existing slides and paste them into the desired positions very easily.

- *Slide show*. You can view your presentation by clicking on the Slide Show icon (🖳) in the bottom-left.

Creating, selecting and using text and graphics components

Slide layout

It is possible to design your own slides from scratch, or to choose one of the layouts provided by PowerPoint. The *Slide Layout* option will display the different layouts from which you can choose. By pointing to each picture you can see a description of the slide.

The layouts are divided into different categories – *Text Layouts*, *Content Layouts*, *Text and Content Layouts*, and *Other Layouts*. Figure 164 shows the different layouts, which allow a range of components to be included in a slide: text (including bulleted lists), charts, graphics, sound and video (referred to as *media clips*).

PowerPoint allows you to click on icons to add the appropriate content for a slide. For example, Thomas Tripp would click on the **Insert Picture** icon to insert a digital photograph in his presentation (Figure 165).

Figure 164 The slide layout options

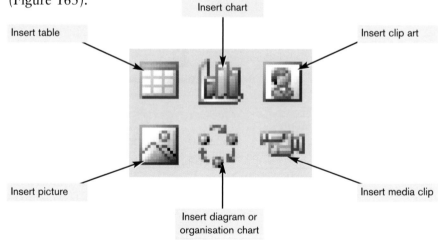

Figure 165 The components available

Using boxes/frames

The design of each slide is broken down into areas called *boxes* (sometimes referred to as *frames*). Each box/frame holds an object. The object can be, for example, a list, a title, text, a piece of clip art, or a chart. A box can be copied, moved and resized in the same way as you would a piece of clip art, and can even be rotated.

200

You can either use one of the slide layouts provided by PowerPoint, or start with a blank slide and insert objects wherever you like on the slide. These objects are automatically held in boxes.

Editing text on slides

Many of the features that you may be familiar with from using other applications – such as Word or CorelDraw – can be applied to text in PowerPoint by selecting **Format** on the *Standard* toolbar (Figure 166). You can format text to bold, italic, underlined or shadowed, and align text to the left, centre, right or justify it. You can change the colour of text and choose from a wide range of fonts and sizes.

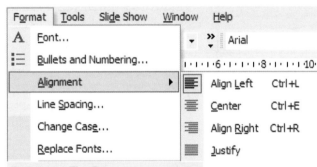
Figure 166 The Format menu options

Using the *Line Spacing* dialogue box from the **Format** menu, you can adjust the line spacing, not only between lines, but before and after paragraphs, just as you can in Word.

Some slide layouts allow for text areas that are specifically for lists. When you start typing in one of these, a bullet will appear before the text. You can format the bullets to different styles, in the same way as you would in Word.

Skills check

Refer to page 91 for information on formatting text.

TiP

PowerPoint includes a spellchecker. All Microsoft Office applications use the same dictionary file to check spellings. If you add a word to the dictionary in Word, PowerPoint will also recognise it.

Skills check

Refer to page 97 for information on formatting bullet lists.

TiP

Take care always to use a font size that can be read easily. Font size 24 or above is a good size to read. Font size 12 or 14 may be fine for a handout, but it would be impossible to read from the back of a room!

Go out and try!

Format the first slide for the presentation you planned in Activity 1.
○ From the menu, select **Format**, **Slide Layout**. The *Slide Layout* task pane appears (see Figure 164).
○ Choose an appropriate layout for your first slide. *Title and Text* is often a good choice.
○ Type in a title and some descriptive text based on the first slide in your plan. Use formatting (e.g. bold) where appropriate.

Open your 'Presentation software' file. Create a new bold heading called '**PS Activity 3**' and write a short paragraph describing the skills you have demonstrated in this activity when editing text in a PowerPoint presentation. 🖫 Save the file.

Skills check ▶▶

The Artwork and Imaging skills section of this book covers editing techniques which you can use when modifying images for a PowerPoint presentation.

Skills check ▶▶

Positioning, cropping, resizing, grouping and borders are controlled in the same way as in Microsoft Word. See page 127 for details.

Editing and using graphics

The graphics you include in a presentation could be a photograph taken with a digital camera, some clip art, a drawing, or perhaps a logo such as the Travelbug logo.

❓ Think it over ...

Have you heard the expression 'a picture is worth a thousand words'? Including graphics in a presentation will ensure that it is more interesting, often easier to understand and – most importantly – more memorable.

You may decide to use a specialist editing package or the *Picture* toolbar in PowerPoint (Figure 167) to edit a graphic. For instance, Thomas Tripp might decide to adjust the colour and resolution of a digital photograph using Coral Photo-Paint or Microsoft Photo Editor rather than use the more limited options supplied with PowerPoint.

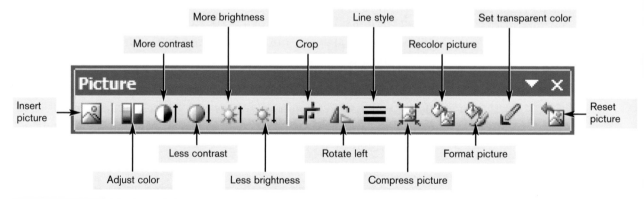

Figure 167 The Picture toolbar

Inserting clip art

Inserting clip art into a slide is very easy – PowerPoint comes with a gallery (Figure 168). If you have an Internet connection, you can click on the **Clips Online** button on the menu bar. This will connect you to Microsoft's database of free clip art. You can also buy a CD-ROM full of pictures you can use.

TiP

*The Internet is a wonderful source of graphics that you can download. However, whatever the source of your graphics, it is important to remember to check that you are allowed to use them. If the creator says that a picture is in the **public domain**, then this means that the copyright on it has been waived and it is free to use. Otherwise you may have to get permission.*

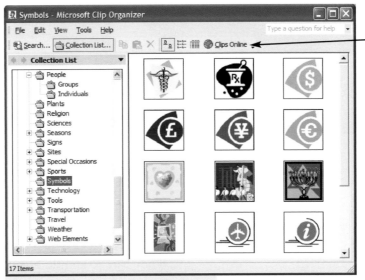

Click here to access Microsoft's Clips Online.

Figure 168 The Microsoft Clip Organizer

TiP

*You can combine a number of images together to make a new image using the **Group**, option on the Drawing toolbar (see page 121).*

Go out and try!

Build a new slide which forms part of the presentation you planned in Activity 1. Include a graphic.
- Click on the **New Slide** button in the *Formatting* toolbar.
- Change the layout to one of the *Content Layouts* using the *Slide Layout* task pane.
- To add some clip art, click the **Insert Clip Art** button (or double-click the area, depending on which version of PowerPoint you are using).
- Double-click the image you would like to use.
- You may decide to insert a photograph and use the editing techniques you have learned to crop and adjust the colour and resolution within PowerPoint.
- Display the *Picture* toolbar (click on an image in your presentation or select **View**, **Toolbars**, **Picture** from the menu).
- Click the **Insert Picture** button (see Figure 167).
- Navigate to the picture you want to add, then double-click it.
- 💾 Save your work.

Open your 'Presentation software' file. Create a new bold heading '**PS Activity 4**' and write a short paragraph describing the skills you have demonstrated in this activity when editing graphics in a PowerPoint presentation. 💾 Save the file.

Adding more features

Inserting lines and simple shapes

An example of a rotated callout with text inside

Figure 169 Using a callout

There are many ways to improve a PowerPoint presentation. You can add lines and shapes, fill the shapes with colour, outline them and make them look three-dimensional. The **Autoshapes** button on the *Drawing* toolbar provides a menu of types of shape, each type having its own sub-menu showing all the shapes available. There are over 150 different shapes to choose from!

Callouts are designed to hold text within the shape. They can be simple boxes with lines pointing from them or 'word and thought' balloons (Figure 169). As with other text boxes, you can resize a callout, and rotate and format its text.

Wrapping text

By default, text inside a shape is wrapped so that it does not spill over the border. If you need to turn this setting off, double-click the shape to display the *Format AutoShape* dialogue, and untick the **Word wrap text in AutoShape** option in the *Text Box* tab (see Figure 170).

Click here to turn off word wrap

Figure 170 Turning off text wrapping in an AutoShape

Inserting WordArt

As with other Microsoft Office programs, such as Word and Excel, you can use the *WordArt* tool to create a logo, or to make text more interesting. One very useful feature is that a design you make in one Office application can be used in any of them. Therefore, if you have used WordArt in Word to create a logo, for example, you could use the same logo in a PowerPoint presentation.

Think it over ...

Look at the two sample slides in Figure 171. One of these has WordArt for the text, and the other does not. Which do you think looks more appealing?

WordArt used for text

Normal text

Figure 171 A comparison of WordArt and normal text

Go out and try!

1 Build a new slide which forms part of the presentation planned in Activity 1. Include lines or shapes.
  ○ Click on **New Slide**.
  ○ Choose a *Blank* or *Title Only* slide layout.
  ○ If the drawing toolbar is not visible, select **View**, **Toolbars**, **Drawing**.
  ○ Click on **AutoShapes** on the *Drawing* toolbar and choose a shape.
  ○ Drag out the shape on the slide.
  ○ Use the formatting icons on the toolbar to change the colour, border, shadow style and 3-D style until you are happy with the result.

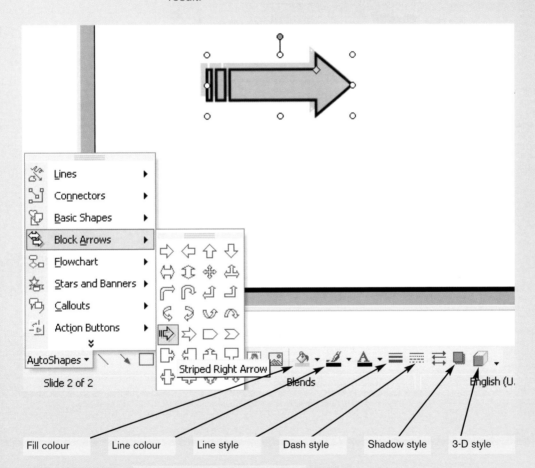

Figure 172 The Drawing toolbar

2 Build a second slide which includes WordArt.
  ○ Click on **New Slide**.
  ○ Click on the **WordArt** button on the *Drawing* toolbar. The *WordArt Gallery* dialogue appears.

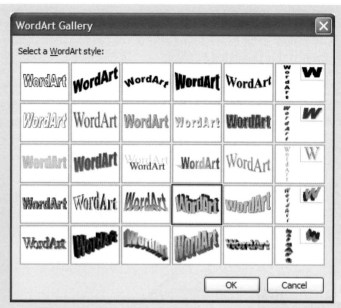

Figure 173 WordArt styles

- Click on a style and then click **OK**. The *Edit WordArt Text* dialogue appears.

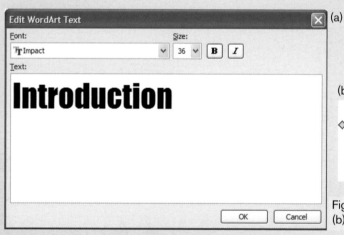
(a)

(b)

Figure 174 (a) Before and (b) after setting the WordArt text

- Type your text and then press **OK**.
- Use the handles to move, resize and rotate the WordArt as necessary.
  - Save your work.

Open your 'Presentation software' file. Create a new bold heading '**PS Activity 5**' and write a short paragraph describing the skills you have demonstrated in this activity when using simple lines, shapes and WordArt in a PowerPoint presentation.
Save the file.

TiP

Remember not to try to include too many sounds. Be careful what you choose – you may enjoy listening to heavy metal, but will your audience?

TiP

Remember the copyright issues you have learned about text and images also applies to music and sound files.

Inserting sounds

Sound can enhance a presentation when used carefully. You can use one of the sound clips provided with PowerPoint, record your own sounds, play sounds off a CD to accompany your presentation, or download sounds from the Internet.

You can add sound effects to your animations. If you wish to, you can even record your own commentary. You cannot, however, use a pre-recorded commentary and another form of recorded sound at the same time.

The final enhancement Thomas Tripp makes to his slide for the Cruise Club presentation is to insert sound. He has chosen 'Sailing' sung by by Rod Stewart. On searching the Internet he finds a free midi (sound) file which he can save to his computer and then insert into the presentation.

Go out and try!

Build up a new slide which forms part of the presentation planned in Activity 1. Include a sound clip using the following steps:
- From the menu select **Insert**, **Movies and Sounds**, **Sound From File**.
- Navigate to the sound file you want to add, select it and press **OK**.
- You will be asked whether you want the sound to play when the slide loads or when the user clicks the sound icon. Make your choice.
- Test your slide show to make sure that the sound plays as you expected.
- 💾 Save your work.

Open your 'Presentation software' file. Create a new bold heading '**PS Activity 6**' and write a short paragraph describing the skills you have demonstrated in this activity when using simple video and sounds in a PowerPoint presentation. Save the file.

Navigation between slides

The default navigation route of a PowerPoint presentation is linear. However, the Action Settings feature will allow you to link to another slide further on in your presentation, to another PowerPoint presentation, to a file, or even to a website (Figure 175). You can add settings to text or to an object in your presentation.

Figure 175 Dialogue box for action settings

The Autoshapes button on the Drawing toolbar also includes a number of action buttons which you can include on slides. This feature can be useful when you wish to move to another part of your presentation, or even to another file.

Thomas Tripp has built a slide which gives examples of what Travelbug can offer their customers (Figure 176). He has also used the action settings facility to link to slides in a different part of the presentation (Figure 177).

By clicking here, the presentation moves out of sequence to show the Cruise Club slide.

Figure 176 Slide with links to different parts of the presentation

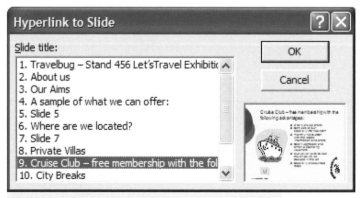

Figure 177 Adding a hyperlink from slide 4 to slide 9

Finally, Thomas has included an action button which he has set to return to the last slide viewed.

Go out and try!

Use the Action Settings feature of PowerPoint to assist in the navigation between slides in your presentation.
- Use the *Drawing* toolbar to insert an AutoShape on the slide you want to link from.
- Right-click the AutoShape and choose **Action Settings** from the menu that appears.
- Select the **Hyperlink to** option and choose which slide you want to link to. Choose **Slide** to link to a particular slide, or **First Slide** to jump back to the beginning of the presentation.
- Test your slide show to make sure that the navigation works as expected.
- 🖫 Save your work.

Open your 'Presentation software' file. Create a new bold heading '**PS Activity 7**' and write a short paragraph describing the skills you have demonstrated in this activity when using actions settings in a PowerPoint presentation.
🖫 Save the file.

Using animation

PowerPoint has a clever feature that will allow you to make words and pictures on your slides appear and disappear when you want. This is called *animation*. Instead of being visible immediately when the slide appears, the object that you animate – text, a picture, or a piece of clip art for example – comes in afterwards, appearing in a special way.

Animation controls how an object is brought on to the slide. An object can appear automatically, or wait until the user clicks the mouse button before appearing. If you have more than one animated object on a slide you can control the order in which they appear. The object will always end up where you put it when you were designing the slide.

The simplest way to animate your presentation is to use one of the animation schemes that PowerPoint provides. You have a choice from such things as *Appear and Dim* (Figure 179), *Dissolve In*, and *Spin*. PowerPoint lets you preview how the animation of your text and objects will appear for one slide or for the whole presentation.

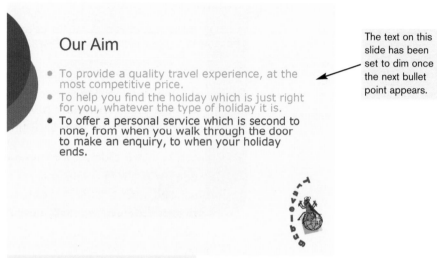

The text on this slide has been set to dim once the next bullet point appears.

Figure 179 Using animation in a slide

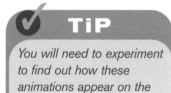

For the more adventurous, there is the *Custom Animation* option, which provides more control of your animations. You can use a lot more animation effects, pick the sound that goes with each animation, choose the order in which animations take place, and set the amount of time to wait between animations. You can decide what happens to an object once it appears, such as making it disappear or change colour.

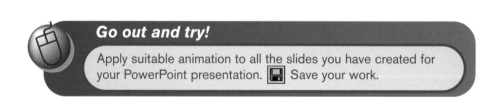

Go out and try!

Apply suitable animation to all the slides you have created for your PowerPoint presentation. Save your work.

Open your 'Presentation software' file. Create a new bold heading '**PS Activity 8**' and write a short paragraph describing the skills you have demonstrated in this activity when using animation in a PowerPoint presentation. Save the file.

Think it over ...

You will have seen examples of transitions all the time, without realising it. For example, a transition happens when you are watching the television and the scene changes from one shot to another.

Creating slide transitions

When you are showing a PowerPoint presentation and move from one slide to the next, this is referred to as *slide transition*. When you design a PowerPoint presentation, each slide has a transition associated with it. The transition will tell PowerPoint how to change the display from one slide to the next.

The latest version of PowerPoint offers over 50 different transition styles from which to choose – examples are *cut*, *dissolve* and *wipe right*. If you prefer, you can choose a random transition, so that a different style and direction will be used each time you move on to a new slide.

You can adjust the speed for slide transitions to be slow, medium or fast. Furthermore, you can make the transitions occur on the click of a mouse or automatically after a set period of time. You can even set up a presentation to show continuously until the **Esc** key is pressed. Thomas Tripp could use this feature for the slide show he wants to show at a travel exhibition.

Go out and try!

Apply suitable slide transitions to all the slides you have created for your PowerPoint presentation. Save your work.

Open your 'Presentation software' file. Create a new bold heading '**PS Activity 9**' and write a short paragraph describing the skills you have demonstrated in this activity when applying slide transitions to a PowerPoint presentation. Save the file.

TiP

*It is possible to blank the screen when running a presentation. This is useful if you want to catch the audience's attention. By pressing **B** on the keyboard the screen will turn black, and on pressing **W** the screen will turn white. You just press these keys again to return to the presentation.*

Producing speaker's notes and handouts

Speaker's notes

PowerPoint has a facility called *speakers notes* which allows you to include notes with a slide. This feature gives a text display for each slide. You can add anything you want in these notes (Figure 180).

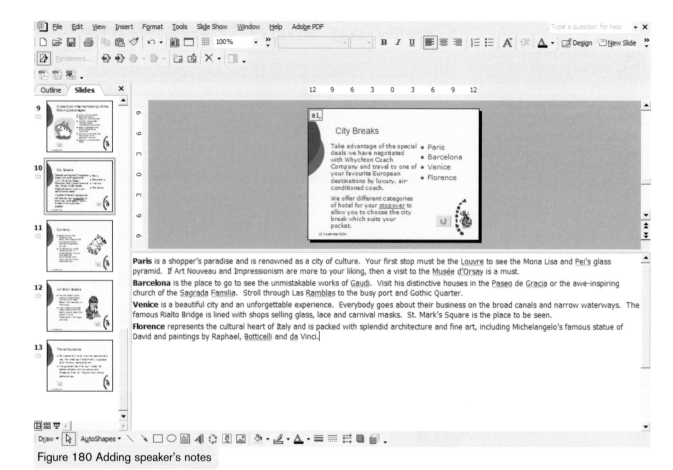

Figure 180 Adding speaker's notes

For example, Thomas Tripp of Travelbug can use this facility to give extra details on the different cities shown on the City Break slide of his presentation. The slide, together with the notes, can be printed out to give to prospective customers.

Handouts

Another feature of PowerPoint is that you can print a presentation as a *handout*. You have the option of choosing how many slides per page to print, up to a maximum of nine. If you choose three slides per page, as shown in Figure 181, PowerPoint automatically adds lines to the right-hand side of each slide so that the audience can write their own notes during the presentation.

Select number of slides per page.

Select the Handouts option.

Shows how the slides will appear when printed.

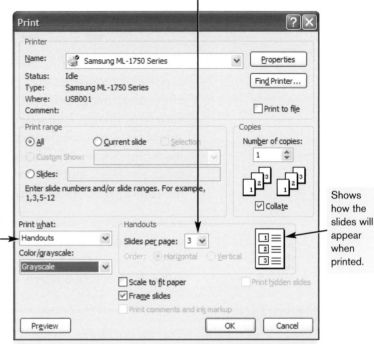

Figure 181 Options to choose from when printing handouts

Go out and try!

Use the skills you have learned to produce Speaker's Notes and Handouts to accompany your presentation. Save your work.

Open your 'Presentation software' file. Create a new bold heading '**PS Activity 10**' and write a short paragraph describing the skills you have demonstrated in this activity when producing Speaker's Notes and Handouts. Save the file.

Artwork and imaging software

With the power of the modern computer and its ability to select, capture or modify images, you don't have to be an artist to create interesting, imaginative and effective artwork. This book contains a variety of images and artwork: some are screen prints of the computer, some are photographs and some are drawings; some are in black and white and others are in colour. They are all intended to make the book more interesting to read and to help you understand the topics you are studying.

Sometimes a graphical representation can stand alone without any words at all, and at other times the image makes the words much easier to understand, or vice versa. For example, it would be very difficult to describe charts and graphs just in words.

LEARNING OUTCOMES

You need to learn about

✓ selecting and capturing images

✓ modifying images

✓ choosing appropriate resolutions and file formats.

Selecting and capturing images

There are a variety of methods to select and capture images that can then be used to improve the presentation of your e-portfolios. You can select images that are already prepared (such as clip art), create your own using drawing tools, or acquire images electronically by scanning them or downloading photos from a digital camera.

Using clip art and library images

Images can be imported into your documents from libraries on CD–ROM, the Internet, or packaged with the software. Word contains its own selection of images, but far more are available from other sources. Many of these clip art libraries are free.

You can enter a topic in the search field and the computer will find relevant pictures available in the library. A search for 'Australia' produced many results. The search was then refined to show only images first in clip art format and then in photo format. Two images of Sydney Opera House were selected, and copied and pasted into the text for this chapter (Figure 182).

Figure 182 Sydney Opera House in clip art format, and in photo format

Go out and try!

Find two images (one from clip art and one from a photo library) to represent a European country of your choice.
- Open a new blank document in Word.
- From the menu, select **Insert**, **Picture**, **Clip Art**. The *Insert Clip Art* task pane appears.
- In the search field, key in the name of your chosen European country (Figure 183).
- Select one suitable image and insert it into your document.
- Search for a photo of your chosen country, from a photo CD or the Internet. Insert the photo using **Insert**, **Picture**, **From File**.
- 🖫 Save the document containing the images as 'Graphic images 1' in your 'Artwork and imaging software' sub-folder.

Figure 183 Clip art search

Start a file called 'Artwork and imaging software'. Create a bold heading '**AIS Activity 1**' and write a short paragraph describing the methods you used to capture these images. 🖫 Save this file in your 'Artwork and imaging software' sub-folder.

215

DiDA

Figure 184 A scanner

Using a scanner

A *scanner* allows you to add pictures from other sources – such as a magazine, book or photograph – into your documents (Figure 184). The scanner reads the information and converts it into digital format.

The document is placed inside the scanner. Once the image has been scanned, it can be stored in the computer and used intact or edited as required. The scanned image is stored in picture format, even if it is text – unless text recognition software is available, in which case the text is stored as data that can be edited using a word processor.

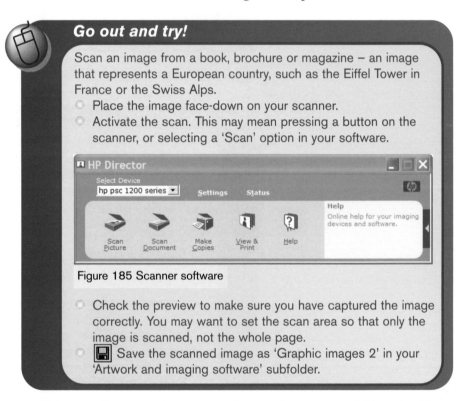

Go out and try!

Scan an image from a book, brochure or magazine – an image that represents a European country, such as the Eiffel Tower in France or the Swiss Alps.
- Place the image face-down on your scanner.
- Activate the scan. This may mean pressing a button on the scanner, or selecting a 'Scan' option in your software.

Figure 185 Scanner software

- Check the preview to make sure you have captured the image correctly. You may want to set the scan area so that only the image is scanned, not the whole page.
- Save the scanned image as 'Graphic images 2' in your 'Artwork and imaging software' subfolder.

Open your file called 'Artwork and imaging software'. Create a new bold heading called '**AIS Activity 2**' and write a short paragraph describing how you scanned the image and viewed it on screen. Save the file.

Using a digital camera and downloading images

Digital cameras look very similar to traditional cameras (Figure 186), but most of them allow you to view the image on a small liquid-

Figure 186 A digital camera

crystal display (LCD) screen built into the camera. As soon as you take a picture, you can view it on the screen and decide whether to keep it or to retake the shot. With a traditional camera the picture is recorded on film, so you have no idea how good or bad the photograph is until the film has been processed.

With a digital camera, light intensities are converted into a digital form that can be stored on a memory card or stick. The images can then be downloaded into the computer, viewed on screen, saved and imported into a document or printed on special photographic-quality paper. The digital images can also be taken to photographic shops and printed in the same size formats as standard photographs taken on film.

Go out and try!

1 Use a digital camera to take a picture of a friend, and ask your friend to take a picture of you.
   ○ Make sure you are happy with the pictures. Delete them and retake them if necessary.
   ○ Transfer the images from the digital camera to your computer (following your manufacturer's instructions). The software will assign numbers to each shot, e.g. Img_0822.
2 Save each image in your 'Artwork and imaging' subfolder.
3 Open a new document and insert both photos into the document.
4 Save the document as 'Graphic images 3' in your 'Artwork and imaging' subfolder.

Open your file called 'Artwork and imaging software'. Create a new bold heading '**AIS Activity 3**' and write a short paragraph describing how you captured and downloaded the images. Save the file.

TiP

*When grouping images, if you click on an image to highlight it and then click on another image, you lose the first highlight. In order to group two or more images, click on the first image, hold down the **Shift** key (the up arrow under the **Caps Lock**), click on each other image in turn, then select **Group** from the Drawing toolbar.*

Modifying images

Once an image has been captured electronically, it is possible to modify the image to suit your purpose exactly.

Grouping and ungrouping

Several different images can be combined to make a new image. The logo designed for Travelbug (Figure 187) was created using WordArt for the text, combined with two clip art images: the world plus an insect sitting on top!

Once the two images were positioned correctly, they were grouped together using the *Drawing* toolbar (Figure 187). The WordArt was resized, rotated to fit around the image, and the colour of the letters changed to blend in. All three elements of the logo were then grouped together.

When the images have been grouped in this way they can be manipulated as one image. If you then wish to change part of the image, you can click on the image and this time select **Ungroup** from the *Drawing* toolbar. After the necessary changes have been made, the individual images can be regrouped to make one image. It is much easier to work with a grouped image because all the elements move together and can be resized in proportion.

Figure 187 WordArt and clip art images are highlighted and grouped to make the logo

Go out and try!

Using clip art and WordArt, combine three separate components to create a logo for a travel company specialising in holidays to your chosen European country.
- Open a new document.
- Use WordArt to create one component for a logo for the travel company.
- Insert two clip art images that suit the name of the travel company.
- Position the three components into a single logo image.
- Group the three images into one logo: click on one, and holding down the **Shift** key, click on the other two. Then right-click on one of the images and select **Group**.
- Save the logo file as 'Graphic images 4' in your 'Artwork and imaging software' subfolder.

Open your file called 'Artwork and imaging software'. Create a new bold heading '**AIS Activity 4**' and write a short paragraph describing how you grouped the images to create your logo. Save the file.

✓ TiP

Images can be reduced or enlarged by dragging the 'handles' at their corners.

Cutting, pasting, cropping, trimming and resizing images

Sometimes you find that what you require is part of a bigger picture. For example, the Sydney Opera House scene shown in Figure 182 (page 215) included a lot of water and sky. If you wanted only the actual opera house, you could cut out that section by using the 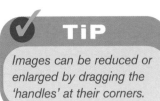 crop (trim) tool to remove the unwanted sections (Figure 188).

Figure 188 Sydney Opera House cropped and resized

Another method of cropping an image is to use the mask tools ( ) that are typically available in graphics software.

- The first mask enables you to draw a rectangular shape around the area you wish to keep.
- The second mask enables you to draw a circle around the area you wish to keep.
- The third mask enables you to draw a freehand shape around the area you wish to keep.

Once the area to be kept has been identified, the image can be cropped to the mask.

To obtain the image of these mask tools, a screen print was made showing the toolbars in Corel Photo-Paint (Figure 189). The rectangular mask was used to select the mask icons and, once the image was 'cropped to mask', the rest of the screen print was removed leaving just the three mask tools.

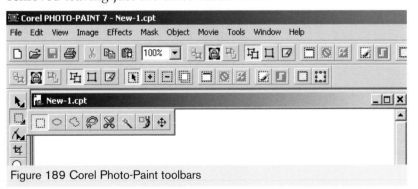

Figure 189 Corel Photo-Paint toolbars

DiDA

Go out and try!

Choose two images from those you have already saved. Copy each of the images into one new file. Crop or trim one image, and resize the second image.

- Open a new document.
- Insert the two images you have chosen.
- Crop one of the images: select the image and clip on the crop tool [𝄃], then drag the edges to cut off the part of the image you want to lose.
- Resize the other image:
  - Select the image and drag the corner handles of the image until it is the size that you want.
  - If you want to be more precise, right-click the image and choose **Format Picture**. In the dialogue box, on the *Size* tab, enter the dimensions for *either* the **Height** or **Width**, tick **Lock aspect ratio** and **Relative to original picture size**, and click **OK**.

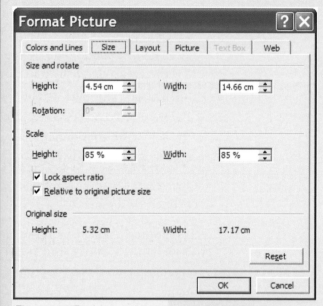

Figure 190 Resizing a picture

🖫 Save your document as 'Graphic images 5' in your 'Artwork and imaging software' subfolder.

Open your file called 'Artwork and imaging software'. Create a new bold heading '**AIS Activity 5**' and write a short paragraph describing how you copied and edited the images. 🖫 Save the file.

Format Picture

Colors and Lines | Size | Layout | Picture | Text Box | Web

Size and rotate

Height: 4.54 cm   Width: 14.66 cm

Rotation: 0°

Scale

Height: 85 %   Width: 85 %

☑ Lock aspect ratio
☑ Relative to original picture size

Original size

Height: 5.32 cm   Width: 17.17 cm

Reset

OK   Cancel

Aligning, rotating, and flipping images

Aligning an image

The **Align or Distribute** options on the *Drawing* toolbar allow you to place an image in a particular position on the page (Figure 191).

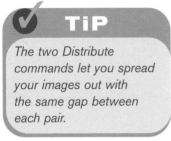

TiP

The two Distribute commands let you spread your images out with the same gap between each pair.

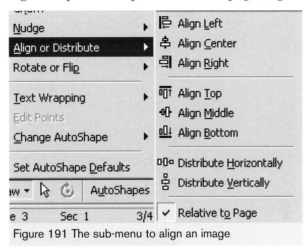

Figure 191 The sub-menu to align an image

This facility can be very useful if, for example, you wish to position the image exactly in the middle of the page, which is quite difficult just by dragging the image into position. Click on the image, select **Relative to Page,** and then **Align Middle** – the image will be placed in the centre of the page.

When drawing a diagram, you may wish to draw a series of boxes the same size and then arrange them to line up evenly on the page. It can be quite difficult to do this just by dragging the boxes into position (Figure 192). Instead, select the boxes and choose **Draw, Align or Distribute, Align Left** from the *Drawing* toolbar.

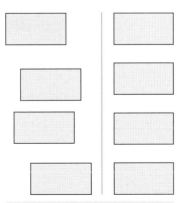

Figure 192 Boxes unaligned, and then aligned and spaced evenly

Figure 193 The AutoShape arrow rotated in various directions

Rotating an image

An image can be rotated to the left, to the right or freely. The *AutoShape arrow* points to the right, but suppose you need an arrow pointing upwards. Select the arrow and rotate left, which changes the direction to point up. If you select free rotate, then the arrow can be angled to any direction you choose (Figure 193).

Flipping an image

If you flip an image, you reverse the direction in which the image is pointing. For example, suppose you need a picture of a horse facing to the right. You have found a good picture but the horse is pointing to the left. You can use the picture and flip it to the right (Figure 194) using **Draw, Rotate or Flip, Flip Horizontal**.

Figure 194 An image flipped horizontally

You can also flip an image vertically so it turns upside down (Figure 195).

Figure 195 An image flipped vertically

Go out and try!

1. Open the file called 'Graphic images 4'; it should contain your logo for a travel company specialising in holidays in your chosen European country.

2. Copy the image and paste *one* copy into a new file. Insert a page break and paste *four* more copies on to the second page. The steps are as follows.
   - Copy the logo into the clipboard.
   - Close the file called 'Graphic images 4'.
   - Create a new document and paste the logo.
   - Select **Insert**, **Break** and select **Page break**.

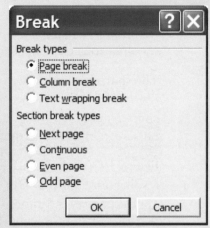

Figure 196
Inserting a page break

   - Paste the logo four times on to page 2.

3. Align the logo on page 1 so that it is centred on the page, as follows.
   - Use the **Draw**, **Align or Distribute** menu on the *Drawing* toolbar. You may need to turn on **Relative to Page**.

4. On page 2, rotate the first logo to the left; rotate the second logo to the right; rotate the third logo using the free rotation tool; and flip the fourth logo.
   - Use the **Draw**, **Rotate or Flip** menu on the *Drawing* toolbar.

5. On page 2, align the four logos so they are vertically distributed and in the centre of the page, as follows.
   - Select all four logos.
   - Use the **Draw**, **Align or Distribute** menu on the *Drawing* toolbar.

6. Save the file as 'Graphic images 6' in your 'Artwork and imaging software' subfolder.

Open your file called 'Artwork and imaging software'. Create a new bold heading '**AIS Activity 6**' and write a short paragraph describing the skills you have learnt. Save the file.

Choosing appropriate image resolutions and file formats

Optimising image resolution for print and digital publications

There are two basic types of images on a computer:

- bitmaps
- vectors.

Bitmaps

A *bitmap* image is made up of dots, whereas a *vector* image is made up of various elements such as lines, curves, circles and squares.

The sharpness or clarity of a bitmap image is determined by its *resolution*, which is measured by the number of *pixels* (or dots) it contains per inch (dpi). A general 'rule of thumb' is to use 72dpi for on-screen images and up to 300 or 600dpi for printed images.

Figure 197(a) shows a bitmap image of a bird with a clear resolution. Figure 197(b) shows the same image increased to approximately 3.5 times the original size, and you can see clearly that the resolution has deteriorated. Figure 197(c) shows an enlarged section of the bird's beak. Notice that the edge of the beak is now looking very ragged and uneven. Figure 197(d) shows the same enlargement including the gridlines. The individual pixels are clearly visible, which is very useful if you wish to edit a picture.

TiP

As a bitmap image is enlarged, the quality becomes poorer. There will be a point beyond which the quality is unacceptable for all normal uses.

TiP

If you want to create an image as a bitmap then it is important to design it at the size it should be printed.

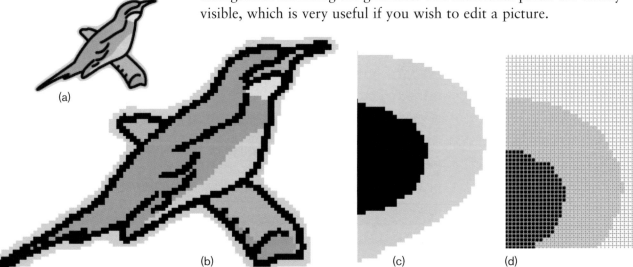

Figure 197 (a) Bitmap image of a bird. (b) The same image enlarged about 3.5 times. (c) An enlarged section of the beak. (d) An enlarged section of the beak showing the individual pixels and gridlines

Vector graphics

In vector graphics, objects are treated as collections of lines rather than patterns of individual dots. This makes it easier to enlarge the image without reducing its sharpness or quality (Figure 198). However, many people believe that bitmap images provide more subtlety in shading and texture.

Figure 198 A vector image: notice that the enlargement retains the quality

Go out and try!

1 Choose a vector/clip art image, such as the one shown in Figure 198, and insert it into a new Word File.
2 Copy the image in Word, open Paint and paste in the copied image. (This turns the vector image into a bitmap image.)
3 Select **View**, **Zoom**, **Large Size** from the menu in Paint.
4 Select **View**, **Zoom**, **Show Grid**. You will now see the individual pixels.
5 Use the Select tool to select just the image, then copy it to the clipboard.
6 Paste the bitmap into the Word file under the vector image.
7 Enlarge each of the images and compare the clarity. You should find that curved and diagonal lines are jagged in the enlarged bitmap image and smooth in the enlarged vector image.
8 Save the Word file as 'Graphical images 7' in your 'Artwork and imaging software' subfolder.

TiP

You can find the Paint *program by clicking on the Windows* **Start** *menu, and selecting* **Programs**, **Accessories**, **Paint**.

 Open your file called 'Artwork and imaging software'. Create a new bold heading '**AIS Activity 7**' and write a short paragraph describing the quality of the four resized images. What conclusions can you draw from this? Save the file.

Digital sound

In the early days of the World Wide Web, websites consisted of text, but little else. DVDs and CD–ROMs were unheard of, and 40 MB of storage capacity was exceptional. Newer technologies have led to audio, video and other multimedia being used on many websites and other platforms such as DVDs and CD–ROMs.

LEARNING OUTCOMES

You need to learn about

✓ capturing sound clips

✓ editing and using sound clips.

Capturing sound clips

Jargon buster

A **WAV file** (with extension '.wav') is the most common format for sound files. All recent browsers can open WAV files. However, these files can be very large: a one-minute WAV file is over 10MB.

If your computer has a sound card, you will be able to capture sound in a digital format and create a *WAV file*. You can use Microsoft Sound Recorder to do this very easily. The source of the sound can be from any playback device, such as a CD player, DVD player, tape recorder and so on. Alternatively you can record the sound live from a microphone or several microphones using a mixing device.

If you want to include a WAV file on a website, it is best to *compress* it. MPEG 3 (MP3) is a popular audio compression that will compress a WAV file to about one-tenth its original size.

You will need to connect the source of the sound to the sound card. In Figure 199 you will see an example of a headset, microphone and two connectors. The pink connector has a picture of a microphone on it and the green connector has a picture of the earphones. You will need to plug these into the correct sockets on your sound card, which are normally at the back of your computer. If you using a microphone to record speech, the speech will go through the pink connector into the sound card and be played back through the green connector to the headset.

Figure 199 Headset, microphone and connectors

Recording a sound file

Microsoft Sound Recorder allows you to record, mix, play and edit sounds. A mixer, such as the one shown in Figure 200, will allow you to adjust the level to ensure that the sound is not too high and distorted, or too low and hard to hear. The vertical sliders allow you to control the volume of the sound: move them up to increase the volume of the signal or down to decrease it. The Balance controls allow you to adjust the sound between left and right.

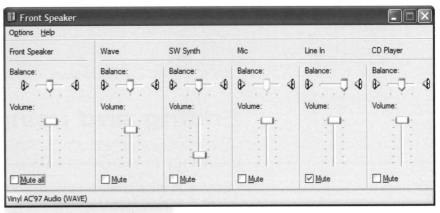

Figure 200 A mixer panel

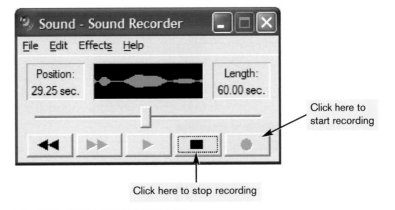

Click here to start recording

Click here to stop recording

Figure 201 Recording a sound

To record a sound, simply make sure you have an audio input device, such as a microphone, connected to your computer and then select **File, New** to create a new file (Figure 201). Click on the start button to commence recording, click on the stop button when you have finished, and finally remember to save the file.

Go out and try!

Select a sound from a suitable source such as CD, DVD, or voice input via microphone). Using Microsoft Sound Recorder, record the sound, adjusting the balance for the sound using the mixer supplied with Microsoft Windows if necessary. 🔲 Save the sound file with a suitable name.

Create a new file called 'Digital video and sound' and save it in your 'Digital sound' sub-folder. Create a new bold heading called '**DS Activity 1**' and write a short paragraph describing the skills you have demonstrated in this activity.
🔲 Save the file.

Editing and using sound clips

Editing a sound file

Once you have recorded a sound, you are able to edit the file in a number of ways. You can

- add sounds to the file
- delete part of the file
- change the playback speed
- change the playback volume
- change the playback direction
- add an echo
- change or convert the sound file type.

Figure 202 Editing options with Sound Recorder

If you wish to mix the sound file with another sound file, you will need to select **Edit, Mix with File** (Figure 202). Alternatively, by moving the slider to the place in the file you want to cut, you can choose to delete all the sound before the current position or after the current position. You can also add echo to an uncompressed sound file by selecting **Effects, Add Echo**.

TiP

*Fortunately, if you change your mind you can undo your changes to a sound file by choosing **File, Revert**.*

If you wish to insert a different sound file, move the slider to where you would like to insert the file and select **Edit, Insert File**. You can only insert a sound file into an uncompressed sound file. When there is no green line in Sound Recorder, the file is compressed and you cannot modify it unless you first adjust the sound quality (Figure 203).

This file has been compressed, therefore there is no green line here.

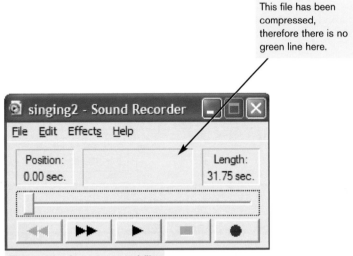

Figure 203 A compressed file

When you are satisfied with your recording, you can compress the file by saving it in a different format, such as MP3. Sound Recorder allows you to save in several different formats (Figure 204).

Jargon buster

Compressing a file means reducing the file size so that it requires less storage space. This will allow it to be transmitted over the Internet more quickly. Unfortunately, the more you compress a digital sound or video file, the more the quality is reduced.

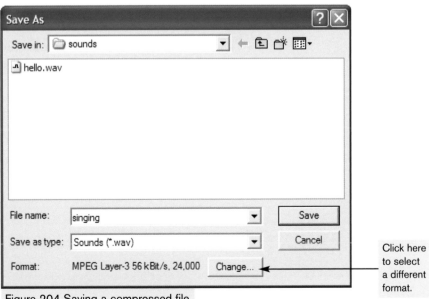

Click here to select a different format.

Figure 204 Saving a compressed file

Using alternative audio software

Microsoft Sound Recorder is an ideal way to record and edit a sound track when you are first starting out. However, as you become more experienced, you will no doubt find that it can be limiting in its features. It is possible to download free audio editing software such as Audacity (see www.heinemann.co.uk/hotlinks (express code 0050P) for more). You can use this software to edit sound in a wide variety of ways. Figure 205 shows the Audacity window.

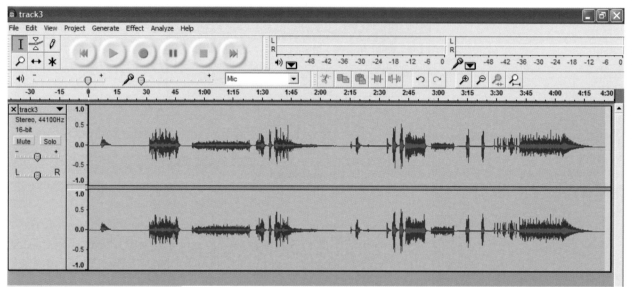

Figure 205 The Audacity window

This software programme includes two excellent online tutorials to work through, which will equip you with the skills to do more advanced editing of sound tracks.

Figure 206 shows a sound track that has been highlighted prior to an effect being applied to it. As you can see, there are a large number of possible effects available with this software.

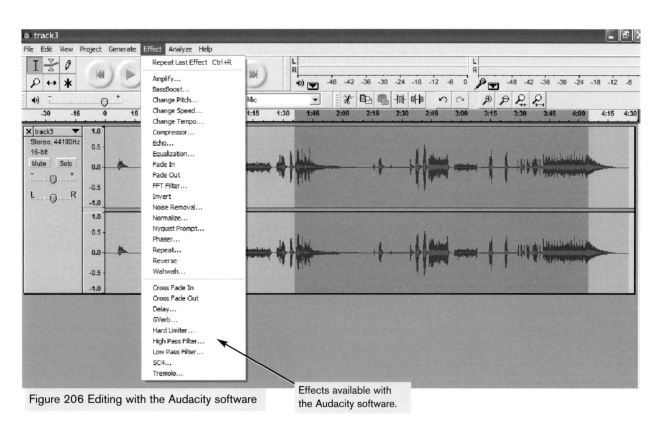

Figure 206 Editing with the Audacity software

Effects available with the Audacity software.

Go out and try!

Using some or all of the techniques you have learned, edit the sound file you recorded in Activity 1. You may decide to record another sound and then mix it with this file, add echo, or increase or decrease the speed. Add the sound file to the presentation or website created for your project. 💾 Save your work.

Open your 'Digital sound' file. Create a new bold heading '**DS Activity 2**' and write a short paragraph describing the skills you have demonstrated whilst modifying a recorded sound. 💾 Save the file.

Internet and intranets

In your studies you will need to research information from a wide variety of sources. A huge amount of information can be obtained if you carry out a search on the Internet or an intranet. However, be warned: there are millions of websites on the World Wide Web (WWW) and, unless you have the skills to carry out an effective search, you may find it difficult to find the exact information you need.

Jargon buster

The **Internet** is the world's largest computer network, connecting millions of organisations and people across the globe.

An **intranet** uses the same technology as the Internet but is an internal communication system for a particular organisation or company. It can be accessed only by authorised users. It allows secure email communication and distribution of data.

The **World Wide Web** is a part of the Internet. Multimedia documents are connected together using **hyperlinks**. Each document is called a **web page** and a set of web pages make up a **website**.

LEARNING OUTCOMES

You need to learn about

✓ using features of browser software

✓ using search engines and portals.

Jargon buster

Broadband is the general term given to the latest in high-speed Internet access technology, which is much faster than using a dial-up modem. An Asymmetric Digital Subscriber Line (ADSL) is an example of always-on broadband technology. It uses an ordinary telephone line to allow you to access the Internet and talk on the telephone at the same time.

Using features of your browser software

The special software which enables you to search the Internet or an intranet is known as a *web browser*. A web browser enables you to view web pages and to click on links – known as *hyperlinks* – to other web pages and websites. The most common web browsers are Microsoft Internet Explorer and Netscape Navigator.

When you double-click on your browser to start it up, you can access web pages only if you are connected to the Internet via your *Internet Service Provider (ISP)*. You may have an 'always on' *broadband connection*, or you may have a 'dial-up' connection (which means that your modem has to dial to your ISP before you can access the Internet).

The home page

When you launch a web browser while connected to the Internet, the default web page – the *home page* – will be loaded and appear on screen. This can be the intranet of the company whose computer you are using, the website of your ISP, or any website you have chosen.

Finding a website

If you know the *website address* (URL) you can go directly to it by typing it in the Address box of the browser and clicking on **Go**. If you don't know the address of a company or organisation, try guessing. It is often possible to guess correctly, as organisations usually try to include their name in the address. You don't even have to type 'http://www' because the browser will add that for you. Figure 207 shows the toolbar and Address box in Internet Explorer.

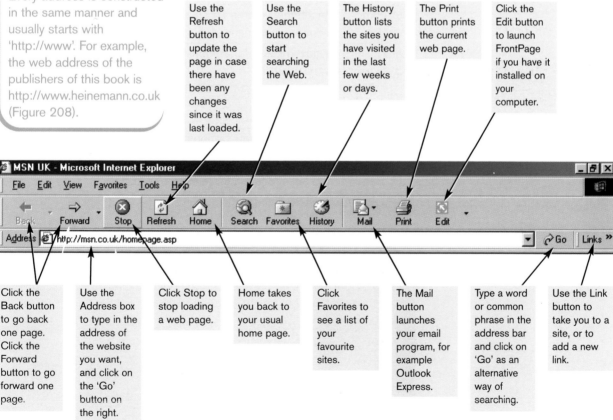

Use the Refresh button to update the page in case there have been any changes since it was last loaded.

Use the Search button to start searching the Web.

The History button lists the sites you have visited in the last few weeks or days.

The Print button prints the current web page.

Click the Edit button to launch FrontPage if you have it installed on your computer.

Click the Back button to go back one page. Click the Forward button to go forward one page.

Use the Address box to type in the address of the website you want, and click on the 'Go' button on the right.

Click Stop to stop loading a web page.

Home takes you back to your usual home page.

Click Favorites to see a list of your favourite sites.

The Mail button launches your email program, for example Outlook Express.

Type a word or common phrase in the address bar and click on 'Go' as an alternative way of searching.

Use the Link button to take you to a site, or to add a new link.

Figure 207 The Internet Explorer toolbar

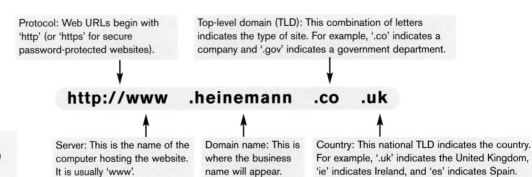

Protocol: Web URLs begin with 'http' (or 'https' for secure password-protected websites).

Top-level domain (TLD): This combination of letters indicates the type of site. For example, '.co' indicates a company and '.gov' indicates a government department.

http://www   .heinemann   .co   .uk

Figure 208
The Heinemann
URL explained

Server: This is the name of the computer hosting the website. It is usually 'www'.

Domain name: This is where the business name will appear.

Country: This national TLD indicates the country. For example, '.uk' indicates the United Kingdom, 'ie' indicates Ireland, and 'es' indicates Spain.

Top-level domains (TLDs) indicate the type of site. Examples of useful top-level domains to know are listed in Figure 209.

.ac	A university, college or academic department
.co	A company
.com	A commercial organisation
.uk.com	An alternative area for UK registrations, often used if the .com or .co.uk name is not available
.gov	A government department
.me	An individual
.mil	A military site
.net	A network-related site
.org	generally a charity or non-profit-making organisation
.sch	A school
.tv	The latest domain for television websites

Figure 209 Top-level domains

Go out and try!

Open your web browser and try to find the following companies' websites by guessing their addresses:
1 Argos
2 Pizza Hut
3 Dixons.
○ Start Internet Explorer (or your installed Internet browser program).
○ In the address bar, key in your guess of the website address.
○ Click 'Go' or 'Search' at the end of the address bar.
○ Repeat for each website address.

Start a new file called 'Internet and intranets' and save it in your 'Internet and intranets' sub-folder. Create a new bold heading called '**II Activity 1**' and write a short paragraph describing the skills you have demonstrated in this activity. Save the file.

Jargon buster

A **hyperlink** is a link on a web page or document which, when you click on it, opens another web page within a website, a different website or a file. Hyperlinks are usually underlined and in another colour, but can also be graphics.

Television

• Pick: **Himalaya with Michael Palin**
  9pm **BBC One**

• BBC TV schedules

Popular programmes:
EastEnders | Smile | TOTP | Lottery

Figure 210 Hyperlinks

Jargon buster

Internet Explorer calls bookmarks **favorites** (spelt the American way).

 TiP

If you share a machine with several people, it is a good idea to create a folder for each person. You can then keep your own favourites separate and easy to find.

Hyperlinks within websites

Many companies have very large websites, starting with a home page and panning out with many pages about different aspects of their company. These pages are connected together by hyperlinks. When you move your mouse pointer over a hyperlink, the arrow changes to a pointing hand. When you click on the hyperlink you will be connected to this link.

It is very easy sometimes to get lost within a company's website, but a well constructed site will always have a link that takes you back to the home page. There will usually be hyperlinks to return you back to the top of a page and to the other main areas of the site. Figure 210 shows some examples of hyperlinks.

Large organisations, such as the BBC, will usually include a search facility for their own site, so that you can quickly find the information you require. The site even has a 'search help and tips' page to help you find the information easily. The BBC's website is a good one to bookmark in your favourites – you will find a host of useful resources to help you with your studies.

Bookmarks

In the same way as you can put a bookmark in a book to return to a page quickly and easily, you can bookmark your favourite websites. You can create folders in which to file these bookmarks, in the same way as you organise and save your files on your hard drive.

Rather than having to remember the address of a website, you can easily return to a site by selecting the name from the favourites list. If there is a specific page within a website that you know you will want to return to on other occasions, you can bookmark that page, rather than the home page of the site.

| Favorites | Tools | Help |

Add to Favorites...

Organize Favorites...

📁 digital applications book ▶
📁 Jenny ▶
📁 Ian ▶
📁 Colin ▶
📁 Ray ▶

Figure 211 Internet Explorer's Favorites folder

235

By using the **Organize Favorites** option, you can add, rename and delete folders. You can also change the order in which you view your favourites so that websites that you visit on a regular basis appear higher in the list.

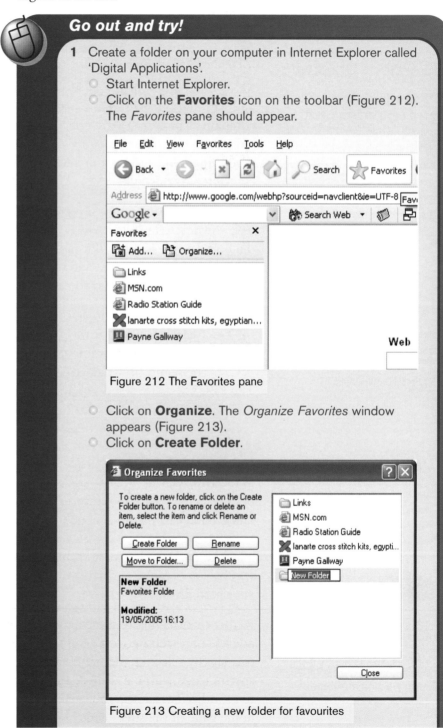

Go out and try!

1   Create a folder on your computer in Internet Explorer called 'Digital Applications'.
   ○ Start Internet Explorer.
   ○ Click on the **Favorites** icon on the toolbar (Figure 212). The *Favorites* pane should appear.

Figure 212 The Favorites pane

   ○ Click on **Organize**. The *Organize Favorites* window appears (Figure 213).
   ○ Click on **Create Folder**.

Figure 213 Creating a new folder for favourites

○ Key in the new folder name 'Digital Applications'.
○ Click **Close**.
2 Visit the website of the BBC through www.heinemann.co.uk/hotlinks (express code 0050P) and bookmark it in the folder within your favourites.
○ Click on the website to be connected.
○ Click **Add** in the *Favorites* task pane.
○ Click **Create in**. The *Add Favorite* window appears (Figure 214).

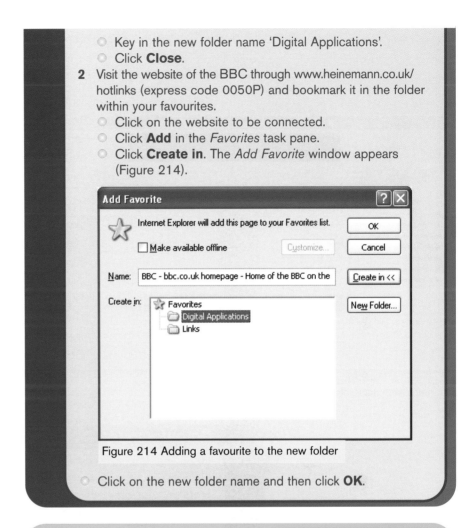

Figure 214 Adding a favourite to the new folder

○ Click on the new folder name and then click **OK**.

 Open your 'Internet and intranets' file. Create a new bold heading '**II Activity 2**' and write a short paragraph describing the skills you have demonstrated when bookmarking a website to a folder. Save the file.

The Back and Forward buttons

All the time you are online, your browser is storing copies of the pages you have recently used in a memory area called *cache*. If you wish to return to a page you visited before, click on **Back** until you reach the page you require. Because the browser program does not have to go back to the Internet, but simply has to look into its internal cache, the page will appear more quickly than it did the first time. You can click on the **Forward** button to return to the web page you were on before you clicked **Back**.

The Refresh button

When you use the **Back** and **Forward** buttons, any changes that may have occurred since you first visited the relevant page will not appear, because the browser has not gone back to the online web page but has merely loaded that page from its internal cache. Clicking on the **Refresh** button will update the page in case there have been any changes since it was last loaded.

For example, by visiting the British Airports Authority plc's (BAA plc) website through www.heinemann.co.uk/hotlinks (express code 0050P), it is possible to check when flights have landed. When you first visit the site, the flight may be shown with its expected arrival time (Figure 215). By clicking on the **Refresh** button at regular intervals you will be able to check when it has actually landed.

Figure 215 The BAA website, which is being constantly updated with flight information

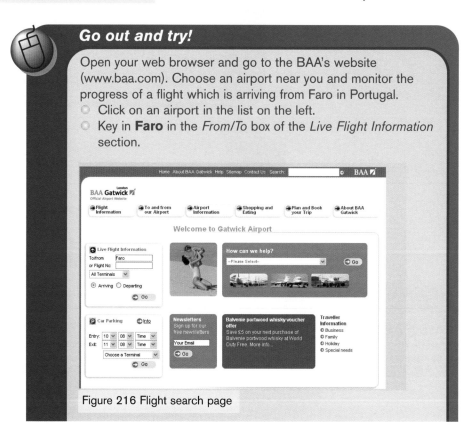

Go out and try!

Open your web browser and go to the BAA's website (www.baa.com). Choose an airport near you and monitor the progress of a flight which is arriving from Faro in Portugal.
- Click on an airport in the list on the left.
- Key in **Faro** in the *From/To* box of the *Live Flight Information* section.

Figure 216 Flight search page

○ Click on **Submit**.

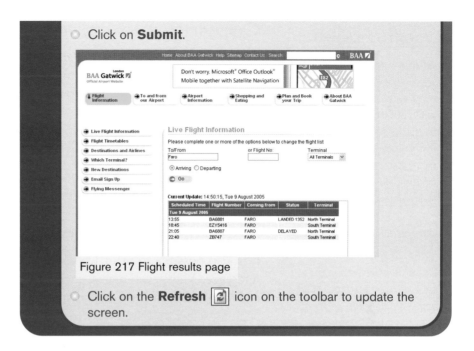

Figure 217 Flight results page

○ Click on the **Refresh** 🔄 icon on the toolbar to update the screen.

Open your 'Internet and intranets' file. Create a new bold heading '**II Activity 3**' and write a short paragraph describing the skills you have demonstrated in this activity. 💾 Save the file.

History

Your browser will store a history of all the websites you have visited over the last few days or weeks. This can be helpful if you have

Figure 218 The History list

forgotten to bookmark a particularly useful site. It is also useful if you have been surfing the net for some time, and you want to return to a page that you previously visited during the current session.

One way to go back to the page is to click the **Back** button, but this can be quite slow if you have visited quite a few pages. Another way is to use the *History* list to select the site (Figure 218).

TIP

Selecting a site from the history list is a quick way of returning to it.

Jargon buster

Offline refers to a way of working with web browsers or email software without being connected to the Internet. **Online** refers to a computer or other device that is connected to the Internet.

TiP

Do remember when you save or copy text from web pages to take into account the copyright issues (see page 81). Some web developers protect their pages so that images and web pages cannot be copied (see Figure 219).

Figure 219 Example of a copyright message

Copying and saving web pages

You can copy text from a website and paste it into another document using the same techniques as you would in Word or Excel. You can also save whole web pages and images from a website on to your computer.

When you save a web page it will be saved in *HTML* (hypertext mark-up language – see page 256). Once you have saved a web page, you can view it through your browser even when you are offline.

Selecting and printing pages

It is also possible to print web pages that you wish to keep for future reference. Many web pages, such as the one shown in Figure 220, include their own print hyperlink. However, you can also print a page by selecting **File, Print** from the menu in the usual way.

The selected text can be printed.

Click here to print the whole page in a printer-friendly format.

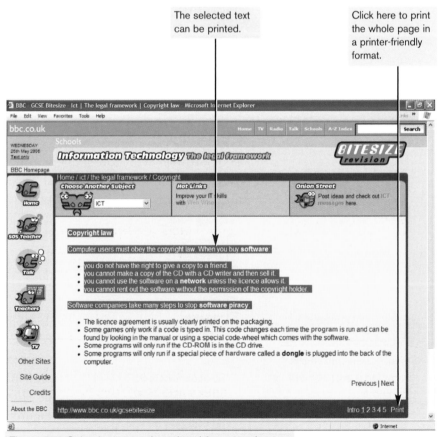

Figure 220 Selecting text to be printed from a web page

Sometimes when you print a web page you find that the material on the right-hand side is cut off. If this happens you will need to change the orientation of the page to landscape using **File, Page Setup** from the menu. You will have practised these skills already with a word processor.

If you want to print a small section of the page, again you can use the skills you have already learned when using other applications such as Word. Select the text you want to print (see Figure 220) and then choose **File, Print** and click on **Selection** before pressing **OK**.

The Go button

You can use the **Go** button on the Address bar to search for web pages. If you type a common name or word in the address bar and click on **Go**, Internet Explorer will either automatically display the web page or list those that are the most likely match.

For example, if you type 'virgin trains' in the Address bar and click on **Go** you will automatically be directed to the Virgin Trains website. However, if you type 'record shops' in the Address bar, a list of possible web pages will be displayed.

TiP

It is worth remembering that search tools are produced by businesses in competition with each other. Do not let the adverts and banners distract you from the real search results.

Jargon buster

A **portal** is a website that offers news, weather information or other services, set up as an entry point to the Web. Most portals are also search engines.

Using search engines

The Internet is the world's largest source of information. However, as you have probably already discovered, there are millions of websites, so it is sometimes quite hard to find the information you want.

If you want to find a particular company, or a certain piece of information, you will need to use a *search tool*. There are several different search tools, the main types being search engines, subject directories, meta-searches and name directories. Figure 221 explains what these are.

You might well be thinking that not only is there a huge amount of information to search, but also many different ways of searching, and you would be right! Choose one search tool and just use that one for a while. If you are not sure which one to choose, ask your friends or your teacher or tutor. When you are used to how it works and what sort of results you get then try another search tool.

- **Search engines** are indexes that work by keywords and context. Popular search engines include Altavista, Ask Jeeves and Google (see www.heinemann.co.uk/hotlinks (express code 0050P) for more). Search engines use a program called a *spider*, *robot* or *crawler* to index huge collections of Internet files. Use search engines when you want to find large numbers of related documents or specific types of document such as image files, MP3 music files or discussion lists.

- **Subject directories** are similar to search engines, but are smaller collections of Internet files grouped by subject headings. These files are not found by software, but chosen by humans. These directories are ideal if you wish to research a general topic and you want to avoid all the irrelevant files that search engines can find. An example of a search directory is Open Directory Project (see www.heinemann.co.uk/hotlinks (express code 0050P) for more).

- **Meta-search engines** send searches to several search engines at the same time. Within a few seconds, you get back results from all the search engines that were queried. Meta-search engines do not own a database of web pages; they send your search terms to the databases maintained for other search engines. You can download and install a meta-search engine to work alongside your browser. Copernic is an example of a meta-search engine which can be downloaded from www.copernic.com (see www.heinemann.co.uk/hotlinks (express code 0050P) for more). Use meta-searches when you want to get an overall picture of what the Internet has on your topic and to check whether the Internet really is the best place for you to search.

- **Name directories** such as Yell (see www.heinemann.co.uk/hotlinks (express code 0050P) for more) are used when you want to search for people by name, telephone number, email address, postcode and so on.

Figure 221 Search tools

Successful searching

As mentioned earlier, sometimes searching can be difficult because, if you do not narrow your search in some way, you can be presented with a large number of irrelevant results. There are ways to overcome this, but these differ between search engines: look at their help pages for tips. Check out the number of hits a search produces, and, if necessary, refine your search to limit the number.

Imagine you are searching for a holiday villa to rent in the Dordogne region of France.

- If you entered *holidays* in the search box of a search engine this would be an example of a *single-criterion search*. It is important to choose the words you are searching on very carefully in order to reduce the number of results you are likely to get. This simple search produced more than 21 million results in Google, so it is unlikely that you would find the ideal holiday from using it!

- You could try typing the words *holiday villas to rent*. This *refined search* narrowed the number of hits to 668 000.

- You could reduce the number of hits further by putting double quotations marks before and after the search words. You will get more accurate information by doing so. This will find websites that include the exact phrase "*holiday villas to rent*" rather than any websites that include *any of the words in any order*. This search reduced the number of hits to 12 700.

- You can limit the number of hits further by using the + sign to show that the word must appear in the results. Typing "*holiday villas to rent*" *+France* reduced the number of hits to 4470. This is an example of *multiple criteria*, the first criterion being "*holidays villas to rent*" and the second being *France*.

- Some of the results included holiday villas in other countries, so typing "*holiday villas to rent*" *+France –Spain* will exclude all sites that have the word *Spain*. This reduced the number of hits to 1560.

- Finally, adding *+Dordogne* to the search, so that it became "*holiday villas to rent*" *+Dordogne +France –Spain* reduced the number of hits to 889.

Using wildcards

To make sure that you do not miss a good website by using the wrong words in your search, you can use *wildcard* matches.

You can use right-hand or left-hand wildcard searches. Entering *water** would produce results that include terms such as 'waterside' and 'waterfront'. Entering **bus* would produce results that include terms such as 'bus', 'minibus' and 'trolleybus'.

Figure 222 is a summary of search techniques.

TiP

Unfortunately Google does not allow the use of wildcards.

- **Single-criterion searches** – single word searches or words grouped together by the use of quotes.
- **Multiple-criterion searches** – multiple word searches that are not grouped together by the use of quotes, or searches that are refined by using logical operators (+ or –).
- **Wildcards** – some search engines (but not Google) allow the use of * as a wildcard. For example, entering *villa** will search for sites including the words 'villa' and 'villas'.

Figure 222 Summary of search techniques

Go out and try!

The search outlined in the bullet list on pages 242–243 was done using Google. First of all, try the different searches again using Google to see how the number of hits has changed since each search was originally carried out in late 2004. Then repeat the searches using different search engines (see www.heinemann.co.uk/hotlinks (express code 0050P) for links to some suitable search engines).

Open your 'Internet and intranets' file. Create a new bold heading '**II Activity 4**' and write a short paragraph describing the skills you have demonstrated when searching the Internet. 📼 Save the file.

Logical operators

The earlier example of searching for holidays used two logical operators: + and −. Those and other operators are explained further in Figure 223.

Operator	What is does when used in a search	Example	What it means when used in a search
+ (AND)	Place this in front when you want a word to be present in the results of your search.	+Dordogne +France	The words *Dordogne* and *France* must appear somewhere in the results.
− (NOT)	Place this in front when you want to exclude a word from the results of your search.	+Dordogne +France −Spain	The words *Dordogne* and *France* must appear somewhere in the results, but all pages also with *Spain* should be excluded.
OR	Use this when you want either word to be included in the result.	France OR Spain	Web pages are included in the results if either or both search terms appear.
" "	Use this when you want the words to appear together in the same order.	"Holiday villas to rent"	The words must appear in this order.

Figure 223 The principal logical operators you will need to refine searches

It is important to remember that different search engines will produce different results, so it is a useful exercise to compare the results achieved from different search engines. Most search engines will have an advanced search option which will prompt you to refine your search (Figure 224).

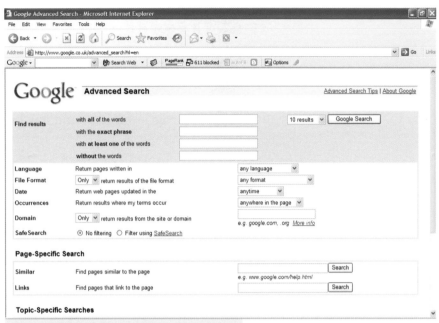

Figure 224 The Google advanced search tool

Also, some search engines, like Ask Jeeves, will allow you to type in direct questions. For example, you could type in *Where can I find information about holiday villas to rent in the Dordogne region of France?*

A warning!

There is no single individual or organisation controlling the information that is published on the Internet. This means that the information you find may not always be correct. It may appear convincing and correct but, in fact, be completely wrong or at least misleading. Protect yourself from inaccurate information in these ways:

- Check whether there is a date on the site, and when it was last updated.
- Look to see whether it is possible to contact the site's developer. Is there an email address to contact?
- Try to work out (or at least be aware of) whether the site was developed by someone or some organisation that wants to put across its message – for example a political (sometimes an extreme political) view.

Email

You will probably have used email at school and often at home. When you start your first job after school or college, or if you go on work experience, you will find that email plays an extremely important role in business and few businesses would be able to function without it.

An email is like an electronic letter, sent in most instances via a computer instead of the postal service. Email is a very sophisticated method of electronic transfer, where messages and documents can be sent from one computer to another using a communications link such as a modem and a telephone line. You can receive and send the electronic equivalent of letters, pictures and sounds, and if you have a webcam attached to your PC you can even send a video email.

Documents prepared on a word processor or other software package, or a document scanned into the computer, can be attached to an email.

LEARNING OUTCOMES

You need to learn about

✓ receiving an email

✓ sending an email

✓ using folders to store and organise emails and attachments.

Hardware and software requirements

To send or receive emails you need

- access to a computer
- a phone line
- a modem (an *analogue modem* if you are using an ordinary phone line, or a *broadband modem* if you have an ADSL line)
- an account with an Internet Service Provider (ISP)
- email communication software, such as Microsoft Outlook Express.

Many businesses use more powerful email programs, such as Microsoft Outlook or Lotus Notes.

The ISP will provide an *email account*, a *password* and a *mailbox* on their server. You will be given an *email address*. The address is a short code, often made up of the user's name, followed by the ISP's domain name – but this can vary. In the example in Figure 225 you will see that three email addresses have been used.

ISP = AOL

ISP = BTInternet

ISP = Freeserve

Text box

Figure 225 Three ISPs represented in this email

When you are connected to the Internet, you can send your email to the ISP's server. From there it is transmitted to the recipient of the message via another server, this time run by the recipient's ISP. It is stored on that server in a *mailbox* until the person you have emailed logs on to check whether he or she has received any new messages.

Many companies have internal email systems so that all their employees can communicate easily with each other. In this case their email address will usually reflect the company name. For example, Thomas Tripp at the Travelbug travel agency has the email address *Thomas.Tripp@travelbugonline.co.uk*.

You may find that the email address of your school or college includes its name (possibly abbreviated) followed by '.ac.uk'. The '.ac' indicates that you are using an academic network that links all colleges and universities in the UK.

Many people have their own web-based email address through companies such as Hotmail (see www.heinemann.co.uk/hotlinks (express code 0050P) for more). By logging on to the Hotmail website and entering a user name and password, you can access your email wherever you are in the world. Also, more and more ISP's will allow you to log on to the same email account that you usually use at home to check your email using any computer with Internet access.

Sending an email

The format of an email depends on the program you are using, but the most basic features of an email message include the following:

- **From:** This is where you enter your own email address.
- **To:** This is where you enter the address of the recipient of the email.
- **Cc:** This is where you enter the address of someone else who you would like to receive a copy of the e-mail.
- **Bcc:** This is where you enter the address of someone else who you would like to receive a copy of the e-mail *without the other recipients knowing that this copy has been sent* (the B stands for 'blind').
- **Subject:** A short description of what your email is about.
- A text box for the body of the message.

This is demonstrated in Figure 226, which shows an email message ready to be sent.

To send an email using software such as Outlook Express, you would do the following.

- Prepare your message offline (to save on telephone charges, unless you have an always-on connection).
- Click on the **Send** button to store it in the *Outbox* (containing outgoing mail).
- Connect to the Internet via your ISP.
- Click on the **Send and Receive** option.
- You may have to enter a password to access your mailbox at your ISP's server. In Outlook Express and most other programs you can configure the software to store and automatically enter the password.

Jargon buster

'**Cc**' means **carbon copy** and is an expression from the days when carbon paper was used to make copies.

Attach button

Click on Send to store
the email in the Outbox.

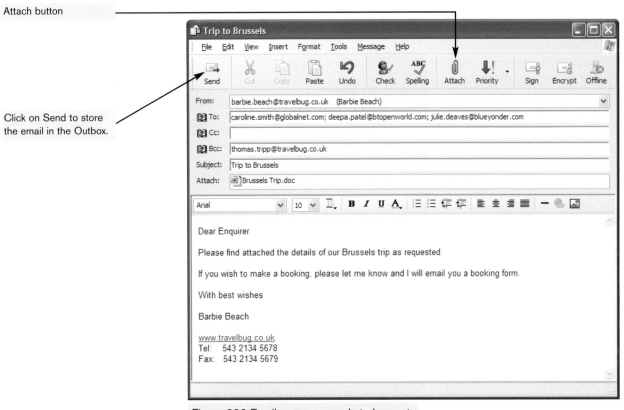

Figure 226 Email message ready to be sent

Your email will be sent to the server at your ISP, and from there to the recipient's ISP.

Sending an email to a group of people

In Figure 226 there is more than one email address in the 'To:' line. Email software will allow you to send emails to more than one person at the same time. In the example, Barbie Beach wants to send details of the Brussels trip to three prospective clients. Note that the email addresses are separated by semicolons (;). You can also Cc or Bcc more than one person in the same way.

Sending an attachment

The **Attach** button allows you to attach (i.e. to send with your email) copies of files stored on your computer. The files can be text, sound, graphics, or even video. In the example in Figure 226, a Word document – Brussels Trip.doc – has been attached.

When you click the **Attach** button, a dialogue box appears, allowing you to locate the file you want to attach (Figure 227).

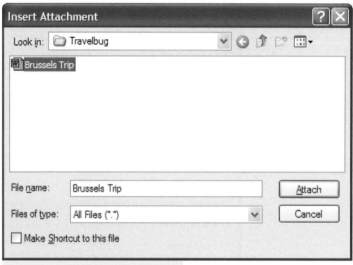

Figure 227 Adding an attachment

Replying to emails

When you receive an email from someone, you might want to reply to it. The simplest way to do this is to click on the **Reply** button (Figure 228). Alternatively, by clicking on the **Reply All** option, your reply could be sent to both the sender and the other recipients of the email – in this case, Molly Wishhusen. In addition, there is usually the option to forward the email on to someone else.

Figure 228 The Reply and Reply All buttons

Click here to reply

When replying to an email, you can choose whether or not to include the original message. Most email software packages will let you set up your system so that the original email is automatically included when you click on the **Reply** button.

Go out and try!

1 Find out the email addresses of five of your fellow students. Send three of them a copy of the file 'WP Activity 1', which you created earlier (see page 90). Include a Cc and Bcc to the two other people.

- Start your email program.
- Click on **New Message**.
- In the **To:** box type the email addresses of the three students, separated by semi-colons.
- In the **Cc:** box type the email address of one of the remaining two students.
- In the **Bcc:** box type the email address of the one remaining student.
- In the **Subject**: box type a brief phrase, such as 'See my attached file'.
- In the main part of the window type any message that you want to send to these students.
- Click on the **paperclip** icon on the toolbar to attach the file.
- Locate the file 'WP Activity 1.doc' in your 'Word processing' sub-folder and click **Attach**.
- Click **Send** to send the email to your Outbox.
- Click the **Send/Recv** button to actually send the email over the Internet.

2 When you receive an email from one of your friends, reply using the **Reply All** feature to let them know you received it.

- Open the email.
- Press the **Reply All** button.
- Type a message such as 'thanks for the file'.
- Send the reply as before.

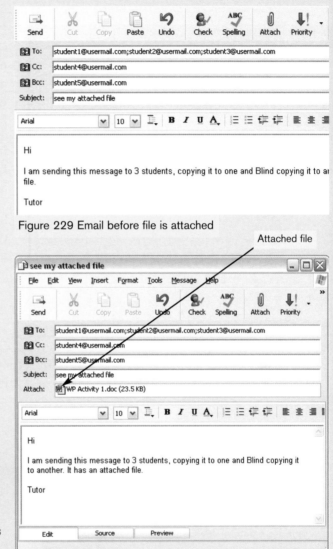

Figure 229 Email before file is attached

Figure 230 Email after file is attached

Create a new file called 'Email' in your 'Email' sub-folder. Create a bold heading called '**E Activity 1**' and write a short paragraph describing the skills you have demonstrated in this activity. Save the file.

Storing and organising emails and attachments

Using folders

Figure 231 Creating a folder

It is important to create folders to help organise your emails, in the same way as you manage any other files such as word-processed documents. Most email software will allow you to create folders and sub-folders to help you organise your emails.

In Figure 231 a new folder called 'Using the Internet' is being created as a sub-folder in the 'digital applications' folder.

Once a folder has been created, you can transfer any emails to it by clicking on the message in the message list and dragging it to the folder, as shown in Figure 232.

TiP

The more emails you send and receive, the harder it can be to find them. It is good practice to spend some time each week deleting emails that are out of date – for example, an email sent to you by a friend reminding you of a music concert, the date for which has now passed.

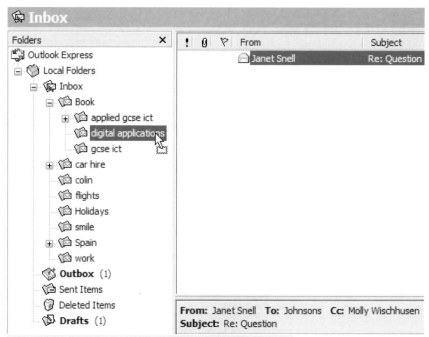

Figure 232 Dragging and dropping to organise emails into folders

To make it easier to locate emails, folders can be sorted by date, name of the sender, or subject. If you sort a folder by sender, you can easily find all the messages from one particular person.

It is possible to set up rules to automatically store received emails directly into folders *at the time they are received*. This means that your Inbox remains tidy, and emails are easy to find.

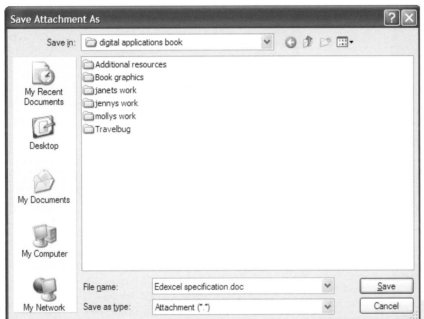

Figure 233 Saving an attachment

When you receive an email with an attachment, it is good practice to save the attachment to a folder in the directory where you keep all such files. This folder could be in your user area if you are at school or college, or it could be in *My Documents* on your home computer. In Figure 233 the Edexcel specification is being saved to the folder 'digital applications book'.

Go out and try!

1 Create a folder called 'Digital Applications Book' within your email software.
- Right-click on the *Inbox* folder name.
- Choose **New Folder** from the menu that appears.

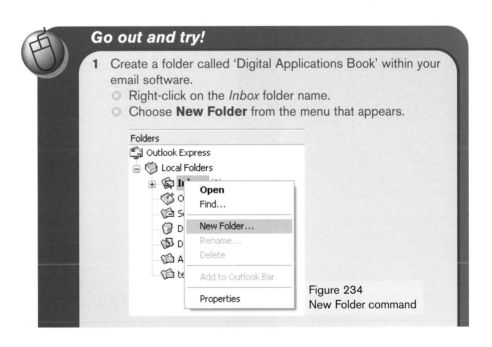

Figure 234
New Folder command

○ Key in the folder name 'Digital Applications Book' and click **OK**.

Figure 235 Naming the new folder

2 Move the emails you received from your fellow students in the first activity to this folder.
   ○ Click on the Inbox to display its contents.
   ○ Drag the emails from the Inbox to the new folder.

3 Save any attachments you received to your 'Email' folder within your user area on the school or college network.
   ○ Open the email with the attachments you want to save.

Figure 236 New folder created under Inbox

   ○ From the menu, select **File**, **Save Attachments**.
   ○ Click on the **Browse** button to specify a folder.

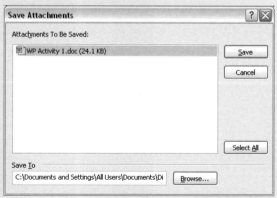

Figure 237 Saving attachments

○ Click the **Save** button.

Open your 'Email' file in the 'Email' sub-folder. Create a new bold heading '**E Activity 2**' and write a short paragraph describing the skills you have demonstrated in this activity. Save the file.

Using a drafts folder

If you wish to prepare an email to send sometime later, most email software packages allow you to save it. For example, in Outlook Express you can save to the Drafts folder by selecting **File, Save** (Figure 238). This will allow you to review the content of the email and send it when you are ready to do so.

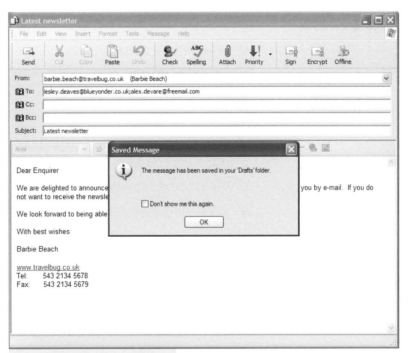

Figure 238 Saving a draft email

Web authoring software

Most organisations and businesses would benefit from having a website. The Internet is an extremely good way of advertising goods and services, and many websites allow customers to order goods online. The Travelbug travel agency have decided that it is very important for them to have their own website to promote their business. They will be designing one using Microsoft FrontPage, a very popular website authoring application. This chapter will follow in detail the construction of their site.

LEARNING OUTCOMES

You need to learn about

✓ creating simple web pages

✓ using colour schemes

✓ creating and modifying tables

✓ editing text

✓ editing graphics

✓ adding lines and simple shapes

✓ using hyperlinks to link pages

✓ using text wrapping

✓ using animation options.

Before we consider website authoring software, it is important to understand what a website actually is.

HTML (hypertext markup language)

A *website* is a collection of related web pages. A *web page* is an electronic document that can contain text, images, forms, graphics, and other multimedia elements such as animation. Web pages are created with computer code known as *hypertext markup language* (*HTML*) and then viewed via web browsers, such as Internet Explorer and Netscape.

HTML is in the form of *tags*, which are used around blocks of text to indicate how the text should appear on the screen. The author of a web page designs the page and links all the material together using HTML. When the page is viewed (either by the author or someone viewing a published web page), the web browser software interprets the HTML language and displays the text exactly as the author intended.

HTML enables you to create *hyperlinks* within the text. When the viewer clicks on a hyperlink with a mouse, he or she is taken automatically to another part of the page or to another page on the Internet. A hyperlink might be represented by a word, a button or a picture.

Requirements for creating a simple web page

Most modern word processors enable you to produce HTML pages without the need to understand the coding. You can also use *web authoring tools*, such as Microsoft's FrontPage or Macromedia's Dreamweaver. We shall be looking at this method of creating web pages later in this chapter. However, it is important to know the basic concepts of HTML, so we shall first be looking at how Travelbug can create a web page manually.

In order to create a web page, Travelbug will need at the very least a simple text editor (like Notepad) to write the HTML. Alternatively, a dedicated HTML text editor (such as Allaire's HomeSite) could be used. There are many alternatives that they could use, including dedicated authoring tools. They could also use standard application software such Microsoft Word, which includes a 'Save as HTML' option. There are also many online wizards that will guide you step-by-step through the process of creating a web page – many ISPs offer online tools, for example.

Travelbug also needs at least one web browser – a dedicated software application that will enable them to view their own web pages as they are written.

Although it is possible to rely on a web authoring tool to create web pages, it is a good idea to learn the codes (or tags) used to format and structure the text.

Finally, and perhaps most importantly, good design and presentation skills are required.

TiP

Figure 240 on page 259 gives a list of common HTML tags.

TiP

Word processors such as Microsoft Word are less effective for writing HTML than basic tools such as Notepad. This is because advanced word processors tend to add extra formatting that interferes with the HTML coding.

Go out and try!

Look at a range of websites on the Internet. Find a page that particularly interests you. Read the page to familiarise yourself with its contents.

You can see how the page has been constructed with HTML code by viewing the *source code*: select **View**, **Source** (or **Document**, **Source**) from the menu of your web browser.

```
www.google.co[1] - Notepad                                    _ □ ☒
File  Edit  Format  View  Help
<html><head><meta http-equiv="content-type" content="text/html; char
body,td,a,p,.h{font-family:arial,sans-serif;}
.h{font-size: 20px;}
.q{color:#0000cc;}
//-->
</style>
<script>
<!--
function sf(){document.f.q.focus();}
function clk(el,ct,cd){if(document.images){(new Image()).src="/url?s
// -->
</script>
</head><body bgcolor=#ffffff text=#000000 link=#0000cc vlink=#551a8b
<form action=/search name=f><script><!--
function qs(el) {if (window.RegExp && window.encodeURIComponent) {va
// -->
</script><table border=0 cellspacing=0 cellpadding=4><tr><td nowrap>
;<a href=/advanced_search?hl=en>Advanced Search</a><br>  <
<script>
//<!--
if (!hp.isHomePage('http://www.google.co.uk/')) {document.write("<p>
//-->
</script></font><p><font size=-2>&copy;2005 Google - Searching 8,058
```

Figure 239 The HTML source of a website

The source code is what the author used to design the page. Can you pick out some of the text you read on the actual page? The code will probably look very complicated because it might have been written by an expert in HTML and will include many advanced concepts.

Create a file called 'Website software' in your 'Website software' sub-folder. Create a new bold heading '**WS Activity 1**' and write a short paragraph describing the skills you have demonstrated in the activity. Save the file.

HTML tags

When you viewed the source code, did you notice words or letters inside the < and > marks? These are known as 'tags' and are the way the web browser knows how to display the document. For example, tags tell the web browser where to start a new paragraph or print a line of text.

Tags usually come in pairs, with the second tag of the pair beginning with a slash symbol (/) to show that the effect of the first tag should now stop. As an example, the **<h1>** and **</h1>** tags indicate where a main heading begins and ends.

The first tag of any document is **<html>**, which tells the web browser that you a beginning a page of information written in HTML. The closing tag **</html>** is put at the end of the document. Figure 240 lists some other very common tags.

Tag		What it does
<html>	**</html>**	Indicates the beginning and the end of an HTML page.
<head>	**</head>**	The head section of the web page.
<title>	**</title>**	The text that will appear on the title bar.
<body>	**</body>**	All the text in the document is between these tags.
<h1>	**</h1>**	Inserts a heading in the largest font. Other sizes are h2, h3, h4, h5 and h6, which is the smallest.
****	****	Displays characters in bold.
<i>	**</i>**	Displays characters in italics.
<center>	**</center>**	Everything between these tags is centred.
** **		Inserts a line break.
<p>	**</p>**	The text between these tags is treated as a separate paragraph.

Figure 240 Common HTML tags

Not all tags come in pairs. The **
** tag, used to create a line break, comes on its own. The **</p>** tag (end of paragraph) is optional, but it is good practice to include it.

Comment tags

If you want to write something in your HTML page that you don't want to appear on your web page, you use a *comment tag*. The tag that turns the comment on is **<!--** and the tag that turns the comment off is **-->**.

Structure of an HTML document

There are always two parts of an HTML document – the *head* and the *body*.

- The first part of any document is always the head. Information in the head is enclosed between the **<head>** and **</head>** tags. Elements in the head area are not displayed in the web page. The most common element is the document's title, bracketed by the **<title>** and **</title>** tags.

- The body of the document begins after the head and is enclosed within the **<body>** and **</body>** tags. The body will contain all the parts of the web page displayed in a web browser's viewing window.

Colour of the background and fonts

You can include between the **<body>** and **</body>** tags different attributes for the style of the text or the background on the web page.

There are 16 colour names that you can choose from (Figure 241). There are also many different combinations of colours that you can achieve by typing what are called alphanumeric codes. Examples of these are **#FFFFCC** for a pale weak yellow, and **#CCCCFF** for a pale weak blue.

Black	Silver	Green	Lime
Gray*	Olive	Yellow	White
Maroon	Navy	Red	Blue
Purple	Teal	Fuchsia	Aqua

Figure 241 Colour names that can be included in HTML code   *Note the American spelling

When altering the font, beware not to use strange fonts. If the font does not exist (is not installed) on the computer of whoever is viewing your page, their browser will choose the 'next best' font, which might destroy the effect you wanted to achieve.

Font type and size

Standard headings come in sizes from H1 (the biggest) to H6 (the smallest). It is possible also to choose the font size of standard text. The default size is 3, but using the tag **<font size=4>** will increase the font size.

The default font type in Internet Explorer is *Times New Roman*. By using the tag **<font face=arial>** the font on the web page can be changed to Arial, which is a very popular sans serif font.

Go out and try!

1 Open the text editor *Notepad* on your computer and key in the HTML code in Figure 242, exactly as shown.
   ○ From the *Start menu*, select **All Programs**, **Accessories**, **Notepad**.
   ○ Key in the text shown in Figure 242. You will need to press **Enter** to go to a new line.

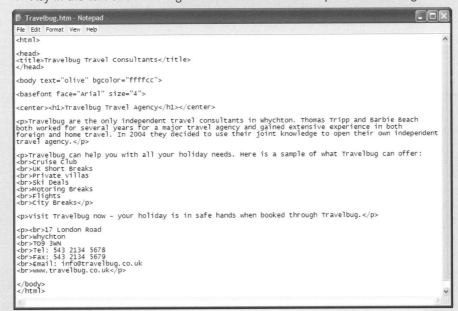

Figure 242 Simple HTML code, written between the <html> and </html> tags

2 Save the file in your 'Website software' sub-folder as 'Travelbug.htm'.
   ○ Select **File**, **Save** and key in 'Travelbug.htm' in the *Filename:* box.
   ○ Click **Save**.
3 View the file in a web browser.
   ○ Browse to the saved file on disk.
   ○ Double-click the file to open it in your web browser.
4 Referring to Figures 240 and 241, which show common HTML tags and colour names, experiment with making changes to the code.
   ○ Edit the 'Travelbug.htm' file in *Notepad*.
   ○ Save the file after each change.
   ○ Click the **Refresh** button in your web browser to see the end result.

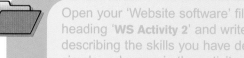
Open your 'Website software' file. Create a new bold heading '**WS Activity 2**' and write a short paragraph describing the skills you have demonstrated while creating a simple web page in the activity. 💾 Save the file.

Skills check ▶▶

There is an opportunity to learn more about storyboards and structures in Unit 2.

Jargon buster

The **navigation route** is the way the visitor to the site will be taken (by means of links) to achieve maximum effect.

❓ **Think it over ...**

Have you ever been looking at a website and then found that you do not know where you are within the overall site, so that you are effectively lost within it? If you don't plan the structure and navigation route before you start creating your website, you could end up with a site that is very difficult to navigate. Visitors will become 'lost in hyperspace'!

Jargon buster

A **web** is FrontPage's name for a set of pages contained within a folder in the software.

Although it is important to understand how to create web pages manually, it is usually quicker to use web-authoring software. The remainder of this unit will show you how to use the features of Microsoft FrontPage to develop web pages.

Establishing the structure of a website

Before you begin creating pages for a multiple-page website, it is important to plan on paper how you want the site to appear. In the same way as when you plan a presentation, you should plan the structure of a website which clearly shows the *navigation route*, and create a *storyboard* that shows the layout and content of each page. A well-designed website will have a clear structure and be easy to navigate.

Using wizards

Most authoring tools will include wizards to make designing a website or web page an easier process. Certainly, for the beginner, you can create a professional looking site by following one of the wizards provided. A wizard will take you step by step through the process, giving you options from which to chose at each stage.

For example, you can see from Figure 243, the New Web Site wizard in FrontPage, provides a range of different designs from which to choose. Furthermore, you can create the folder in which to save the *web* at the same time.

Go out and try!

1 Investigate which authoring tool your school or college uses and the wizards that come with the software. Which wizard do you think Travelbug should choose for their website?
2 Plan a website about one of your hobbies. Create a storyboard and the structure. You should plan a website that will allow you to practise all the skills you will learn about in this chapter.

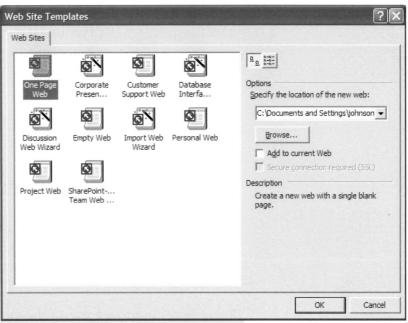

Figure 243 FrontPage's New Web Site wizard

Open your 'Website software' file. Create a new bold heading 'WS Activity 3' and write a short paragraph describing the skills you have demonstrated in this activity. Save the file.

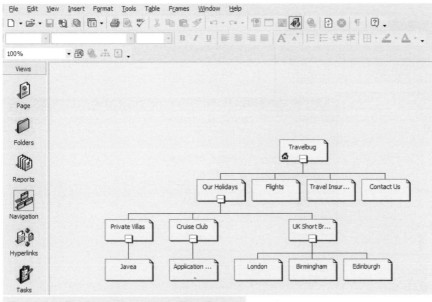

Figure 244 The Navigation view in FrontPage

Thomas Tripp of Travelbug could decide to use the Personal Web wizard in FrontPage to create a website for the company. This wizard will automatically create a basic website with a home page and several pages that link to the home page. The structure will not necessarily be the same as his paper design, but Thomas will be able to amend it very easily. In *Navigation view* it is possible to add or delete pages and rename existing pages.

Figure 244 shows the navigational structure of the Travelbug website with the pages renamed to meet Thomas's needs. It is the construction of this website that you will be following throughout the remainder of this chapter.

The next step will be for Thomas to build each web page in turn. However, unlike when a website is coded from scratch in HTML, screen prompts are given on how to continue.

Using colour schemes

Using the themes supplied with FrontPage allows you to create a consistent website. You can either use the colour schemes as they are or make changes that will be reflected on individual pages or throughout the entire website.

If you prefer not to use one of the themes supplied, you can still easily change the background colour, or even include a graphic, by selecting the **Background** option from the **Format** menu.

Also, you can change the text styles used, either in a theme or in a web page you are designing without a theme. For example, if Thomas Tripp decides to change the font style and size for normal text on his website (called 'Body' text), he can click on the **Text** button of the *Themes* dialogue box to do so (Figure 245).

Figure 245 Changing font styles

Using and editing text

Whether you have decided to build a web page from scratch, or to use one of the templates supplied with FrontPage, you will need to add text. One of the benefits of using a web-authoring tool is that you do not need to use HTML to add text. You simply enter the text you want and format it using the normal formatting tools, just as you would in Word. As you are doing this, FrontPage is creating the HTML for you.

Once you have keyed in your text, changing the font type, size and colour is far easier than in HTML. Simply select the text and change the font type, size and colour, just as you would do in Word. You can create bulleted lists and change paragraph formatting – justification and line spacing – again, just as you would do in Word. In FrontPage you can choose the option you require from the **Format** menu (Figure 246).

Skills check ▶▶

See page 91 for a reminder of how to format text in Word.

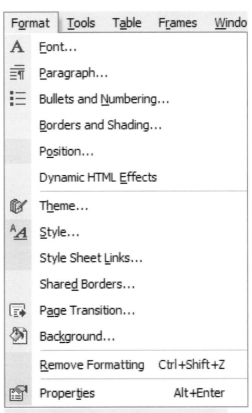

Figure 246 The Format menu in FrontPage

Figure 247 shows FrontPage dialogue boxes used to format text. You will see that they are very similar to those used in other packages – just remember to select the text first before applying the different formatting.

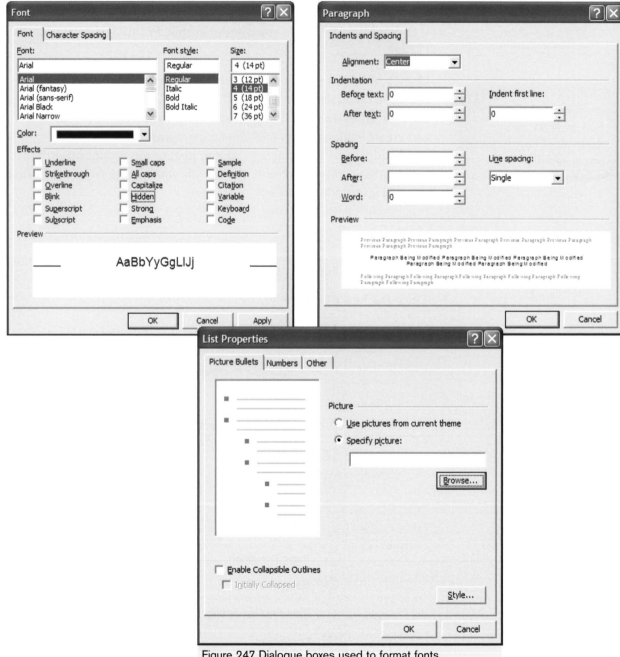

Figure 247 Dialogue boxes used to format fonts, paragraphs and bullets in FrontPage

Figure 248 shows a possible home page for Travelbug's website, which is still under construction. There are three view buttons – **Normal, HTML** and **Preview**. Use **Normal** view to edit the page, **HTML** view to view or edit the HTML code, or **Preview** view to see how the page will look in a web browser.

Banner

Navigation bar

Main section

Different views

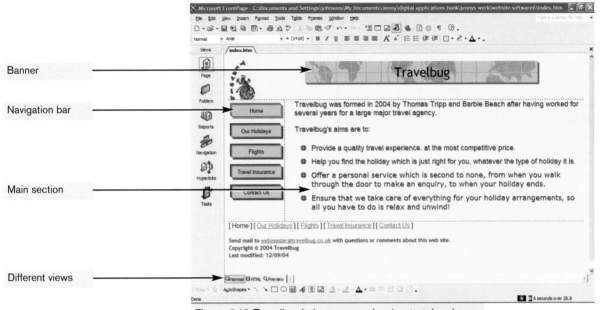

Figure 248 Travelbug's home page begins to take shape

Page Banner refers to the text and graphic that goes across the top of each page, as in Figure 248. The banner graphic remains the same but the text heading changes on each page. This would be quite a complex task to code using HTML alone, but by using FrontPage the process is extremely simple.

Creating and modifying tables

You have probably guessed by now that if you want to include a table in a web page, it will be more complicated if you do so by writing HTML code than by using FrontPage.

Many of the skills you have learned for creating a table in Word can be applied to FrontPage. You can create a basic structure by using the **Table** menu on the *Standard* toolbar, and then add text or graphics in the cells (Figure 249). You can even include tables within tables! You can merge cells, change their height and width, and apply different borders just as you would in Word.

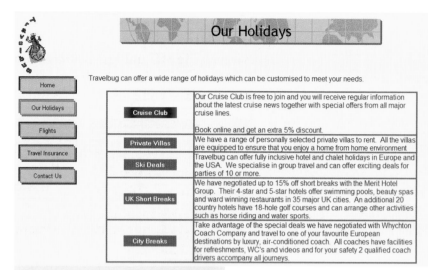

Figure 249 A table created in FrontPage

Skills check ▶▶

See page 114 for a reminder of how to format tables in Word.

You can create more complex tables by selecting **Table, Draw Table** from the menu. Once you have drawn a table, you can erase rows and columns from it using the eraser tool.

Tables can be used for arranging information in rows and colums, or for displaying text and graphics on a page. In fact, tables are extremely useful for designing a web page layout. Often tables are used for some or all of a page's layout, although you may not be aware of this when looking at a web page (Figure 250).

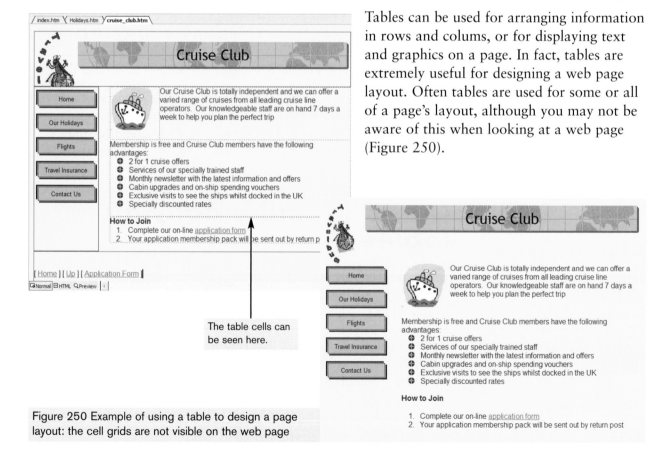

The table cells can be seen here.

Figure 250 Example of using a table to design a page layout: the cell grids are not visible on the web page

Using and editing graphics

Graphics are an important part of any website as they can communicate a lot of information very easily. It is a simple process to insert a graphic into a website being created in FrontPage.

Sourcing the images

The graphics can come from a number of sources, which you will have already learned about in the chapter on artwork and imaging software (page 214).

- Graphics applications allow you to create your own pictures. Examples are CorelDraw, Windows Paint and Adobe Photoshop.
- Clip art is available from various sources.
- You can scan existing photographs or pictures to put into your work.
- Digital still and video cameras allow you to take photos and videos which can be included on your website.

Inserting an image

Thomas Tripp wants to include the Travelbug logo on his newly designed website. To do this he selects **Insert, Picture** from the **File** menu (Figure 251). The **Set Transparent Color** option from the *Picture* toolbar will allow Thomas to remove the white background so that the logo blends nicely into the page.

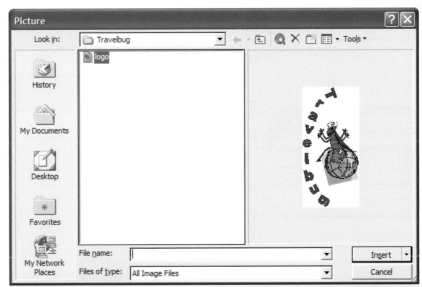

Figure 251 The picture called 'logo' has been selected from the Travelbug folder, and a thumbnail is displayed

TiP

When you create a page using FrontPage, the download time *is shown in the bottom right-hand corner of the screen. The download time will depend on the modem used by the computer. Most modern modems used for dial-up to the Internet have a maximum speed of 56 kbps. Many people and organisations have broadband connections, which offer download times at much higher rates.*

Skills check

For information on choosing the most appropriate image resolution for print and screen, see page 224.

Just as in other applications, FrontPage's *Picture* toolbar will allow you to make changes to a graphic, such as rotating it, adjusting the brightness or even creating an automatic *thumbnail*. Thumbnails are often used on web pages to decrease download times – the visitor to the website can decide which images to see in full size, usually by clicking on them.

Another useful feature of FrontPage is that you can create a *photo gallery* of pictures very quickly by using **Insert, Web Component** and then selecting **Photo Gallery**. You can choose from four different layouts. In each case, thumbnail images of your files are created automatically (Figure 252).

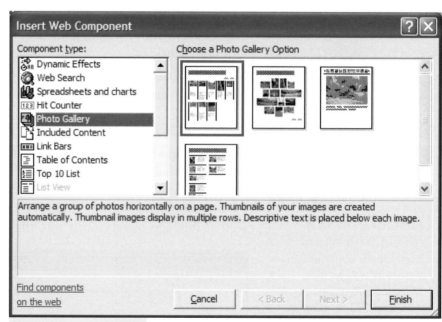

Figure 252 A photogallery

An advantage of producing a photogallery automatically with FrontPage is that the file sizes of the images are reduced substantially when the thumbnails are created. In the photogallery in Figure 253, each thumbnail is 4 KB, whereas the original images were all in excess of 1000 KB.

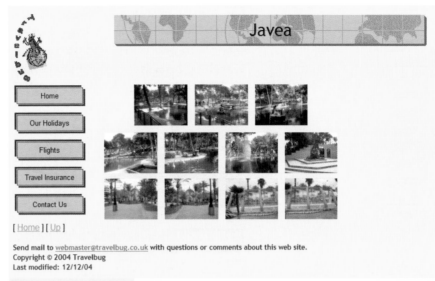

Figure 253 Thumbnails

Wrapping text

You can change the properties of an image to control how text wraps around it.

Figure 254 Changing how text wraps around an image

Double-click the image to display its *Picture Properties* dialogue. Click on the *Appearance* tab and make your selection for the **Alignment**, as shown in Figure 254.

Adding lines and simple shapes

You can add lines and shapes, fill the shapes with colour, outline them and make them look three-dimensional. The method in FrontPage is the same as in PowerPoint and the other Microsoft Office tools.

The **Autoshapes** button on the *Drawing* toolbar can be used to add shapes, including lines, a flowchart, stars, banners and callouts. It is possible to add borders to text and objects, as shown in Figure 255: Travelbug have used a *callout* on their Contact Us page, and have used a border around the text on their Insurance page.

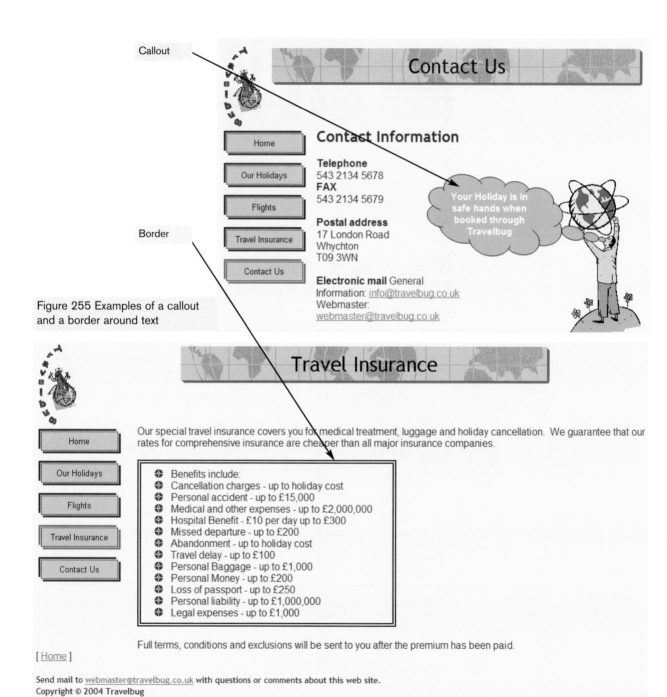

Figure 255 Examples of a callout and a border around text

Go out and try!

Using skills you have gained, experiment with creating some simple web pages that include text, tables, lines and simple shapes, and graphics. Try out different ways of formatting the text. Try using a table to organise a web page. Add graphics, shapes and lines in the most appropriate way for your project.

- Open your web page in FrontPage.
- Enter any text you require and format it as you would in Word.
- Use the **Insert** menu to add any graphics that you think will enhance the look of your page.

Figure 256 The Insert menu

Open your 'Website software' file. Create a new bold heading 'WS Activity 4' and write a short paragraph describing the skills you have demonstrated when using text, tables, shapes/lines and graphics when creating web pages.

Save the file.

Inserting hyperlinks

Click here to
add a ScreenTip

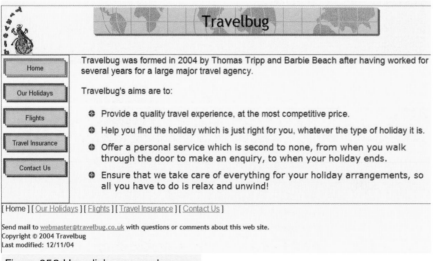

Figure 257 Adding a hyperlink and a ScreenTip

FrontPage will allow you to add *hyperlinks*, which allow visitors to the website to move from one page to another easily. Hyperlinks can also be used to move to different parts of a page or even to a different website.

You have the option of using text, buttons or pictures as hyperlinks. For example, on the Cruise Club web page, Thomas Tripp has created a hyperlink to the online application form (Figure 257). He has done this by typing the text, selecting it and then choosing **Insert, Hyperlink** from the menu.

Furthermore, when you are creating a set of web pages (a 'web') using certain wizards, FrontPage automatically creates a *navigation bar* that has hyperlinks to the other pages in the web. These hyperlinks allow the visitor to move to a different page when the appropriate link is clicked. In Figure 258 the main navigation bar shows user-friendly *button hyperlinks*, whereas the hyperlinks at the bottom of the web page are examples of *text hyperlinks*.

TiP

✓ *It is helpful to add a* **ScreenTip** *which pops up when the user points at the hyperlink with their mouse. Figure 257 shows the button that allows you to add this feature.*

Figure 258 Hyperlinks on a web page

Including sounds

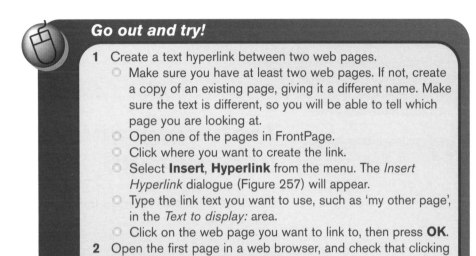

Figure 259 Adding a sound to a web page in FrontPage

FrontPage allows you set a background sound for a web page. With your mouse, right-click on the page area while in Normal view and select **Page Properties** from the pop-up menu. The sound can be set to loop a set number of times, or to play the entire time the user is viewing a page.

Thomas Tripp of Travelbug decided to set the background sound of the company's Cruise Club page to the sound file 'Sailing', which he included in his PowerPoint presentation (see page 207). The Page Properties dialogue box he used is shown in Figure 259.

Sound can be attached also to 'hover buttons' and other dynamic effects.

If you have a microphone and sound card, you may decide to record the sound in a digital format on your computer using Microsoft Sound Recorder. You might choose to save the recorded sound as a

WAV file, which is the most common format for sound files and the easiest for users to play, since all recent browsers can open WAV files.

Including animation (movement)

There are a number of ways in which you can include animation on your website.

Scrolling text

FrontPage allows you to add what it calls *marquees*. These are text areas that will *scroll* across the screen repeatedly. They are useful for getting a message across. Travelbug could include a marquee on its Cruise Club page: 'Don't delay ... join now!'

Animated GIFs

You could include an animated GIF file, which consists of a series of static GIF images that are displayed in succession to create the illusion of movement. It is possible to download the Microsoft GIF Animator for free use in order to create animated GIF files for a website.

Dynamic HTML

You can use the *dynamic HTML* facility within FrontPage to animate text in a number of ways. For example, you could animate text to fly in from the right when a page is loaded, or you could format the text to change size when the mouse is moved over it. Figure 260 shows the *DHTML Effects* toolbar.

Allows you to select the event that will trigger the effect.

Available effects are displayed here.

Allows you to set any properties that are available for the effect.

Click here to remove the effect.

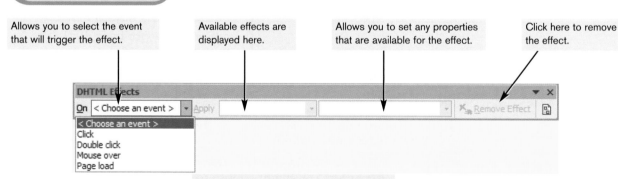

Figure 260 The dynamic HTML toolbar

Using transitions

As in PowerPoint presentations, you can apply transitions. FrontPage allows you to apply transitions to a web page for when a user enters or exits a page, or when the user enters or exits your website. You are able to choose the transition effect that you want, or choose random transition, so that the effect will change each time a user enters or leaves your website or web page (Figure 261).

Choose Page Enter, Page Exit, Site Enter or Site Exit here.

Set the duration here.

Choose the effect here.

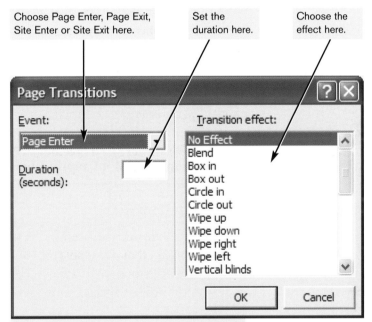

Figure 261 Dialogue box for page transitions

You can also set the time for the transition in seconds by entering a value in the *Duration (seconds)* text box.

Go out and try!

Add a variety of sounds and animations, as appropriate, to the web pages you have created. Remember to take into account the warnings about file sizes and how this will effect download times.

Open your 'Website software' file. Create a new bold heading '**WS Activity 5**' and write a short paragraph describing the skills you have demonstrated for this activity. 💾 Save the file.

Publishing the Web

In FrontPage, a 'web' does not become a website until it has been published and can be viewed by other people. A *web host* is the name given to the company that provides space on a web server for you to publish your site. Many companies will offer to publish websites free of charge on condition that they display some advertising banners at the top of each page. Alternatively, your school or college may have their own web server onto which you can publish your site.

Your own ISP may offer limited free space to publish your site. If you wish to publish your 'web' as it has been created in FrontPage, you need to find out whether your ISP supports FrontPage Server Extensions.

The steps necessary to upload the files that make up your website can vary from one ISP to another, but it is normally quite a simple process.

Section 3 Project planning

All projects have a number of common characteristics:

- clear objectives
- a definitive outcome
- a fixed period of running time
- the possibility of being broken down into a sequence of smaller tasks.

Most things you do, no matter how simple or complex, require careful planning and preparation in order to be successful.

Before you start it is essential to

- read the whole project brief carefully
- decide/understand what you have to do
- create appropriate directory/folder structures to organise your e-portfolio.

Even something as straightforward as baking a birthday cake needs planning to ensure you have the exact ingredients, the right size of baking tin and sufficient time for it to bake in the oven.

An example

Organising a holiday requires careful planning. Frankie and Sam would like to go on holiday together. Before they visit Travelbug to make their booking they must have a clear idea of where they would like to go, what they would like to do, and how much time they can afford to spend away from home.

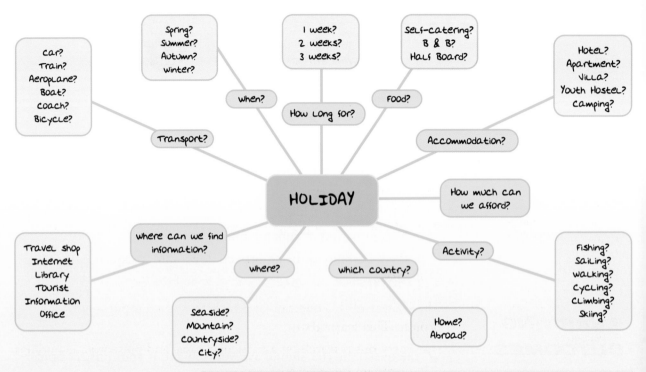

Figure 262 Frankie and Sam's spider diagram records all their suggestions and ideas

They both have so many suggestions and ideas that they decide to write them all down to be sure everything will be taken into consideration before reaching a final decision (Figure 262).

After much discussion they agree on a two-week camping and sports activity holiday in the French Alps. Now that they have a clear goal, they can really begin the preparations for their holiday. These preparations will include

- researching the holiday market and booking the holiday
- obtaining passports
- arranging travel insurance and medical insurance
- preparing for the sports activities – perhaps by getting fit and buying suitable clothing and footwear
- buying foreign currency
- arranging for their pets to be cared for
- arranging transport to the station or airport.

By the time they leave, Frankie and Sam will have put considerable effort into the planning and preparation of their holiday, so it should be a great success.

The same is true for the projects you will be completing in order to achieve your Certificate or Diploma in Digital Applications: if the projects are not planned carefully they are unlikely to be successful!

Your project brief

A well-written brief will enable you to identify the key features of the project. Spend time reading the project brief to familiarise yourself with its contents. After studying it, you should be able to provide answers to the following questions, which will eventually form the basis of your overall plan.

What have I been asked to do?

The answer to this question will reveal the overall purpose of the project. This may be to

- carry out research on a particular topic and present your findings
- create multimedia products
- produce images and artwork
- explore and plan for a business activity.

What do I have to produce?

When you are clear about the overall aim of the project, you should study the project brief more closely and make a list of all the separate items you must produce. These may be a combination of text, graphics, images or sound. For example, you may have to produce a letter, a web site, a presentation, a graphic image, a leaflet and a report. The items in your list will become the *objectives* of the project.

Why am I doing it?

Once you have established what you have been asked to do and what you are going to produce, you should think about *why* you are doing the work. This will ensure that your 'products' are entirely suitable for their purpose.

There will usually be a specific reason for producing the product:

- writing a report to convince people that something should change or remain the same

Assessment Hint

You will be provided with a detailed summative project brief (SPB) for both of the modules that comprise the Certificate in Digital Applications, or the modules that comprise the Diploma in Digital Applications.

Jargon buster

Objectives are the practical tasks that will enable you to achieve the overall aim of the project. Good objectives are said to be **SMART**:

Specific
Measurable
Agreed
Realistic
Time-constrained.

In other words, you should make sure that the tasks you set are achievable in terms of your own skills, the resources that are available to you and the time you have to complete them. Keep this in mind when you start to plan your project in more detail.

- producing a series of publications to educate people about a topical issue
- producing a multimedia product to convey a message to the public
- producing a graphic image to promote a product or event.

If you are unclear in your own mind as to the reason you are doing the work, it is highly likely that your audience will also have difficulties in understanding your message. To be successful you must make sure that your products convey the message in the most appropriate way.

Who are the target audience?

Another important point to consider is what type of people your product is directed at. In other words, who are the *target audience*? You would be expected to choose different methods for conveying the same information to children compared with adults.

For example, a poster aimed at children should be quite simple and straightforward, whereas you might use a more subtle approach for adults. If you were producing a written report for technical experts it would be quite acceptable to use technical language. However, you would have to reduce the level of technical jargon if the same report were to be presented to members of the general public.

It is important that you choose an appropriate style for your audience whilst at the same time ensuring that your finished product is also fit for its intended purpose.

Make sure you allocate some time to dealing with the unexpected. It is very unusual for everything to go smoothly, so there will almost certainly be unforeseen problems and delays along the way.

When do I have to have it finished?

Think about your timescale and how you will fit everything in. You should expect to spend a total of about 30 hours on each project. Take into account the time you will spend on planning and preparation in addition to actually producing your products.

Include time to review your work, and allow other people time to test your products. You will almost certainly need to modify or amend your work, and this must *all* be completed within the time allocated for the project.

If you wish to use a photograph that somebody else has taken, you must remember the law relating to copyright and obtain written permission to use the image. This will also take time.

Allow time to locate and order multimedia components, such as video and audio recordings from film libraries or video collections, if you need to include these in your project.

TiP

If a resource is going to be difficult to access, it might be worthwhile considering if there is an alternative way of achieving the same outcome.

Assessment Hint

You must ensure that your work complies with the technical specification outlined in the summative project brief. Make sure you follow the guidance given about file formats, download times and the overall size of the e-portfolio.

It is important that you do not take on something too ambitious that you will not be able to finish properly because you run out of time!

What resources can I use?

Each of the summative project briefs will include links to relevant websites or titles of textbooks that may help you. You will clearly have to use other resources too.

Some resources – such as school or college library books, the Internet, computers and printers – are probably readily available to you, but others may not be. For example, you may need to use specialist software or equipment that is available only at school or college, and you might need to share it with 20 or 30 other students. Alternatively, you might need to obtain books or other media from an outside source such as a library. This can take time to arrange.

If you know that something is going to be difficult to get hold of or restricted in use, you must keep this uppermost in your mind when planning your project. Furthermore, you must remember to record details of the sources of all the materials you use and to include these as evidence in your e-portfolio.

What else do I need to consider?

If you are working on artwork and images, you will also need to consider how the image is to be published. Consider, for example, whether it is to be published on screen or printed on paper. You can clearly see how an image will be viewed as part of a screen-based publication, but it is more difficult to visualise an image incorporated in a paper-based document. Carefully check the size of the image, the position on the page, and so on.

How will the success of your project be judged?

Your work will be presented in an e-portfolio that will be reviewed by your assessor and the moderator from the examining body, Edexcel. You will not be there to show them where to find the evidence of your work, so *your e-portfolio must be well structured and easy to use*. Follow the advice on creating e-portfolios given in the summative project briefs and in Skills section 5 (page 298).

You will be assessed against a number of activities, including

- planning and managing your project
- reviewing your project
- presenting evidence in an e-portfolio.

The other activities differ for each project, and more information is given in the appropriate chapters. Each activity carries a range of marks, and the marks are awarded according to the complexity of each activity.

The questions the assessor or moderator will have in mind when assessing your work are

- Is the product fit for the purpose?
- Is the product fit for the intended audience?

The safest way to make sure the assessor or moderator can answer 'Yes' to these questions is to make certain your work is reviewed throughout production and that you take notice of any points your reviewers make.

Who will review my work, and when?

It is very easy to get sidetracked and to lose sight of the original objective when you are working under pressure. A fresh pair of eyes can sometimes help to show where you have gone adrift. So for this reason you must make sure that you ask someone to look at your work at regular intervals to ensure it is fit for both the purpose and the intended audience.

You could ask your teacher, or maybe your friends or a member of your family, to help you. You could find someone who falls into the target audience category and ask him or her for an opinion.

You should show your product to a variety of different people and welcome their opinions. Constructive feedback is very valuable and is not a criticism of your work but is offered to help you improve your work and thereby achieve better marks. Listen to what other people say and consider their ideas carefully. You may not always agree, but a second opinion is always worth thinking about.

Getting started

When you have read through the summative project brief, ask your teacher or tutor to explain anything you do not understand. In this way you will avoid wasting valuable time by starting work on something that is not required!

✔ **TiP**

Remember that when you start to plan your project in detail you must ensure you allow time for other people to look at your work during production as well as at the end.

You might find it helpful to produce a table, similar to the one in Figure 263, where you can make notes as you work through the project brief. It will help to ensure that nothing important is overlooked. It will also form the basis for the detailed project planning that must be done before you start work.

What have I been asked to do? This is the overall aim.		
What do I have to produce? These are the objectives.	Why am I doing it? This will help you focus on the purpose.	Who are the target audience?
1	1	1
2	2	2
3	3	3
4	4	4
5	5	5
6	6	6
7	7	7
8	8	8
9	9	9
10	10	10
When do I have to have the project finished?		
What resources can I use?		
Who will review my work?		

Figure 263 A chart to help you organise your thoughts

Project ideas

You are now almost ready to embark on your project, but you are still not ready to switch the computer on! There are a few more issues to be considered.

First you need to come up with some ideas. One of the most successful ways of doing this is to hold a brainstorming session with a group of friends – just like Frankie and Sam when they were planning their holiday! Record everything you can think of so that nothing is forgotten or overlooked.

Some people find a simple hand-written list is a good method of keeping track of ideas. One of the most popular methods is to produce a *mind map*. Mind maps help you organise your thoughts on one page so that you can see the relationship between one idea and another, and your ideas can flow from one topic to the next. Simple images can help you focus your ideas in a fun way.

Record the main topic at the centre of the page. From there, branch out and add the major themes around the main topic. Add associated ideas with further branches. Once your mind map is finished you can weigh up the pros and cons of the various ideas before coming to a decision.

Figure 264 Mind map for planning an 18th birthday party

This mind map (Figure 264) was used to help plan an 18th birthday party.

Be SMART (see page 281) and don't get carried away by grand ideas that go off at a tangent. Always keep the target audience and project objective in mind. Some good advice is to keep things relatively simple – think 'quality' rather than 'quantity'!

Your project plan

After preparing a list of objectives from the summative project brief, your next job must be to rearrange the list into a logical sequence, remembering that some tasks may have to be finished before others can be started.

List the key milestones in each project, and, where possible, try to finish one thing before getting too involved in the next. Number the tasks in the order you will complete them.

Now look at each task in turn and break it down into a sequence of smaller tasks so that you know exactly what has to be done. Give each of the smaller tasks a number. Remember to include time to ask your reviewers to give you feedback on your work.

For example, if the first task is to produce a poster, you might come up with a list like this:

1 Produce a poster
    1.1 Take digital photos
    1.2 Sketch out my design and show it to my teacher
    1.3 Transfer images from digital camera to computer
    1.4 Produce poster on the computer
    1.5 Proofread and print in colour
    1.6 Ask family to review poster
    1.7 Modify design if necessary

Assessment Hint

Your project plans must be included in your e-portfolio as supporting evidence for each project. For this reason it is important that you record your progress as you go along.

Decide how much time to allocate to each part of the project and write down when you plan to start and finish each task. Remember that you should also include time to deal with anything that might go wrong.

You should repeat this process for each of the objectives you have identified. The flow chart in Figure 265 can be used to remind yourself of the steps to take when planning each project.

When you have planned your project in detail you might find it helpful to record this information in table format similar to Figure 266. Ask your teacher or tutor to approve your plan before you start any work on the project. As you complete each task, tick it off. Keep a record of any changes you had to make to the plan, and say why.

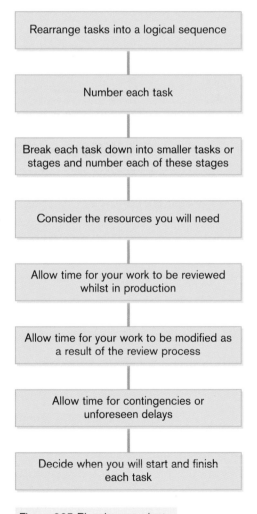

Figure 265 Planning a project

Summative Project – Unit 1		Project Start Date: 16 February			Project End Date: 25 March		
What will I produce?	**How will I go about it?**	**How long will it take to complete?**	**When will I start?**	**When will I finish?**	**Done** ✓	**Record your progress and note any changes you make to the plan and why.**
Task 1 **A poster** To encourage new students to join the activity clubs	**Task 1a** Take digital photos at Wednesday activity clubs.	1 hour	16 February	~~16 February~~ 23 February	✓	The battery in the camera was not charged and I had to delay taking the pictures for one week. This meant that I could not start work on the computer until 24 February.
	Task 1b Sketch out my design and show it to Mr Stewart.	1 hour	At home on 19/20 February	20 February	✓	
	Task 1c Transfer photos to my computer and produce poster in my IT class.	1 ½ hours	In my IT lesson on ~~22~~ February 24	~~22~~ February 24	✓	My teacher, Mr Stewart, suggested some small changes to my design. I showed the poster to my friends and family over half term but they did not make any suggestions and I did not need to modify it.
	Task 1d Proofread to check details are accurate and print in colour.	½ hour	In my IT lesson on ~~22~~ February 24	~~22~~ February 24	✓	
	Task 1e Show poster to my friends and family for their comments.	½ hour	25 February	10 March	✓	
	Task 1f Modify poster if necessary.	1 hour	10 March	10 March		
Task 2 **Leaflet** To promote healthy lifestyle	**Task 2a** Research, using the Internet and library, to find out what activities are available locally	2 hours	17 February	19 February	✓	
	Task 2b Summarise information gathered and design draft leaflet.	4 hours	21 February	17 March		

Figure 266 A chart to monitor progress

Use the plan to help you meet your deadlines and finish your project on time. Every time you need to modify your plan you must save the plan with a new filename so that you can provide evidence of the development of your project from the beginning to the end. Don't be tempted to produce the plan after you have finished your project! Keep in mind that your teachers and the moderators who will look at the plan in your e-portfolio are very experienced and can usually discover the shortcomings!

The chart should include headings for the tasks and sub-tasks. These should be in the order in which you will carry them out, and should show how much time you will spend on each and when you will ask your reviewers for feedback. You should also include

- task descriptions
- start dates
- finish dates
- times allowed
- notes to record progress and changes made to the plan.

When you have a complete list of all the tasks, you might also find it helpful to show the proposed timing on a chart similar to Figure 267. This style of chart is called a *Gantt chart*. It helps you to see at a glance how you have spread the workload and how you can modify the plan if you run into difficulties. It is a good way of reviewing the progress of your project so you can rearrange the rest of your work if necessary. The chart in Figure 267 was produced using a table but you could also consider using a spreadsheet.

NAME								TIME PLAN

Summative Project – Unit 1	Project Start Date: 16 February	Project End Date: 25 March

Notes:
Task 1 – Poster
Task 2 – Leaflet
Task 3 – Power Point presentation

Duration of Project

		1	2	3	4	5	6
Week No		1	2	3	4	5	6
Month		Feb	Feb	March	March	March	March
Date							

Half Term

Tasks to be completed	Time required
1a Take photographs	1 hour
1b Sketch design	1 hour
1c Transfer images to computer/produce poster	1¼ hours
1d Proof read/check/print	¼ hour
1e Review with family/friends	¼ hour
1f Modify	1 hour
2a Research local activities	2 hours
2b Summarise information and prepare draft leaflet	4 hours
2c Check design ideas with my teacher	¼ hour
2d Modify design	1 hour
2e Produce design on computer	3 hours
2f Proof read/check/print	¼ hour

Time Allocated
Time Extended

Page No 1 of 2

Figure 267 A Gantt chart

Assessment Hint

Don't forget to include in your e-portfolio demonstrations of how you used different software tools in your project. Screen captures can be useful for this.

Use one colour to show the time you plan to spend on each task. If necessary, you can amend it to take account of any modifications to your timescale, showing them in a different colour.

If you have access to Microsoft Works on your home computer, you may perhaps consider using the Project Planner to list each task of the project (Figure 268). You can also record the due date and make notes to remind you of what you have to do, or to record any reasons for modifying your project plan.

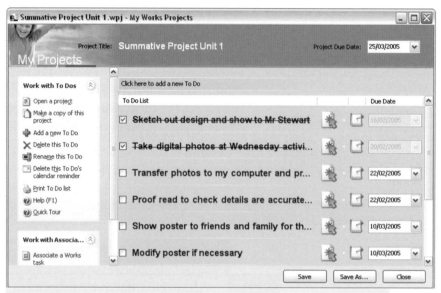

Figure 268 Microsoft Works includes this simple project planning software

Skills check ▶▶

The designers of large, commercial projects often use special project management software to help them plan and monitor the progress of their work. If you study for Unit 4 you will learn to use specialist project planning software to help you develop your plan and produce a Gantt chart. You will be able to check that the progress of the work follows the plan and, if necessary, update the plan to take account of any unforeseen delays or problems. In this way the plan will become a reliable, working document that you can refer to at any time to see what still has to be done. If you work alongside the plan and keep it up to date, it will help ensure your project is completed within the given timescale.

Hints and tips

Before embarking on your project work, you will have studied the skills chapters on word processing, spreadsheets, databases and so on. It is important that you make full use of these skills in order to create documents and on-screen publications that convey the message in the most effective way possible.

Here are some other hints to help you along the way:

- Remember to plan your e-portfolio before you start. Decide on the filenames you will use and make sure you know the

TiP

As you are doing an IT course, there is no excuse for presenting work that is inaccurate or poorly presented. If you have worked through the skills chapters in this book you should have picked up a lot of useful tips that will help you produce successful paper-based or screen-based publications.

appropriate format for publication in your e-portfolio. The summative project brief will specify the acceptable formats for each project. Don't waste time as you go along by converting every file into the final published format. It is a good idea to convert only the files that you will be presenting in your e-portfolio. You are less likely to get in a muddle if you do not have too many different versions of each file!

- Don't waste time in class working on things that can be done away from the classroom. Use the time you have with your teacher or tutor to get any help you need.

- Use folders and sub-folders to organise all your project work. Don't forget that you will be required to include evidence of your product from design through to implementation.

- Save updates of your work regularly with different filenames. In this way, in the unlikely event you find yourself with a corrupt file, you can revert to the previous version and you will not have too much work to repeat. This will also help you demonstrate progress in your e-portfolio.

- A USB memory stick is a good way of transferring your work between school or college and home. You will soon find the data files are too large to fit on to a floppy disk. Remember to scan your files for viruses!

- Make regular backup copies of all your data files on CD as a safety precaution. Keep the backup copies in a safe place. It is sensible to save your project work on the school or college computer system as well as at home.

When you are happy that you can put a tick against each of the following points, then you have probably done as much as you can to ensure success:

- Have you followed your plan and used it to monitor your progress?

- Have you recorded and justified any amendments you made to the plan?

- Can the history of the project be clearly seen from your plan?

- Have you kept a record of *all* the resources you used?

- Have you produced everything that you were asked to produce?

- Does your document or presentation have an appropriate layout and structure?

- Is the presentation style (font style, heading style, background colour, slide layout, and so on) consistent throughout?

- Have you used page breaks sensibly?
- Have you made effective use of space?
- Have you chosen an appropriate font size?
- Is it written in an appropriate language style to suit the target audience?
- Have you spellchecked *and* proofread your work?
- Have you used WordArt, clip art and colour in moderation?
- Are the content and images relevant and suitable for the intended audience?
- Are your images clear and a sensible size?
- Are download times acceptable for images in your web pages?
- Does your document or presentation look professional?
- Have you reviewed your work and asked somebody else to test your product?
- Have you listened to their comments and modified your product if necessary? Remember to include evidence of your modified work in your e-portfolio.
- Is the product fit for the intended purpose?
- Do all navigation routes work?
- Have you saved your work in the specified file formats?
- Does the overall size of your e-portfolio comply with the technical specification?

Keep these guidelines in mind and you should be able to produce a first-class product that will meet all the original objectives.

Good luck with all your projects!

Section 4 Review and evaluation

It is important that you undertake a thorough review of your project once it is completed. You should consider

- outcomes (the publications you have produced)
- process (how you worked)
- performance (the skills you have demonstrated).

LEARNING OUTCOMES

You need to learn about

✓ collecting and presenting review evidence

✓ how to analyse the success of your project.

Introduction

Think back to Frankie and Sam and their two-week camping and sports activity holiday in the French Alps (page 279). Did you imagine that when they returned from their holiday they would forget all about it? Of course not! When they came home they would have discussed every aspect of the holiday. It is quite natural to look back on the experience, reflect on the good parts and try to work out why other aspects did not go quite so well. If they decide to repeat the holiday again some time in the future they won't want to repeat the mistakes too – they will want to have an even better time.

This is exactly the same process that you will carry out when you have completed each project. The process of reviewing your work is equally as important as actually carrying out the work in the first place. A thorough and effective evaluation will consider both the *outcomes* (what you produced), the *processes* (how you produced it) and *performance* (your own contribution). You will make your own judgements and will also seek the opinions and views of a variety of other people in order to provide a comprehensive evaluation with suggestions for improvement.

TiP

It is sensible to ask several people who have not seen your work in production to give you their feedback. These are likely to be people other than your teacher and friends at school or college – for example, members of your family or people with a particular interest in the topic you have been working on.

You will have asked several people to review your project whilst you were working on it and you should have acted on their advice. You must also ensure that your finished product is reviewed by yourself and others.

Review evidence and presentation

The evidence you collect to show that you and other people have reviewed your project should be included in your e-portfolio. It may be presented in a variety of different ways.

For example, you may have provided a questionnaire for people to complete, so you could present the results graphically, drawing your conclusions from their responses. You may have received written evaluations, which could be scanned and presented as on-screen documents. Perhaps you have spoken to several people and can include a recording of your interviews. You may decide to prepare your own written evaluation, summarising the feedback you have received from other people together with your own thoughts. You might also consider producing your evaluation as a multimedia presentation or a video or audio diary. Your evidence is likely to be a combination of two or more of these suggestions.

Most things we do show that we all have strengths and weaknesses. Sometimes things turn out well and sometimes they are not so good. For example, one day we bake a cake that turns out to be rather flat, slightly burnt and generally disappointing. We show the cake to someone who has more experience, and he or she suggests that we might have used the wrong type of flour or had the oven temperature too high. We try again and next time the cake is much better.

Perhaps it will be obvious to you that some things did not go as well as you had planned and you recognise that there are weaknesses. In this case you will usually be very receptive to suggestions for improving it. However, it is more difficult to accept criticism when you think everything is all right, but do listen to what your reviewers have to say and do not be afraid to acknowledge weaknesses and to act on their suggestions for improvement.

Three important words to keep in mind when you are evaluating your work are *explain*, *justify* and *improve*. Imagine you are looking at a poster you have produced to make people aware of a

Assessment Hint

The Edexcel moderators recognise that, with a limited amount of time in which to complete a project, things do not always work out exactly as planned. This in itself is not a major problem, provided you recognise where and how things went wrong, and can explain what you would do differently another time.

forthcoming meeting. On reflection, you feel the font size you used was too small and not easy to read. In your evaluation don't just say 'The font size was too small' – instead *explain*, *justify* and *improve*! You might say 'The font size was too small for the poster to be read from a distance, and as a result it was not an effective publication. I should have used a font size of at least 72 point so that people passing by were aware of the date, time and place of the meeting. In addition I could have made better use of white space to make the important points stand out.'

When you were first given the summative project brief, you studied it and found answers to a series of questions:

- **What** have I been asked to do?
- **What** do I have to produce?
- **Why** am I doing it?
- **Who** are the target audience?
- **When** do I have to have it finished?
- **What** resources can I use?
- **Who** will review my work, and when?

In your evaluation you should consider whether you achieved everything you set out to do. Do not just answer 'Yes' or 'No' in each case – *explain* and *justify* your answers. What went wrong and why did it go wrong? On the other hand, what did you consider to be particularly successful and why was it a success? Were you able to make use of knowledge and skills that you already had? Alternatively, what new skills did you have to learn?

Consider the resources you used:

- Were some especially helpful and others not so useful?
- Did you have any difficulty in finding useful material?
- Were you able to use specific hardware and software successfully?
- Did you choose the most appropriate hardware and software?

Remember to *explain* and *justify* any statements you make.

- EXPLAIN who 'tested' your product during its production stages, why you asked that particular person and what their comments were. As a result of this feedback, what did you do to IMPROVE your product. Remember your 'product' might be a document, an image, a multimedia presentation or an on-screen publication. JUSTIFY your reasons for modifying your product or not modifying it.

Assessment Hint

You will not achieve the highest possible marks if you do not make at least two constructive and convincing suggestions for improvement.

● EXPLAIN why you asked for feedback from the people who looked at your finished project. Provide evidence that they have looked at your project, that you have considered their feedback and say whether or not you agreed with their comments. JUSTIFY your reasons for reaching your conclusions.

● How would you make sure things didn't go wrong again? What could you do better next time? Think about what you could do to IMPROVE things!

Finally, consider what you have learnt from the whole experience? Was your time plan realistic? Which areas of the project took longer than anticipated and why? Were there aspects of your own skill-base that were weak? Why? How would you rectify the weakness?

A successful evaluation will consider the project from every aspect. In particular, your assessors will be looking to see that you have reviewed the outcomes, the processes and your own performance.

Outcomes

✓ To what extent have the project's objectives been met?

✓ How effective are the final products?

✓ Are they fit for purpose?

✓ How could they be improved?

✓ Does the mix of components enhance the message you are trying to convey?

✓ Is the information organised in an appropriate manner?

✓ How well do your multimedia products function?

✓ Do you think their structure and mix of components work?

✓ How easy are they to use?

✓ Are the file formats and image resolutions suitable?

✓ Does your artwork convey the intended message?

Process

✓ How well did you plan your work?

✓ Did you manage your time well?

✓ Did you meet the deadline?

✓ What, if anything, went wrong?

✓ Did you choose the right or best people to review your project?

✓ Would you arrange the project differently next time?

Performance

✓ What have you learned from working on this project?

✓ Did you have appropriate ICT skills?

✓ What additional training do you feel you need?

✓ How well did you communicate your ideas to others?

✓ How could you further improve your work?

✓ What have you learned about yourself whilst working on this project?

✓ Were you able to draw on knowledge or skills you have acquired in other subjects?

✓ Are you proud of your achievements?

Section 5
Creating an e-portfolio

You will create an e-portfolio to present evidence of your achievements. The assessor and the moderator will use your e-portfolio to judge your work, so you must make sure that it is self-explanatory and easy to use.

LEARNING OUTCOMES

You need to learn about

✓ what to include in your e-portfolio

✓ how to structure your e-portfolio

✓ how to test your e-portfolio.

What is an e-portfolio?

For most students, the idea of presenting coursework in electronic form rather than on paper is something quite new and challenging.

An e-portfolio is a multimedia stage designed to present your work. In this instance, the assessor and moderator must be able to find evidence of your achievements easily.

This is an innovative and exciting way of showing what you are able to do. Your work can come alive with graphics, animations and sound. It is environmentally friendly, saving pages and pages of paper, as well as being a very convenient way of taking your work from place to place. Ultimately your e-portfolio will contain additional information about you, your education and career and, in the longer term, is likely to be looked at by a wide range of people.

You may use Microsoft FrontPage to produce your e-portfolio or you may use one of the many commercial e-portfolio systems available. Your teacher or tutor will provide you with more detailed information on the system you will be using. However, ideally, you should be able to access your work from any PC wherever you choose: at school or college or at home.

> ### ⭐ Assessment Hint
>
> *All the work you produce as evidence towards your Certificate or Diploma in Digital Applications will be presented for assessment and moderation in an e-portfolio. You will not be required to submit any documentation on paper.*

You have already looked at a wide variety of websites and are familiar with the features that make them pleasing to look at, easy to use and effective. You have evaluated their impact and appropriateness for the intended audience and looked at the combination of text and graphics, download times, and so on. Your aim is to replicate the successful features so that the assessor and moderator can easily find their way around your work. When you study each of the summative project briefs, notice how buttons and links take you from one section of the project to another, and how they also direct you to pages of hints and tips and back again to the main sections. Each one has been designed to make it easy for you to find your way around. Similarly, your e-portfolio must clearly guide users through your work.

Organisation of your e-portfolio

TiP

You will find it much easier if you plan the development of an e-portfolio alongside the planning of each project. In this way it is unlikely that important elements will be overlooked.

You must keep in mind that the people who will look at your e-portfolio will not have you at their side to help them find the evidence they will be looking for. The user interface is therefore an important element of any e-portfolio: it is essential that your e-portfolio be well organised, and structured so that anyone can find their way around it efficiently and without difficulty.

The skills you developed in Presentation software and web authoring software are equally applicable to your e-portfolio. Developing a storyboard, structure and flow charts will help ensure that suitable links are in place to make the e-portfolio easy to navigate and user-friendly.

The overall appearance of the e-portfolio is equally as important as the content. You must make sure that it is pleasing for users to look at, as well as being easy to use. Include a variety of interactive components such as buttons, hotspots, and links.

Content of your e-portfolio

The content will reflect the tasks set in the summative project briefs, so each e-portfolio will therefore be different from another. The project brief

will set out in detail what should be included, but the basic structure of each e-portfolio will be similar and will include the following

- home page
- contents page or menu
- the final work you have produced, which may include letters or reports, presentations, web pages, images, etc.
- evidence and explanations of the work you carried out, such as
  - project planning and monitoring
  - the development stages of your work – images, presentations, brochures, web pages, and so on – with comments justifying any modifications made
  - references to sources of documents or graphical components
  - evidence of data collection
  - supporting evidence of database structures or spreadsheets
  - evidence of market research or surveys
  - storyboards, structure charts and flow charts
  - review and evaluation of the project process and outcomes
  - feedback from your reviewers and suggestions for improvement
  - bibliography
  - copyright information, including acknowledgements and permissions where applicable.

TiP

It is a good idea to leave the actual compilation of the e-portfolio to the very end in case you need to modify your work, and so that you will know exactly which files to include. The summative project brief will outline the file formats that should be applied to each project, and will specify the maximum size of each e-portfolio.

Saving your work

It is quite likely that people viewing your e-portfolio may not have access to the same software that you used to produce your documents, images, presentations and so on. For this reason it is essential that you save the work in your e-portfolio in suitable formats as outlined in the summative project brief. For example, paper-based documents are most likely to be in PDF format, whereas screen presentations such as web pages will be HTML files. Images will normally be saved as JPEGs, and multimedia presentations converted to Flash SWF format.

Accessibility and testing

When your work is finished and your e-portfolio is complete you must make sure it works properly. Do not rely solely on checking it for yourself – you know the way around your work and will not be able to provide totally unbiased feedback. Let somebody else who is not familiar with the contents look at it.

As a result of this feedback, it might be necessary to modify your e-portfolio. The important thing to remember is that it must be user-friendly so that the assessor and moderator can use it without help.

In particular you should check that

- the content is complete and includes everything detailed in the summative project brief
- the e-portfolio is clearly presented, easy to use, attractive and effective
- every link goes where it should go with no dead-ends
- the e-portfolio can be displayed correctly in different browsers (e.g. Internet Explorer and Netscape)
- download speeds are acceptable
- other people can use the e-portfolio without help.

> ## ✔ TiP
>
> *Sometimes it is helpful to give the person testing your e-portfolio a list of questions and ask him or her to find the answers. That person will have to rely on the links, instructions and explanations you have set up in your e-portfolio.*

Authentication

Finally your teacher or tutor must provide authentication to confirm that the work is your own.

Go out and try!

This is an opportunity for you to produce a small e-portfolio to display evidence of the various skills you have learnt. It will also enable you to learn how to save files in suitable file formats and to check download speeds for images.

When you worked through the other skills sections you saved separate files describing the skills you had been using. You included headings for each of the activities and wrote a short description of the skills you had learnt. Can you use the headings to provide a link to the examples described?

Task

1 Design an e-portfolio that contains a home page which will direct users to three of the skills pages, and from there to two of the files that illustrate the skills described. Make sure that some of the pages include graphic images so that you can test the download speeds of the images.

For example, the flow chart in Figure 269 would result in a home page with three distinct buttons to link to the word-processing, spreadsheet and database skills files. From there, links would be set up to show the worked examples of the first two activities in each.

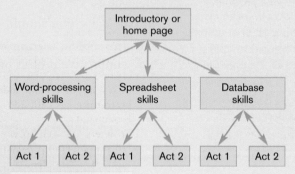

Figure 269 Flow chart

Before you create the e-portfolio, think about the file formats you should use to ensure your work can be viewed on any computer, such as using .pdf files for text pages. Ask your teacher to check that you have not forgotten anything important.

2 Ask your friends to test this e-portfolio. Consider any suggestions they make for improvement and modify your structure if necessary.

3 In turn, look at what your friends have produced and compare ideas. Think about why some e-portfolios might appear more user-friendly than others. Do you think your e-portfolio is the best possible showcase in which to display your achievements? How might you improve on your ideas when you produce the e-portfolio for your first assessment? Write a list of the improvements you might make and say why you think they are necessary – if you don't do this now you will almost certainly forget the improvements by the time you do your assessment! Save the list so that you can refer to it later.

Index

Page numbers in italics refer to illustrations.

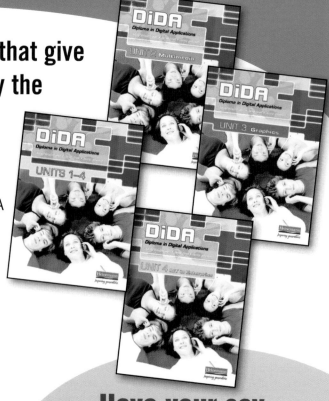